IN IT
FOR THE
LONG
RUN

MUSIC IN AMERICAN LIFE

*A list of books in the series
appears at the end of this book.*

JIM ROONEY

IN IT FOR THE LONG RUN

A MUSICAL ODYSSEY

UNIVERSITY OF ILLINOIS PRESS
URBANA, CHICAGO, AND SPRINGFIELD

Library of Congress Cataloging-in-Publication Data
Rooney, Jim, 1938– author.
In it for the long run : a musical odyssey / Jim Rooney.
pages cm. — (Music in American life)
Discography (pages).
ISBN 978-0-252-03823-5 (cloth : alk. paper)
ISBN 978-0-252-07981-8 (pbk. : alk. paper)
ISBN 978-0-252-09606-8 (ebook)
1. Rooney, Jim, 1938– 2. Sound recording executives
and producers—United States—Biography. 3. Popular
music—United States—History and criticism. 4. Folk
music—United States—History and criticism.
I. Title.
ML429.R67A3   2014
781.64092—dc23 [B]   2013031281

To Jack "Cowboy" Clement
for opening his door to me.

To Carol Langstaff
for opening my senses and my heart.

CONTENTS

PART II
FINDING
MY OWN
VOICE

PART III
FOLLOWING
MY OWN
PATH

PART IV
THE LONG
RUN

ACKNOWLEDGMENTS

The journey of this book began back in 2003 at the annual Folk Alliance Conference, where I was the subject of an oral history interview by Scott Alarik, who covered the Boston folk music scene for many years for the *Boston Globe*. Scott asked me to talk about various times in my journey from the *Hayloft Jamboree* to the Club 47, Newport, New Orleans, Woodstock, and Nashville. And talk I did for more than an hour. Afterward, my old friend Michael Melford came up to me and said that he felt my story had the makings of a book in it. I demurred, saying something about writing books was no fun—especially if it was about me and my wonderful life! However, Mike followed up and wouldn't let it go. I respected his judgment. I'd first known him as a mandolin picker and then as a record producer who earned a Grammy for his work with my good friend John Hartford. He had long been a lawyer, representing, among others, NPR's auto gurus Click and Clack. (Mike is connected to the renowned law firm of Dewey, Cheatem & Howe). We obtained a transcript of the interview, which I showed to another good friend in Nashville, John Lomax III. Between them, John and Mike put together a package to show to potential publishers, but, to make a long story very short, there were no takers.

By now, however, I had decided that even if no one else was interested, I would see what I could do about telling my story to satisfy myself. I certainly had lived through interesting times and had been part of some important musical scenes. Eyewitness accounts are important elements of history making, so I plunged ahead and called up P.J. Curtis, a fellow record producer (Maura O'Connell, Altan, and many more) and writer of music history and novels. My wife Carol Langstaff and I were in Ireland for the winter, and P.J. lived half an hour away in his old family cottage in the middle of the Burren in County Clare. I asked P.J. if he'd be willing to be my interlocutor. Thankfully, he didn't hesitate. The following Wednesday morning I showed up at P.J.'s door with my little mini-disc recorder. He sat me down in a chair in his back sunroom, poured me a glass of Irish whiskey, asked me a question and I talked for a couple of hours! Along the way P.J.'s questions, comments, and observations helped me make better sense of my jumbled recollections. He then fed me a big bowl of soup and we went for a ramble on the Burren, which he knew like the back of his hand. We did this every Wednesday for about eight weeks until we were more or less out of stories.

Then came the "no fun" part, which I had dimly remembered from the days of writing *Bossmen* and *Baby, Let Me Follow You Down*. I transcribed all eight of the mini-discs onto yellow legal pads, editing and revising as I went. While in the midst of this process, still in Ireland, I was contacted by Sandy Harsch, a high school classmate of Carol's who had been living in Ireland for many years and was the host of a program called *Countrytime* on RTE Radio 1, the Irish national broadcaster. She had long been a supporter of artists I had produced and asked if she and her producer Aidan Butler could come out to the house and interview me. Once again, I told my story (or stories), which she and Aidan brilliantly edited into three forty-five-minute programs called *In It for the Long Run*. The programs were very positively received, which encouraged me to keep on and add this material to my growing pile of yellow legal pads. THEN I finally started to write on my MacBook laptop.

By this time, thanks to Matt Lindsey, who had been our song-plugger at Forerunner Music, I had been in touch with Albert Lafarge, an agent in Boston, who expressed an interest in what I was doing and offered to help find a home for my book whenever I was ready to let it go. I was still working in Nashville and living in Vermont and Ireland, where I was also doing some work, so months passed; a couple of years passed. Every so often I'd call Albert. He was still there. Patiently waiting. Finally, I sent him the manuscript file. I knew it was too long and so did Albert, and he kindly put me in touch with an editor in New York, Charis Conn. Charis redlined every single page, sent me a dozen pages of notes and suggestions, and sent me back to work. It was a huge help. Of course, for every cut, I found myself adding something I had overlooked, so it was a pretty convoluted process. I was also the beneficiary of some very generous and thoughtful comments after a partial reading of my manuscript from my good friend Peter Guralnick, who took time out from his own serious writing schedule to do it, but I finally got to the place where it seemed to be as finished as it ever would be, and I gave it back to Albert.

Of course, since 2003 the book business had undergone many of the same changes I had seen in the record business, and I was under no illusions about the possibility of finding a publisher. I feel very fortunate to be in the good hands of Laurie Matheson, her assistant Dawn Durante, and editor Nancy Albright at the University of Illinois Press, which has a distinguished list of books about music, and I am looking forward to having my story added to all of those others for whom music has been life.

MUSIC PUBLISHING CREDITS

ATV Music Publishing LLC. All rights for Sony/ATV Music Publishing, LLC administered by Sony/ATV Publishing LLC. Used by permission. All rights reserved. Reprinted by permission of Hal Leonard Corp.

We've Heard It All Before (Pat Alger) © 1993 Universal Music Corp. and Universal-Polygram International Publishing, Inc. Used by permission. All rights reserved. Reprinted by permission of Hal Leonard Corp.

Let the Harvest Go to Seed (Peter Rowan) © Sea Lion Music. Used by permission. All rights reserved.

Bluegrass Boy (Peter Rowan) © Sea Lion Music. Used by permission. All rights reserved.

Going Back to Georgia (Nanci Griffith/Adam Durwitz/Brian Claflin) © Irving Music/Ponder Heart Music/EMI Blackwood Music, Inc./Jones Falls Music/Almo Music Corp/Griffmill Music. All rights reserved.

Rose of Sharon (Eliza Gilkyson) © Gilkysongs. All rights reserved.

Walk through the Bottomland (Lyle Lovett) © 1987/1988 Michael H. Goldsen, Inc./Lyle Lovett. Used by permission. All rights reserved.

Every Drop of Water (Allen Shamblin/Steve Seskin) © 1994 Sony/ATV Music Publishing LLC/David Aaron Music and Built On Rock Music. Sony/ATV LLC rights administered by Sony/ATV Music Publishing LLC; Built On Rock rights administered by BMG Rights Management. International copyright secured. All rights reserved. Reprinted by permission of Hal Leonard Corp.

Streets of Baltimore (Harlan Howard/Tompall Glaser) © 1966 Sony/ATV Music Publishing LLC. All rights administered by Sony/ATV Music Publishing LLC, 8 Music Square West, Nashville, Tenn. 37203. All rights reserved. Used by permission.

Wall of Death (Richard Thompson) © 1996 Beeswing Music administered by Bug Music, a BMG Chrysalis Company. International copyright secured. All rights reserved. Reprinted by permission of Hal Leonard Corp.

Who Knows Where the Time Goes (Sandy Denny) © 1969 Winckler Musik-forlag administered by Irving Music, Inc. Copyright renewed. Used by permission. All rights reserved. Reprinted by permission of Hal Leonard Corp.

Darcy Farrow (Steve Gillette/Tom Campbell) © Rumpole Dumple Music c/o Ruminating Music c/o Wixen Music Pub. Inc./Compass Rose Music c/o Wixen Music Pub. Inc. Used by permission. All rights reserved.

We're Not the Jet Set (Bobby Braddock) © Sony ATV Tree. All rights reserved.

We Could (Felice Bryant) © 1955 House of Bryant Publications/Sony/ATV

IN IT
FOR THE
LONG
RUN

INTRODUCTION

"DO IT YOUR OWN IGNORANT WAY!"

With these words, Gammy—my mother's mother, Julia Flaherty—would dismiss one or the other of us grandchildren as we informed her of how we were about to do something. So that's what I've been doing ever since—going my own way in the world, finding my own voice, following my own path—doing it "my own ignorant way." That path took me on a musical journey from Dedham, Massachusetts, to Cambridge, to New Orleans, to Newport, to Woodstock, to Nashville, to Ireland, to Vermont, and all around the world. I've been making my story up as I went along. Here it is.

PART I

GOING MY OWN WAY IN THE WORLD

TEX AND ABE

They tell us that we carry all kinds of information in us, locked in our genes, passed down through the generations. So when I first heard the sound of the fiddle and banjo coming out of the radio as I tuned in one night, I'm convinced that my Irish genes woke from their slumber and started jangling. Nothing had prepared me for this. It was 1951. I was thirteen years old, living outside of Boston in Dedham, Massachusetts, far from the mountains of Appalachia, farther still from the Emerald Isle, definitely not a musical hotbed.

My parents had moved there to raise their family away from the Irish-Catholic enclaves in Boston. They were raising us to be open to all kinds of people. The focus was on education, and like my brother John before me, I was going to the Roxbury Latin School. After the Ames School in Dedham, where I had been quite the little genius, it was like walking into a stone wall. This was a "classical" education and I was taking Latin, Math, English, History, and Geography for starters. French, Greek and Physics would come later. I begged my parents to take me out, but they kept telling me that I could do it. Education was it. It was not negotiable.

At school I had become buddies with a live wire named Dick Curley. One day Dick told me to turn the radio on to WCOP at 7:45 that night. This band was playing "hillbilly" music. It was the funniest thing he'd ever heard. Songs like "Mother's Not Dead, She's Only Sleeping." It was a riot. I went home that night, took Dick's advice and tuned in. I heard this amazing sound—fiddle, banjo, mandolin, and guitar coupled with a high wailing kind of singing. They called themselves The Confederate Mountaineers, and they were really from the South. Unlike Dick Curley, I wasn't laughing. Something about that sound was familiar; something about it was "right." Was it my Irish genes aroused by this music? Who knows? All I know is that I kept coming back again and again. I was hooked.

But there was more! Right after the Confederate Mountaineers a disc jockey named Nelson Bragg came on with a show called the *Hayloft Jamboree*. He was a great character—"The Merry Mayor of Milo, Maine." He definitely wasn't from the south, but he knew that there were lots of rural New Englanders and people from Quebec and The Maritimes who'd moved to the cities for work and who loved this simple, heartfelt music. Hank Williams sang "Honky Tonk Blues," Lefty Frizzell had "If You've Got the Money, Honey (I've Got the Time)," Hank Snow did "A Fool Such as I," Webb Pierce sang about a "Back Street Affair." This was a life I knew nothing about. If Dedham had any honky-tonks or back streets I certainly didn't know where they were, but these singers and these songs were reaching something deep inside of me, stirring emotions I didn't even know I had. They were taking me out of the life I knew. I was setting out on the journey of a lifetime.

Once a month the *Hayloft Jamboree* did a big show at Symphony Hall, so Dick Curley and I decided to go. The star was going to be Slim Whitman, who sang in a high, yodelly style and had had big hits with "Indian Love Call" and "Rose Marie." Symphony Hall was full and buzzing. I had been there once before on a school trip to hear the Boston Symphony Orchestra, something I would never forget, but Nelson Bragg lost no time in letting everyone know that there'd be no longhair music being played that night, and we were all invited to let *our* hair down and whoop it up. All the performers were dressed in western outfits except the Confederate Mountaineers who wore riding pants, high boots, and Confederate officers' hats. Slim Whitman *was* a star. When he came out in his black-and-white suit, his black-and-white guitar, and his Clark Gable looks,

FIGURE 1. The Confederate Mountaineers
(*l. to r.*: Everett Lilly, Bea Lilly, Tex Logan, Don Stover).

and hit his first high note the place went wild. I'd never experienced anything like it. It was worlds away from Dedham, from Roxbury Latin. I felt like I had taken a trip to an exotic land, but it was only a bus and trolley ride away.

One day Curley talked me into going into the radio station to see the Confederate Mountaineers play. WCOP took up a good part of the first floor of the New England Mutual Life Building in Copley Square. We entered a large lobby painted with a big mural of "hillbillys" having fun in the style of Al Capp's popular comic strip "Lil' Abner." There was a maze of studios and control rooms beyond the lobby, and as we rounded a corner there in one of the studios we could see the Confederate Mountaineers getting ready to go on the air!

Dick and I stood there in a classic pose, with our noses literally pressed against the glass, watching our heroes. Everett Lilly did all the talking in his high-pitched West Virginia accent. "Thank you just a whole lot there, Nelson Bragg. We'd like to say a great big howdy to all the friends and neighbors! We're going to kindly start off with a good Bill Monroe number, "'Footprints in the Snow.'" And off they went, gathered around the microphone—Tex Logan shouldering his way in with his fiddle, Don Stover driving with his banjo, Everett holding his mandolin up and singing high and clear, and his brother Bea, constantly smiling, steady on his guitar. After a couple of songs, they'd do an instrumental and let Tex and Don loose. Then they'd do a gospel number like "Sinner You Better Get Ready," something my Catholic ears had never heard before and sure wasn't in the hymnal at Roxbury Latin! This was passionate, heartfelt music.

All too soon the fifteen minutes was over. They packed up their instruments, came out, and said hello. They were leaving, so we left with them. Soon we were out in Copley Square, walking along with the four of them in their full Confederate regalia. I'm sure heads must have been turning, but we were oblivious, just happy to be allowed to walk along like we belonged! We crossed Boston Common to The Plaza Bar, and they invited us in to hear a set. It was early, and there was a thin crowd of sailors and other people who definitely didn't live in Dedham, but Curley and I were thrilled. There we were—friends of the people on stage, in a real honky-tonk, like the ones in the songs. Little did I know then how many nights of my life were to be spent this way! The thrill would never leave me.

We spent the summers near the sea in a place called Green Harbor in a cottage my folks had built. One night I found something called *Saturday Night Country Style* on the CBS station. Every week they would broadcast two half-hour live shows from various country music shows around the country. My Uncle Jim Flaherty, God bless him, was visiting and saw me sitting by the radio, strumming along on an old tennis racquet. He must have thought, "That boy needs something else to strum on," and on his next visit he gave me a Roy Smeck ukulele! He also gave me a chord book and showed me how most songs had three or four chords. The book had some songs in it like "Red River Valley," so I just started strumming and trying to change chords where they sounded right. One small detail I didn't notice: I had picked up the ukulele left-handed—upside down. It just felt natural; I wrote with my left hand. No one was around to correct me. I did it "my own ignorant way."

I subscribed to a magazine called *Country Song Roundup*. Every month I got the lyrics to all the songs I was hearing on the radio. By the end of the summer I was singing songs like "Back Street Affair" and "Your Cheating Heart." I had three older girl cousins—the Walsh girls—living down the road. They seemed to think that listening to little Jimmy sing these songs about back street affairs and cheating hearts was the cutest thing they'd ever heard. That was okay with me.

As I listened to the radio every night that fall, my heart was getting touched most of all by the singing of Hank Williams. In addition to "Your Cheating Heart," I started singing "I'm So Lonesome I Could Cry." The lyric to the last verse was so beautiful to me:

> The silence of a falling star
> Lights up a purple sky
> And as I wonder where you are
> I'm so lonesome I could cry.

The sadness in his voice went straight to my teenage heart. I wanted to sing like him. I wanted to be that sad. That Christmas of 1952 my brother Johnny gave me the greatest present—two albums of 78s by Hank Williams: *Moanin' the Blues* and *Luke the Drifter*. I'd camp out in front of our record player listening to these records over and over, probably driving everyone else crazy. I took to practicing in front of the mirror in the front room, trying to figure out how to break my voice like Hank did when he sang "Lovesick Blues" or "Honky Tonk Blues." I guess I figured if I could watch myself stretch my neck somehow, my voice would break easier.

Then came the news. Hank was dead. January 1, 1953. It was so confusing. I had just fallen deeply in love, and now he was gone. Almost immediately there was a memorial album, with a picture of Hank against

FIGURE 2. "Little" Jimmy serenades one of his sister Kathleen's college classmates, while she strums his new ukulele, 1953.

a purple background, edged in black, complete with a letter to Hank in Heaven from Frank Walker of MGM Records. Hank's sister Irene started a column in *Country Song Roundup* about Hank. I wrote her a letter saying I wanted to write a book about Hank and could she give me any inside information. She never answered.

Over the summer there were changes at WCOP. Nelson Bragg went to the big pop station WBZ and The Confederate Mountaineers lost their daily radio show. The live *Jamboree* show moved to John Hancock Hall every Friday night with a new lineup. Elton Britt became a resident "star." He was a fine yodeler and had had a huge hit during the Second World War with a song called "There's a Star Spangled Banner Waving Somewhere." Among the new cast members was a group called "Buzz, Jack & Scotty; The Bayou Boys" featuring a wild mandolinist and singer, Buzz Busby; a show-stopping fiddler, Scotty Stoneman; and Jack Clement, who sang and played guitar. It was my first time to lay eyes on Jack, but it definitely wasn't going to be my last.

Another of my classmates at school, Bob Holland, sold me a little plywood guitar with a canvas case for $12. It came with a fingerpick, which I thought you put on over your fingernail. I took it home and got out one of my Hank Williams songbooks. "Darlin' Let's Turn Back the Years" had only two chords so I gave that a try. It was excruciating. It felt like the wire was carving into my fingers. It was. Since I was playing left-handed, I thought it might be a good idea to change the strings around and play it properly, but the thin strings in the fat grooves just rattled and buzzed, so I switched the strings back. I wasn't trying to be Chet Atkins anyway. I wanted to be Hank Williams and just strum along while I sang about my broken heart.

One day I heard two girls on the *Jamboree* who sounded like two cats on a fence. I said to myself, "I'm as good as they are," screwed up my courage, and headed into the station the next week. All the local "stars" were sitting around the lobby, dressed up in their spangles, hats, and boots (even though they were on the radio). I spotted a guy who seemed to be in charge and asked him if I could audition. His name was Aubrey Mayhew. He was the first kind of music business sharpie I'd ever met. He had slicked back hair, a jacket with pointy shoulders, and kind of a sly smile. He took me into the big studio and told me to play something. So I put on my little plywood guitar upside down, put the fingerpick over my fingernail and launched into Hank Snow's "Music Makin' Mama from Memphis." He told me to do another, so I did Hank Williams's "Honky Tonk Blues." Aubrey Mayhew smiled and said, "Do you want to be on the radio?" I said, "Sure!" So he told me to hang around. Oh my goodness!

I had to find a phone. I called my folks and Dick Curley and announced, "I'm gonna be on the radio!!!"

There was a band on the show called Cappy Paxton & The Trailsmen. Aubrey Mayhew told them what I was going to sing, and they'd back me up. They loaned me a good guitar to play. The whole experience was like being in a dream. Instead of being on the outside looking in, here I was inside the studio with a band all around me singing on the radio! When it was over, everybody was very friendly, telling me that I did great, and Aubrey Mayhew told me to come back the next week. After the next time he invited me to come play on the *Jamboree* the following Friday. I was going to be a "star"! Which meant that I had to get some stage clothes.

I went to my mother and broke the good news. She might have been hoping that this phase I was going through would pass, but she went along with me to a store where we would not be normally shopping. I picked out some powder blue, pleated, slightly pegged pants, which were just coming into style at the time. I also got a checkered shirt and, somehow or another, got my hands on a clip-on red string tie. I was nearly 6'2" and weighed about 125 pounds. I must have cut quite a figure. A dressed-up stick.

I went into the show on Friday. It was sponsored by the Viva Spaghetti Company. They had "Vivaettes" for ushers—girls dressed up in cowgirl outfits with short skirts, which got my attention. The audience was mostly sailors and their girlfriends and guys in leather jackets with D.A. haircuts. Backstage I now blended in with everyone else in my new clothes. Cappy Paxton was a good front man and did a bit of comedy. They had a singer, Jackie Russell, "the boy with the golden voice," who sang smooth Eddy Arnold songs. After a while, Cappy brought me on and I launched into "Music Makin' Mama" and "Honky Tonk Blues." I was too excited to be nervous and gave it all I had, hunched over the microphone just like Hank Williams. The band was right there with me, with the wild, new sound of Ronnie Lee, "King of the Pedal Steel Guitar." When the people cheered at the end I could have gone to heaven right then.

Suddenly my life was very different. At school everybody started calling me "Tex." I would do the *Jamboree* every Friday night, do the live radio show Saturday afternoon, and often we would then go to a school or a small hall for a show. We'd all pile into Cappy's fastback Hudson, with the bass on top and the instruments in the trunk. After the show they'd leave me at a bus or trolley stop, and I'd go back home to my other life. The bass player was a kid about my age. We were talking one day, and he said, "You're good. Why don't you come with us all the time?" I said, "I can't. I'm in school." He looked at me as if that was no good reason, but I just repeated my mantra, "I can't, I'm in school." It was absolutely inconceivable that I could even consider leaving school to go play music in a hillbilly band!

As it was, I was pushing the limits. One Friday I was up in my room putting my powder blue pants on, and my mother said, "What do you think you're doing? Where are you going?" "I'm going to the *Jamboree*. It's Friday." "It's GOOD FRIDAY!" "Well," I said, "we've got a show." The next week my parents decided they'd better come in and see what this "show" was all about. My father was also about 6'2" and always wore a suit and tie. My mother was a very nice looking lady. So they weren't hard to spot sitting in a sea of navy blue and leather among the Vivaettes and their fans. After the show I was signing autographs and acting like a "star." My parents took it all in, but they evidently decided that there was no serious harm being done to my immortal soul, and they let me go on.

At the end of the spring there was a big show at Boston's Mechanics Hall, which seated four or five thousand people. In addition to Elton Britt, the star of the show was Hank Thompson and his Brazos Valley Boys—a full-blown western swing band complete with electric fiddles, trumpet, piano, steel guitar, and electric guitars. Hank Thompson was huge at the time, with his big hit, "I Didn't Know God Made Honky Tonk Angels," and he had two more singers with him—Billy Gray, who was a smooth Texas-style singer, and Wanda Jackson, who was a belter and just about my age. The whole show took my breath away. For my part, Aubrey had me buy a pair of overalls and sit on a bale of hay at the edge of the stage singing "Honky Tonk Blues" while Cappy and some girl did a comedy skit. I didn't care what I had to do. I was in show business!

That was the last show of the year, and soon my family headed off to Green Harbor where I got a job on a nearby farm picking berries and selling vegetables by the side of the road. I was saving up to buy a Martin guitar just like Hank's. However, when we got back to Dedham in the fall, the *Jamboree* was gone! WCOP had totally changed its format, and the whole thing evaporated. I went ahead with my plan anyway and went into the Boston Music Company with my hard earned money and bought a brand new Martin D-18 guitar for $135. What a day in my life! I can remember the smell of that guitar when I took it out of the case. I remember the feel of it in my hands. It was so smooth, so easy to play. The chords sounded so rich and rang so long. When I got it home, I put it on and stood in front of the mirror looking at myself with my Martin guitar. It was definitely a dream come true. But there I was, all dressed up and nowhere to go!

Although I'm pretty sure that my parents were quite relieved to see the end of the *Jamboree*, my mother was sympathetic. She seemed to understand that music and songs had become part of my life and would not be going away. For my birthday in January of '55 she gave me Carl Sandburg's *American Songbag*. I had been reading his biography of Abraham Lincoln for school, and this turned out to be a wonderful gift. I started going through the book and finding songs like "Roving Gambler" and "Kentucky Moonshiner." I would read the words and many times just make up the melodies. Not that I thought of myself as a songwriter; I guess I was becoming a folk singer. At a store near WCOP in Boston called The Book Clearing House they had a little section of records called "folk music." I found "Leadbelly's Last Sessions," "Big Bill Broonzy," Pete Seeger's "Talking Union." I was branching out on my own, following whatever little hunches I had. There was no agenda, no plan. I didn't know anybody who did this other than me. I was opening myself up to whatever music came my way.

With WCOP gone, Dick Curley turned my attention to another station, WBMS. The disc jockey was just as exciting as Nelson Bragg had been, but in an entirely different way. He was none other than "Symphony Sid," whose deep, mellifluous voice introduced me to phrases like "the hippest," "the coolest." I was off into yet another exotic world far from Dedham Square. In the afternoon he played what he called R&B—rhythm and blues. I was hearing Little Richard and Fats Domino, Ruth Brown, and Clyde McPhatter. Then at 5 o'clock he turned into "Brother Sid" and did an hour of gospel music, so I heard Mahalia Jackson, Sister Rosetta Tharpe, and The Five Blind Boys of Alabama. At night Sid turned his attention to jazz, so I was introduced to Dizzy Gillespie, Slim & Slam (Slim Gaillard and Slam Stewart), and Duke Ellington.

One day Sid mentioned that Duke Ellington and his Orchestra would be doing a special matinee on Easter Sunday to benefit the NAACP at a jazz club near Copley Square called "Storyville," run by a man named George Wein. I went in with another friend from school. Several of the Ellington band members were from the area, so their families and friends were all there. As Sid might have said, it was "the hippest, the coolest." We were sitting at a small table about twenty feet away from Duke Ellington at the piano in all his dapper splendor and the full band at its height. One woman got up with her big Easter bonnet on and just about sat on the piano singing "Easter Parade." When she sang, "On the Avenue, Columbus Avenue" the place went wild. Columbus Avenue was to the black community of Boston what Fifth Avenue was to the white community of New York. That was a day of absolute musical joy that would stay with me forever.

Unlike my brother John, I was not good at sports, but music gave me another way to go, a way to express myself. One of my teachers, Richard Whitney, noticed that I was coming out of my shell and encouraged me to try out for the school play, which was Robert Sherwood's *Abe Lincoln in Illinois*. To my great surprise he told me that I would be playing the part of Abe Lincoln! As I got into the part, Hank Williams and Abe Lincoln took me over and conflated into some kind of different person than a person from Boston with that harsh accent. I talked and moved slower. "Tex" and Abe became one.

It was definitely part of my parents' philosophy that you needed to be open to other people in this world. My new explorations into the world of "folk" music would reinforce these thoughts. One of the Folkways Records I found at The Book Clearing House was Pete Seeger's "Talking Union," which was full of songs about the labor unions and what they had gone through in the thirties and forties. My father was a straight Democrat who wept when Eisenhower beat Adlai Stevenson. My mother was an admirer of the Catholic activist Dorothy Day and had voted for Henry Wallace, a Socialist, for president. The music I was listening to and playing was definitely the music of "the people" and not of "the bosses." Country music, Blues, R&B, Jazz, Gospel, Appalachian music, and Folk music all had an energy and vitality that moved me and brought me great joy. All of these streams were flowing together in me and were shaping my outlook on life.

BEATS AND BLUEGRASS
AT AMHERST

After graduating from Roxbury Latin in 1956 I chose to go to Amherst College in western Massachusetts. As I settled in, I discovered other kids like me, who had brought their record albums with them. Many of the people I gravitated toward were into jazz, so I started hearing Miles Davis, Thelonious Monk, and Sonny Rollins. When I went home at Christmas I went into The Book Clearing House, and looked at the jazz section and started buying those records.

I tried out for WAMF and eventually got myself a one-hour weekly program. On my show I decided to play "American" music. The theme song was "Walk, Don't Run" by the guitarist Johnny Smith. (It could have been the theme song for my life!) There were a lot of hipsters at the radio station who were into beat stuff, bebop, Jack Kerouac. I was interested in being a little bit hip myself—listening to stuff that everyone else wasn't listening to. As a result, my "American Music" show covered everything from Hank Williams to Aaron Copeland; from Duke Ellington to Fats Domino; from Leadbelly to Charlie Parker; from Hank Snow to Pete Seeger. Sharing all of this extraordinary music with others brought me great satisfaction.

Of course, in the big picture, music was off to the side. By the time I got to Amherst, I'd had five years of Latin and three years of Greek, so it just seemed to be the path of least resistance to carry on and become a Classics major. In the course of time there were only three of us majoring, and after a two-hour seminar on Aeschylus or Plato we would adjourn to Professor John Moore's house for a meal, washed down with ample quantities of wine, followed by hours of conversation, often joined by other teachers or students. It was a true symposium, and John Moore was the closest person to Socrates I would ever know. At three or four in the morning he would still be in full flight unraveling the mysteries of whatever lay hidden in the material we were studying. At nine the next morning I would run into him bounding up the library stairs, ready to plunge into the day. I might have been a bit groggy myself.

For my first two and a half years at Amherst the only music I was playing was either in my room or at the bar in the basement of my fraternity. Then one day somebody introduced me to a kid in the class behind me who played the banjo. His name was Bill Keith. He was playing a longneck Pete Seeger style 5-string banjo and was learning from Pete's instruction book. The last two pages of the book had an introduction to the Earl Scruggs style of banjo playing. Bill had gotten hold of a Flatt & Scruggs album and was teaching himself this style. When we got together, I said, "I know some of those songs. I used to hear these guys called the Lilly Brothers sing them." Bill and I started getting together, and I also showed him a Folkways album I had picked up at The Book Clearing House called *American Banjo, Scruggs Style*, which Mike Seeger had recorded. Once Bill set his mind to something, he was very thorough. Having someone else around to accompany him and sing some songs gave him the impetus to really get into it.

The Lilly Brothers and Don Stover were now playing regularly at a place called The Hillbilly Ranch in downtown Boston next to the Trailways bus station, so when Bill and I went home for the Easter holiday, I took him there. Naturally, Bill Keith's eyes never left Don Stover's hands. Don was a powerful player. He wouldn't have to be on mic to hear him. He was totally traditional and totally original. He could frail old-time, play driving Scruggs style, or do beautiful pedal steel-like licks on slow tunes. Watching Don was a crash course for Bill. This was something you couldn't learn from books or records. Right here in Boston there was a master in our midst, and Bill was eager to learn all he could from him.

That summer I took a student boat to Europe and traveled around with a classmate from Roxbury Latin, Larry Casson. On my return to Amherst I immediately hooked up with Bill. I had acquired a couple of new albums. One was another of Mike Seeger's collections on Folkways, *Mountain Music, Bluegrass Style*. The other was of Earl Taylor, a singer and mandolin player from Baltimore who had been recorded by Alan Lomax. In the liner notes Lomax described Bluegrass as being "folk music in overdrive." It was the arrival of both of these records that introduced me to the term *Bluegrass*. *Hillbilly* had been replaced by *Country*, and *Bluegrass* was on its own over in left field somewhere near *Folk*. I proceeded to incorporate this mixture into what Bill and I were playing, and I started to adapt some of the folk songs from *American Songbag* to a more bluegrass or "mountain music" style. We worked up "Pretty Polly," "John Henry," and "Kentucky Moonshiner." One afternoon Bill was working at learning a Sonny Osborne banjo tune, "Banjo Boy Chimes." Something about the chord changes stayed with me, and I started to fit them to the words of another song out of the Sandburg *Songbag*, "One Morning in May." In the process I also changed the tempo from 4/4 time to 3/4 time and showed it to Bill. He had just acquired an autoharp and tried playing it on that. It sounded beautiful. Neither of us gave a thought to the fact that we were "arranging" or rewriting the song. We were just following our instincts, and our instincts told us that we had come up with something special.

On one of our trips home, Bill and I called on two college friends, Jon Scott and Tom West, who, as "underachievers" had been invited by the college to take a year off. They were sharing a student slum apartment in Cambridge with a friend of theirs from Martha's Vineyard, Davy Gude. While we were there, a gorgeous girl with dark eyes and long black hair came by for her guitar lesson with Davy. Her name was Joan Baez. It definitely registered that there was more to life than what our secluded life at Amherst had to offer. They told us of a coffeehouse near Boston University called "The Golden Vanity," so we decided to check it out. It had sort of a nautical atmosphere with fishnets hung around the place. They put on "folk" acts like the Chad Mitchell Trio, Rev. Gary Davis, and Sonny Terry and Brownie McGhee. They also had hootenannies on Sundays where anyone could play, so Bill and I did that on one of our visits. There were lots of girls dressed in black. There was one girl in particular who caught my attention named Betsy Minot. She wore the shortest skirts I'd seen to date and could swear like a sailor. She wasn't shy. The folk music scene was getting more and more intriguing.

Back at Amherst, Bill had been listening to the WWVA *Wheeling Jamboree* on the radio and had heard that Jimmy Martin & The Sunny Mountain Boys would be playing in Pittsfield, Massachusetts, so we went over. The banjo player was a skinny kid named J.D. Crowe, who had some tunes like Earl Scruggs, which involved tuning the banjo in midflight. The other member of the band was Paul Williams, who played mandolin and was a fine tenor singer. Though they were just a trio, they had a big sound. Jimmy Martin was a strong guitar player and had a powerful voice and tons of energy. They had really good songs—"Sophronie," "Hit Parade of Love," and "Ocean of Diamonds"—all destined to be classic bluegrass songs. We hung around afterward and got a glimpse into the bluegrass life. They had driven from Louisiana in Jimmy's Cadillac and were headed back to Wheeling that night. J.D. told Bill that he did most of the driving while Jimmy talked or slept. The music apparently made it all worthwhile. It was an eye opener.

We had also gone down to New York City a couple of times to join in the bluegrass jam sessions on Sunday afternoons in Washington Square down in Greenwich Village. One of the ringleaders was a banjo player named Roger Sprung, who had added "Scruggs tuners" to his banjo. Bill was still playing a longnecked banjo, but he now equipped it with additional tuning pegs with "rabbit-ear" extensions so he could play the Scruggs and J.D. Crowe showpieces. Somehow we were asked to play on a television show on WWLP-TV in Springfield, Massachusetts. We worked up a program of folk songs and bluegrass style songs, and the show went off without a hitch. We were a good team. I wasn't shy about performing and doing some talking. Bill let his banjo do the talking.

The tide of music was rising in my life, but I still had to pay attention to my studies. With Professor Moore's help I wrote a senior thesis on the plays of Aeschylus, which focused my attention on this amazing period in Greek history when the Athenians were coming into their own and were attempting to harness the powerful religious, social, and political forces that were swirling about them. There was great energy in these plays which I had no trouble relating to. I also took a seminar on oral poetry taught by a great curmudgeon, Professor Theodore Baird. He liked Shakespeare and the great novels of the nineteenth century. The Norse epics, "Song of Roland," "Beowulf," the English ballads didn't satisfy him as stories. As he put it, "I'm reading along and all of a sudden a wall appears that wasn't ever mentioned before. Where did that come from? What kind of narrative is that?" I plunged into the English ballads collected by Francis Child, as sung by Ewan MacColl and A. L. Lloyd. This wasn't literature; these were sung stories. Baird was a reader, not a listener, and that was why this material was so puzzling to him. Melody and tempo supply the setting for the story and set the mood so that you don't even think to ask the same questions you might ask when reading a novel. Explaining all this in class made me realize that I had joined a very long, deep, and legitimate tradition as a singer and adapter of songs.

INTO THE FOLK
AND BLUEGRASS POOL

Toward the end of my senior year, a folk music promoter named Manny Greenhill came up from Boston. He wanted to put Odetta on in concert at the University of Massachusetts across town. He needed a campus organization to sponsor the concert, so he helped organize The Pioneer Valley Folklore Society. Among the founding members were Bill and me, fellow Amherst students Rick Lee and Jesse Auerbach (later named Josh Dunson), and UMass students Taj Mahal and Buffy Ste. Marie. (The Society is still going!) Manny heard Bill and me play at that time and liked us well enough to ask us to open up for a singer named Charlotte Daniels at a club he had opened in Boston next to George Wein's "Storyville" called "The Ballad Room." We'd get $15 a night for two nights, our first professional gig. We were excited. Our parents came, as well as Dick Curley, Larry Casson, and a few other friends. We wore ties and matching blue shirts and tried to look professional. We played our eclectic set to this select audience and were doing okay. Then, after one particular song, a voice boomed out from the back of the room, "I never heard it better!" It was Odetta. She'd gone out of her way to come and hear us and encourage us. I never forgot that.

Next we headed to Newport for the Folk Festival. Odetta was going to be on the show, as was Earl Scruggs. We had to go! Suddenly we found ourselves in the midst of thousands of others who, like us, had been discovering folk music for ourselves and had started singing and playing on our own. We were no longer alone. All day long there were jam sessions on the green in the middle of town. After the shows, we all went to the beaches and played around campfires. We were welcome to play along and make ourselves heard from time to time. If we slept, we slept in Bill's car or on the beach. I presume we ate from time to time. Nothing mattered but the music.

At Newport, Roger Sprung invited us to join him on a trip down to Asheville, North Carolina, to a festival organized by a man named Bascom Lamar Lunsford, a local folk song collector. Following that was an old-time fiddler's convention in Galax, Virginia. Here it was—1960; I'd been listening to and playing this southern music for eight years or so, but I'd never been south of Washington, D.C.! I'll never forget crossing the Potomac River onto "The Lee Highway." It was like going to another country—a country I'd wanted to go to for a long time. I thought I knew a lot about it, but, of course, I didn't. Everything was exotic—just the way people spoke, inviting you to "come back," wishing you "good mornin.'" Then there was the food—grits, biscuits and gravy, country ham, sweet iced tea. As we drove over hill and dale down the Shenandoah Valley and up into the Blue Ridge Mountains hearing Flatt & Scruggs and Bill Monroe on the radio, we were finally entering the world we had only imagined.

When we arrived in Asheville, Roger took us over to the Municipal Auditorium where he introduced us to Bascom Lamar Lunsford, who was all dressed up in a white linen suit, the very image of a courtly southern gentleman. He was very welcoming. If Roger said we were good enough to be on the show that was good enough for him. He obviously liked Roger, who'd been coming for several years. He introduced Roger to the audience as "a great big friendly Jew from New York," which, of course, he was. There was no malice intended and none taken. The show wasn't a country music show. It was folk musicians from the area—ballad singers, old-time fiddlers, banjo players, and clog dancers. When we finally went on, we did "John Henry" at a pretty torrid pace. I let loose on the vocal, and Bill burned up the banjo. The crowd loved it. We were immediately accepted.

After the show everybody went out to a shopping mall parking lot and picked until two or three in the morning. We started meeting people—Ron and Don Norman, who were both good banjo players from Georgia, and a heartfelt country and bluegrass singer named Walter Butler. Bill had bought a shortneck banjo from Don Stover and this was a chance for him to really get into the Scruggs style and learn. All the picking we were doing was rubbing off on me as well. Walter Butler and the other bluegrass guitar players did these bass runs that seemed to be an important part of playing bluegrass guitar. I got someone to give me a thumbpick and started to figure out how to do some of these runs upside down. We were playing all day and all night, so I started to get the hang of it pretty fast.

The last night of the festival this old-time fiddler, Byard Ray, from Marshall in the mountains west of Asheville, invited us to come home with him. We met him on Monday afternoon and followed him on the paved highway, which ran along the French Broad River, and then on a dirt road up a long holler to the end where he lived in a small farmhouse with his family. We'd only been in the South for a week and now we were as deep into the mountains as you could go. The Southern hospitality was real. There was food on the table seemingly from morning to night, starting with eggs and biscuits, ham and gravy, molasses, grits, and applesauce. After dinner we sat out on the porch and picked a few tunes. Then we went up the road to visit Byard's parents Champ and Rachel. He was a tough old ex-logger; she was a good ballad singer and knew lots of great old songs. Another night Byard took us over to meet Obray Ramsay—an old-time banjo player and singer with a very distinctive, quavery singing style. I'd heard him on one of my records of Southern Appalachian music. Each night we would play and listen and soak up this music, which seemed so much a part of the natural landscape, the streams, the hollers, the mountains.

The drive up to Galax was beautiful. As I looked at the little farms with their split rail fences and cabinlike houses, I'd be humming "Cabin in Caroline." The song was real. Galax was a smaller town than Asheville. It had a main street and one hotel—the Blue Ridge Hotel—which was where we were staying. This was a real old-time fiddler's convention, held in the high school gym or outside on the baseball field. They had contests for fiddle, banjo, guitar, band, and clogging. Afterward everyone would spread themselves around the baseball field picking. The two local heroes were George Pegram and Red Parham. Pegram played the clawhammer banjo and sang; Red played guitar and harmonica and sang. We stayed up picking with them 'til all hours while people clogged in the dirt around us.

During the day, Bill would sit on the bed in the hotel practicing new licks he'd picked up or dreamed up. He'd go over the same notes again and again and again. I'd lie there and think, "There. He's got it." Then he'd do it again. And again. Finally I'd get up and take a walk. There wasn't much to do. I could go to a little diner and have a piece of pie and a cup of coffee. Then I could go to the furniture store where they also sold records by people like Don Reno & Red Smiley, The Stanley Brothers, and Carl Story & The Rambling Mountaineers—things I'd never find in Boston. After a while I'd go back to the hotel. Coming down the corridor I'd hear Bill playing the same lick he'd been playing when I left. He was serious. Finally, we'd have a bite to eat and head back over to the school. On the last night we played until the last clogger clogged. At some point in the proceedings Red Parham borrowed my guitar and did a good job of carving up the back with his belt buckle while he danced around the infield. There might have been some moonshine involved. I was honored that he had put his mark on my guitar. At last we said our goodbyes, got into the car, and hit the road.

We were headed to Silver Springs, Maryland, just outside of Washington, to meet a man named Tom Morgan, who was going to make a banjo neck for Bill's new banjo. By 9 o'clock in the morning we were nearly to Washington when we heard a show being advertised for that afternoon in a place called Watermelon Park in Berryville, Virginia. The show included Bill Monroe, Don Reno & Red Smiley, Mac Wiseman, The Osborne Brothers, and Bill Harrell, among others. We found it on the map about sixty miles west of Washington and just turned the car around and headed there.

When we drove in, a small crowd of a few hundred people was gathering. For the most part they were country people who loved this kind of music. However, there was another group clustered near the front of the stage who had tape recorders with them. We recognized Mike Seeger from meeting him at Newport. The others were young college students like ourselves who were excited by this music. We joined them up front as close as we could get. The highlight of the afternoon came when Bill Monroe, Mac Wiseman, and Don Reno came out and recreated his 1948 band. Hearing them do "Sweetheart Of Mine, Can't You Hear Me Calling" just gave you chills all over. People told us that at the time Monroe didn't really have a regular band. Country music had moved on to a more modern sound, and he wasn't the big draw he had been in the forties and early fifties. Elvis, Rockabilly, and "The Nashville Sound" were making it hard for someone like Monroe to make a living. Be that as it may, the energy coming from him that afternoon was electrifying. He might not have realized it then, but he was singing to what was to become an important new audience for him. The power of his music could not be denied, and we were irresistibly drawn to it.

Excited as we were about music, Bill and I had to return to the academic world—he to Amherst for his final year, and I to an apartment in Boston with two Amherst classmates, John Richardson and Evan Hoorneman. I had been accepted at Harvard as a Classics graduate student and was lucky enough to win a Woodrow Wilson Fellowship. I was serious about my studies, kept my nose to the grindstone, and stayed away from the coffeehouses.

Early in the New Year, Manny Greenhill called to ask whether we'd like to play a concert at Dartmouth College in Hanover, New Hampshire, during their Winter Carnival. They'd pay us $100! I said, "My goodness! They've never even heard us!" "Do you want to do it or not?" he asked. So I said, "Of course." The other person on the show was Joan Baez. I hadn't seen Joan since I met her with Davy Gude, but I had heard that she'd caused quite a stir at Newport in '59 when she was introduced by the well-known Chicago folksinger Bob Gibson, and she was now singing regularly in Cambridge at the Club Mt. Auburn 47 Coffeehouse. Recently she had been part of an album called *Folk Singers 'Round Harvard Square*, so I was pleased that Manny thought enough of us to give us a shot at a real concert gig with someone as good as Joan.

Bill and I stayed outside of Hanover the night before with a banjo-playing friend of his, Sterling Klinck (a great name for a banjo player, it seemed to me). It started to snow, and by morning there was nearly a foot of snow on the ground. The concert was at ten-thirty in the morning. "Nobody's going to be at this thing," I said. "We'll be lucky to get there ourselves." We did make it, though.

Webster Hall at Dartmouth seated about one thousand people. We went downstairs to the dressing rooms under the stage where we couldn't see or hear the audience coming in and started tuning up and running over a couple of songs. Joan arrived, and we quickly decided to do "Banks of the Ohio" and "Bury Me beneath the Willow" together at the end of the concert. Bill and I made our way upstairs. To my amazement, the place was packed to the rafters. Out we went. They gave us a great reception and seemed to like us. We certainly thought we were wonderful. After a short break, Joan went out, and the roof absolutely went off the place. It was like that through her whole set. When we sang together at the end, there was no end to the shouting and applause. Up until now we had been pretty naive and hadn't quite copped to the fact that this "folk" music thing was really beginning to take off. I came away from this concert with a new understanding of this developing phenomenon that we had become part of.

That summer Bill and I returned to Asheville, where we were welcomed back by our many friends there and were even asked to play on a horse-drawn wagon in a parade through downtown Asheville. We had definitely arrived. By the end of the summer I had decided to give in and move to Cambridge. On my very first day there I was down in Harvard Square and ran into my old friend from the Golden Vanity, she of the loud mouth and short skirt, Betsy Minot. She was with her new husband Bob Siggins. Bob was a great character—a biochemist who played banjo in a group I'd heard of, the Charles River Valley Boys. As we were standing there, we were joined by Eric Von Schmidt, who I had seen play at the Ballad Room one time. He had a beard, a gold tooth, and a wild gravelly voice. He had knocked me out that night with a song called "Grizzly Bear" which seemed to sum him up perfectly. After Bob and Betsy introduced me to Eric he said, "I'm going to be showing some Charlie Chaplin films up at my apartment tonight. Come on over." That was the beginning of a long downhill slide in my academic career.

Bob and Betsy had just moved into an apartment on Camden Place. Before long Eric and his wife Helen moved in next door. Between the two places there were almost nightly gatherings. Eric was a few years older than us. He'd actually been to the Library of Congress and had many of Alan Lomax's recordings, as well as the Harry Smith Anthology of American Folk Music on Folkways Records. We were listening to people like Clarence Ashley sing "The Cuckoo Bird," Dock Boggs doing "Oh Death," Mississippi John Hurt playing "Candy Man," and the Carter Family sing "Foggy Mountain Top." Inevitably, a picking session would develop. Eric had a vast repertoire that included all sorts of Leadbelly songs, cowboy songs, ballads, and Lomax prison work songs—all sung with great intensity and emotion. He was more than happy to share this music and was a great source of material for a lot of people, including Joan Baez and, eventually, Bob Dylan, who on his first album acknowledged learning "Baby Let Me Follow You Down" from Eric "in the green pastures of Harvard University."

Eric and Rolf Cahn had by this time been playing regularly at the Club Mt. Auburn 47 for a year or more, as had Joan Baez, who had just moved to California with her family. Because of them, the Club was becoming more and more oriented to folk music. The Charles River Valley Boys were starting to play there as well, and I had hopes that Bill Keith and I could too. On Mondays the girls running the Club, Paula Kelly and Joyce Kalina, started putting on a series of hootenannies in support of the

Committee for a Sane Nuclear Policy called "Sing Out for Sane." I signed Bill and me up to do one of these purely as a way of getting our foot in the door. However, my plan was to be thwarted by the Cambridge police.

When the police looked at the Club they saw a den of iniquity, full of beatniks, pinkos, and subversives, all dressed in black, smoking foreign cigarettes (and who knows what else). Now with "Sing Out For Sane" the girls running the Club were going too far. Possibly there might have been another unstated problem—they weren't "taking care" of the guys on the beat. One night I came down to the hoot only to find a crowd milling around in front of the Club. It had been raided. The police came in and found a guy with a bottle of liquor on him, so they closed it down. Everyone was outraged. If the police thought we would all just go away, they were in for a big surprise. Suddenly the "folk community" came together. A committee was formed, benefits were held, and everyone seemed to be energized by the fight. Our debut at the Club was going to have to wait.

Bill was now in an Air Force Reserve unit stationed in Boston and had moved in with John Richardson and me. Through Manny Greenhill we got some little gigs at Radcliffe College and the Folksong Society of Greater Boston. After our "triumph" at Dartmouth, he had taken the time to write a detailed letter critiquing our performance. His belief in us made us want to get better, and we teamed up with a washtub bass player named Fritz Richmond. The tub had a wire cable on it, but Fritz wore a welder's glove with nickels taped into the fingers, so he had a real sound. He also had great time and a wonderful laid-back style. There was always a beatific smile on his face; he glowed from the inside. His solid foundation made a big difference in our music.

Occasionally we would make a weekend trip to New York to hang out with all the pickers down there. On arrival we would inevitably head for Izzy Young's Folklore Center on Bleeker Street. Izzy was one of those larger-than-life people—full of energy, absolutely committed to folk music as a force for social change. The front of the store had records, songbooks, and instruction books. Izzy had a cramped, crowded office at the back where he would hold court with anyone who happened to come in. Bill and I quickly figured out that if we hung around Izzy's long enough someone we knew—or wanted to know—would come in, and one thing would lead to another. One day there was this kid in the back hunched over Izzy's typewriter, typing furiously. Eventually he took a break, and Izzy introduced me to Bob Dylan. After a while we made our way to a bar called The Dugout, next to The Bitter End, which was the most "professional" folk club in the Village. Bob and I hit it off. Over a few beers we discovered a mutual love for Hank Williams. Theo Bikel was running a hootenanny next door, so we decided to go in and sign up. We were told that the list was full, so we just found a place in the hallway leading back to the kitchen and sang some Hank Williams songs to each other. Probably one of the last times Bob couldn't get in a door!

At one of the little concerts Bill and I did at the Community Church in Boston two guys came up to us afterward and introduced themselves. I recognized one of them from the *Hayloft Jamboree*. He was Joe Val. His friend was named Herb Applin. Joe played mandolin and was really into Bill Monroe's style of singing. Herb played fiddle and guitar and also sang tenor. We started getting together, and suddenly we had a full bluegrass band. We could now work up trios and quartets. Bill had a great ear for harmony, so he could show me baritone parts to sing under Joe and Herb. A whole new repertoire of instrumentals associated with Bill Monroe came into our lives. There was no end to it.

Bill Keith had learned "The Devil's Dream" and "The Sailor's Hornpipe" from a friend named June Hall, who was originally from Nova Scotia. His desire to play the melody notes on the banjo just as they were on the fiddle led him into a chromatic approach that was to revolutionize banjo playing. At the same time he was learning all of Earl Scruggs instrumentals and solos by slowing them down on the record player. As he did so he was starting to figure out a form of written tablature, which would accurately describe how to play each note. You could say it was a total immersion experience.

With all of this going on, it might be hard to believe that I still had an academic career, but I did. Harvard had granted me a teaching fellowship. I was what they call a "section man" in a big freshman Humanities course. The fall semester covered epic poetry, from "The Iliad" to "Paradise Lost." There were two lectures a week by an elegant, charismatic teacher named John Finley. Finley was brilliant at bringing out the truly epic and heroic elements of these poems. The spring semester was taught by an equally charismatic man, William Alfred. Bill Alfred was as rumpled as Finley was elegant. He himself was a playwright (soon to bring out his celebrated "Hogan's Goat.") We started with Aeschylus and wound up with Beckett. In every play Bill would uncover the simple human traits in us all that could lead to disaster or success, tears or laughter, tragedy or comedy. It was my role as a section man to take two groups of about twenty students through a closer examination of what we were reading and to do my best to loosen up the emotions of these young people, many of whom had wound up at Harvard to satisfy their parents' dreams and wishes, but who had not, with a few exceptions, been allowed to spend much time listening to their hearts and expressing their own thoughts and desires. I felt so fortunate that music and song had been helping me do that now for the past ten years, and I was still only beginning.

Early in 1962, the Club 47 reopened. A lawyer named Gerry Gillerman had taken the case pro bono and made mincemeat out of the police case. In his summation he made Harvard seem like a poor second to the Club in the cultural life of Cambridge and the case was thrown out of court. Everyone cheered. Then reality set in. Paula and Joyce decided to move on with their lives, so a board was formed including Manny Greenhill, Betsy Siggins, Victor Oppenheimer, Fred Greenman, and others. The first order of business was to find someone to run the place. Victor came up with the name of Byron Linardos. What a fortunate choice! Byron was a Greek-American townie who had grown up about eight blocks away. He knew how to run a coffeehouse and how to make money out of coffee, tea, and flavored soda water. He also was passionate about life and the arts. He cared. If he was going to be involved in the place he would work as hard as he could to make it THE BEST. And that's what he did.

Every night there would be someone different playing. Tom Rush would be on a Tuesday night, Jim Kweskin on Wednesday, Bill Keith and me on Thursday, The Charles River Valley Boys on Friday, Jackie Washington on Saturday. It was a little thin at first, but after a month or so the business started coming back, and by late spring there were lines down the street.

That summer Bill and I went away for the first time to play other clubs. We first went to the Café Lena in Saratoga Springs, N.Y., which was run by a great mother of a woman, Lena Spencer. Lena's encouragement made us feel that we were now a part of the traveling folk music community. While Lena's was similar to the Club 47 in atmosphere, our next stop was a place called The Purple Onion in Toronto, which was more like a night

FIGURE 3. Keith & Rooney at the Club 47, 1962 (*l. to r.*: Fritz Richmond, Jim Rooney, Herb Applin, Joe Val, Bill Keith).

club. It was in Toronto's version of Greenwich Village and served liquor. The audience was expecting a professional performance. In keeping with that we were also getting paid more than we were used to making. Accommodation was provided upstairs in a small room with a large bed (for the two of us) next to a guy's room who loved to play Jimmy Smith's organ trio records half the night. We didn't care. We were playing a real gig in a big city. We also got to meet the Toronto folkies—Ian & Sylvia, John Wynne, and Gordon Lightfoot. Bill and I were expanding our horizons.

Although there had been no folk festivals at Newport for a couple of years due to a "riot" at the Jazz Festival, a folk festival had started near Philadelphia, so we went to that in early September. They had a banjo contest, which Bill entered and won playing "The Devil's Dream." The prize was a new banjo and a spot on the main stage, along with people like Ramblin' Jack Elliott and Bonnie Dobson, so on we went. I sang a couple, and Bill did his contest winner. There was no money involved, but a lot of pride. The show was recorded and eventually was released on Prestige Records, titled *Hootenanny*, so this was our recording debut. Pretty exciting stuff!

At the end of August we moved to an apartment near Porter Square. One side benefit of our move was that it put me just a few blocks away from where a girl named Carol Langstaff lived. One night that summer I had gone to the Club, and on stage sat a girl singing and playing a mountain dulcimer. Her head was bent and her long blonde hair fell over her shoulders. Her singing was clear and seemed to float on the air. A very fine web settled around me and held me captive. Carol lived nearby with a woman named Nancy Sweezy and her family, so I now became a regular visitor to what Eric Von Schmidt and I came to call "the house of beautiful women"—Carol, Nancy, and her two daughters Lybess and Moophie. Ralph Rinzler brought Doc Watson up to play at the Club and Nancy's house became his home away from home and the scene of many amazing picking parties. Carol was going to the Longy Music School and had lots of young men seeking her company. I took her to Green Harbor for long walks in the autumn mist. She showed me how to make a hot whiskey while we listened to the Irish music of the Clancy Brothers and Tommy Makem, who had been brought together by her mother, the music collector Diane Hamilton. Carol had a spunky side, which would come out in a snowball fight. Her nickname was "Sunshine," and she definitely brightened things up wherever she was. However, there was a virginal aura about her that was beyond me at the time. Perhaps I was too shy and didn't want to burst that illusion. I eventually gave up the pursuit in favor of a beautiful and more accessible waitress at the Club named Rachel, but there was something about Carol that I wouldn't forget.

Another major source of excitement that fall was the fact that we were going to make a record. A fellow named Paul Rothchild, who worked at a record store and was a hi-fi enthusiast, had started coming to the Club and quickly sensed that something special was going on there and got the idea to record it. He made a proposal to the Club board that they start a little record label—Mt. Auburn 47 Records. After the Charles River Valley Boys, Bill Keith and I were next on Paul's list.

In late October we went into Boston to record. The recording engineer was Steve Fassett, a very thorough and patient man, who primarily recorded classical music and had very good microphones and recording equipment. We were in the library of a house owned by Harvard on Beacon Hill that was lined with books two stories high and had beautiful wood parquet floors. Paul and Steve installed a large Ampex recording machine in a small room and set us up in the library in sort of a circle. For the recording we had hired a fiddler named Herb Hooven, who was originally from North Carolina. He had played fiddle on Jimmy Martin's *Good 'n' Country* album, so he was really good. Herb Applin played second acoustic guitar, which he played in a more standard bluegrass style than I did. So there were six of us—the two Herbs, Joe, Fritz, Bill and me.

We recorded seven or eight songs the first Saturday, with Joe and me splitting the lead vocals. All of our playing and practicing together really paid off, and we were able to do everything live. There were no edits. We knew our harmonies and who was going to play what when. If someone made a big mistake, we just did the song again. We came back two or three weeks later, just Bill, Fritz, and me and did some of our folkier songs like "Kentucky Moonshiner," on which Bill played lead acoustic guitar, and "One Morning in May," on which he played autoharp. Most importantly, we recorded "Devil's Dream" and "Sailor's Hornpipe" as one piece. Bill was flawless. It turned out to be a historic recording, because it was the first time Bill's chromatic approach was fully documented. Of course, this was also the first time that Joe Val recorded, and his singing was absolutely thrilling. As for myself, whatever I lacked in terms of finesse or my singing abilities, I made up for with something else—an ability to convey the spirit of the music, which is what people seemed to respond to.

After the recording was finished, Bill got a call from Tom Morgan telling him that Red Allen and Frank Wakefield were looking for a banjo player. Red was a great singer who had made one of our favorite albums with the Osborne Brothers. Frank was an astoundingly creative mandolin player. They were on the WWVA *Wheeling Jamboree*, so this was an opportunity for Bill to get into the "real" Bluegrass world. Since our album was finished and there was a lull in our action, he decided to take it.

Meanwhile, I was trying to move the record album along. Paul Rothchild seemed to be having trouble paying Herb Hooven the $50 we had promised him and got huffy when I called him about it. While I was at it, I checked with Eric Von Schmidt about the cover art. He was waiting for Paul to bring him some pictures of us that Byron had taken. That night I went down to the Club and found Paul sitting at the front desk. I said, "I'm just going to get those pictures from Byron and bring them over to Eric to help move things along." Eric was doing lots of collages for a Joan Baez songbook and there was paper all over his studio. I cleared a place for myself and sat down. Eric offered me some rum and I was telling him my troubles with Paul when we heard some footsteps coming up the stairs. It was Paul! He said, "Jim, this is the second time today you've interfered in my business"—blah, blah, blah. Paul wasn't too big and the next thing I knew Eric had picked him up by the collar and threw him into a big pile of paper and turpentine rags. I shouted, "Eric! Eric! Eric!" as I saw our record deal going out the window! Paul picked himself up, smoothed his ruffled feathers and retreated down the stairs. Now we really had a reason to drink.

So that was that for a long time. The whole label project with the Club ground to a halt, but there was a happy ending. Bob Weinstock from Prestige Records in New York came to visit Manny Greenhill. Prestige had been a jazz label, but they had just recently ventured into folk music with people like Ramblin' Jack Elliott and Dave Van Ronk. Manny got Paul over to his office to play Weinstock the Charles River Valley Boys record and our tape. The next thing we knew, Paul had a job as an A & R (Artists & Repertoire) director for Prestige records and was on his way to New York! Our record would come out on Prestige. All's well that ends well. Within the year Paul recorded Tom Rush, Jim Kweskin, and Geoff Muldaur—even Eric Von Schmidt, just to show there were no hard feelings!

As a result of putting Joan Baez on some concerts with Flatt & Scruggs, Manny Greenhill had established a good relationship with Louise and Earl Scruggs. Earl had been working on a banjo instruction book. Manny knew that Bill Keith had come up with a tablature system and arranged for Bill to meet Earl at a show they were doing in Baltimore. After Bill demonstrated the system to Earl, he was impressed and asked Bill if he could come down to Nashville to work on the instruction book with him. Earl Scruggs was Bill's idol. He didn't have to think about it. Once in Nashville, Earl brought Bill to the Grand Ole Opry. At some point Bill joined a jam session backstage and played "The Devil's Dream" and "The Sailor's Hornpipe." Jaws were dropping. One of them belonged to Bill Monroe! A while later he sent his fiddle player Kenny Baker back to Bill Keith. He said, "If you ever want a job with Bill Monroe, you've got it." So Bill finished his work on Earl's book, wrapped things up with Red and Frank and went to join the Bluegrass Boys.

Meanwhile, I was in for a big surprise myself. Back in the fall I had applied for a Fulbright Fellowship to go to Greece. I didn't really give myself much of a chance to get it, but I applied anyway. When I went in for the interview with three professors from Harvard, I was pretty honest and said, "I've been studying this stuff for eight or nine years, and I think I should go there and see what the place is like." I guess they agreed with me, because, much to my surprise, I got a letter informing me that I was going to be a Fulbright Fellow and would be going to the American School of Classical Studies in Athens! So Bill Keith was going off to Nashville to play with Bill Monroe and The Bluegrass Boys, and I was going off to Athens.

Before I went to Greece I took a trip with Geoff Muldaur and Robert L. Jones, two of the regulars from the Club. They were headed on a pilgrimage to Blind Lemon Jefferson's grave, and I went with them as far as Nashville to visit Bill, who was sharing an apartment with Ralph Rinzler and Del McCoury. Ralph was trying to manage Bill Monroe, and Del was playing guitar and singing lead in the Bluegrass Boys. The day after we arrived we were all sitting around and who should pull into the yard but the man himself, Bill Monroe! Bill came in with his longtime partner, Bessie Mauldin. Bessie was a substantial woman with platinum blonde hair piled on top of her head. She'd brought some mayonnaise that she'd made for the troops. My guitar was out, lying on a couch. Bill Monroe sat down, picked up the guitar, got out a flat pick and started playing on it. He looked up and said, "Whose guitar is this?" I said, "It's mine." He immediately handed it to me and said, "Why don't you play something?" "Oh my God! Oh my God!" I thought. There was nothing to do, but do it, so I put on my thumbpick, picked up the guitar upside down and backward and did "Reuben's Train." I was too nervous to think. When I got through, he said, "You've got a good lick there. Don't change it." A great moment in my life.

Naturally, I was very excited to finally be in Nashville and to start to soak up the atmosphere surrounding the Grand Ole Opry at the Ryman Auditorium. Tagging along with Bill and the Bluegrass Boys backstage I'd be running into the likes of Hank Snow, Ernest Tubb, Porter Wagoner, Loretta Lynn. It was all so down to earth. Everyone seemed to be in a good mood, joking, laughing, visiting—truly a huge family. In addition to the music on stage, there were continuous jam sessions in the two small dressing rooms backstage and across the alley in back where Roy Acuff had his own separate jamming headquarters. Bill Keith had made quite an impression on the Bluegrass contingent and was a welcome addition to sessions with the Osborne Brothers and Jim and Jesse. Earl Scruggs invited us out to the taping of their weekly TV series. Of course, getting a chance to hear Bill Monroe repeatedly at the Opry or at his outdoor park in Beanblossom, Indiana, was thrilling every single time.

One week Bill and I drove over to North Carolina to visit Doc Watson. Doc had been up to play at the Club a few times. Being the musician that he was, Doc appreciated what Bill Keith was doing on the banjo. In the course of his visits to Cambridge, we had become friends, and he had extended an open invitation to visit him at his home in Deep Gap, so we took him up on it. We were reminded of our trips to Byard Ray's. The hospitality and warmth of welcome were the same. Songs and tunes flowed well into the night.

The next day, we went with Doc over to Asheville, where he was to play a concert at the Municipal Auditorium with Pete Seeger. The front page of the local paper featured a lead story about the local American Legion protesting the appearance of the "Communist" Pete Seeger. We could see that there was still some life left in the "red scare," but it didn't seem to scare off the audience. Doc had already become a totally relaxed concert performer. He was the same on stage as on his front porch. His warmth and casual demeanor just served to further highlight his virtuosity on the guitar. He would take your breath away. Needless to say, he got a huge ovation at the end of his set. Then it was Pete's turn. He came out with his longnecked banjo, sleeves rolled up, red socks. His reception was on the cool side, especially in contrast to Doc's. Pete was in no hurry. He played a couple of mountain tunes on the banjo, did a couple of Woody Guthrie songs, got the audience to join him singing "Rock Island Line." Gradually he drew them in until, at the close of his set, he introduced a song he had picked up from a singer named Guy Carawan at a place called The Highlander School in East Tennessee. The song was "We Shall Overcome." Pete started quietly, inviting the audience to join him. Gradually people joined in. He kept encouraging them, finally urging them to get on their feet and join hands. Before long everyone was up, singing, swaying, singing "We Shall Overcome." Indeed, Pete had overcome. With music. I never forgot that performance.

After my sojourn in Nashville I headed for Newport. There had been a two-year hiatus, and this time around George Wein enlisted the help of Pete Seeger to create a nonprofit foundation for the promotion of folk music. That festival gave many of us our first chance to hear in person some of the great older traditional musicians, many of whom had recorded in the twenties and thirties and were now being rediscovered by collectors like Alan Lomax, Mike Seeger, Ralph Rinzler, John Cohen, and others. Hearing and seeing people like Mississippi John Hurt, Roscoe Holcomb, Hobart Smith, Clarence Ashley, and Dock Boggs for the first time was very inspiring. The connections deepened when many of these musicians came to the Club to play. We opened our houses and our hearts to them. There was definitely the feeling that we were privileged to listen and learn from them in person and that a torch was being passed from one generation to another.

After the festival I went back to Cambridge for a short time before heading off to Greece. For some time I had been a member of the Board of Directors of the Club 47. We had come to the conclusion that our storefront space at 47 Mt. Auburn was too small, and we had started looking around for an alternative. One option was an old building just off of Harvard Square. The basement was entirely unfinished, with walls of brick and granite and a dirt floor, so the space could be put together any way we wanted. The rent was $750/month, which was pretty rich for us, but we all decided to take the leap. Nancy Sweezy was now a member of the board. She was a first-class potter and had a good sense of design, so it was left to Nancy and Byron to design the space. I hated to leave just as this exciting new plan was hatching, but I had all the confidence in the world that they would put together something special and lasting. I couldn't have known then how special and how lasting it was to be.

THE LIGHT OF GREECE

The American School of Classical Studies in Athens had a program for graduate students, and we spent the first part of the year going around to various archaeological sites with our guide, Eugene Vanderpool. He knew every inch of the country and every bit of its history from the earliest sacrificial sites on the tops of mountains to the fountain in a town square donated by the Greek-American community of some town in Pennsylvania. Each of us would give a paper to the group about some archaeological site, some battle, some historical event. In the process we covered great swaths of the countryside on foot and got a feel for the life of the people wherever we went.

I totally immersed myself in the program and gave little thought to the music scene I'd left back home. I was right when I'd told those professors interviewing me that I actually needed to see the light, the shape of the land, to get into the everyday life of the Greeks themselves. I was getting much more of a feeling for the real depth of the history of the place and of what an achievement it had been for the Greeks to bring their own wildness under control and give us the art, the theater, the poetry, the architecture, the philosophy that was so original and that I found so compelling.

As we got into the rhythm of our trips, I found some kindred spirits who liked to go exploring and sampling the food and drink wherever we were. One time we pulled into the village of Mycenae, the seat of the Mycenaean civilization. The Homeric poems were about these people. In its time Mycenae had been the site of a huge palace and had been an imposing, impressive place. The modern village, however, was not. There was a small hotel where we were all going to be staying. Across the street was one café and down the road was another one. That was it.

A few of us went across to the café for an ouzo or two. When we came back to the hotel for dinner, there was a carafe of retsina on each table. Once through the meal, it only made sense to go see what was going on at the other café down the road. There wasn't a soul in there, but at the sight of half a dozen young Americans coming through the door, the woman of the place had a 45 record player on the counter in about a minute, along with a bottle of Metaxa brandy to go with it. The very first song was Pat Boone singing "Speedy Gonzales," which she thought would be right up our alley. So off we went. The bottle of Metaxa was bottomless. Eventually, we got her to play some Greek music, so up we got, doing the Greek dances with the handkerchiefs and everything—circling and circling and circling. Eventually I circled out the door. I couldn't stop circling, so I sat down in the road. I could see the hotel light at the end of the road. There was only one solution. I crawled down the road, up the steps of the hotel, through the little lobby, up the stairs, down the hall to my room where I collapsed on the bed. I wasn't dreaming of Helen of Troy that night.

My revels were to come to an abrupt halt in the town of Megalopolis. I was in a café having my morning yogurt and coffee. There was a radio on. It was in English—probably the Armed Forces Radio—and they were talking about some American Senator or other, but I wasn't paying any attention. I went to a kiosk to stock up on my daily supply of biscuits and chocolate before we went on our archaeological exploration. The woman in the kiosk asked me in Greek if I was an American and started to tell me how sorry she was, what a tragedy it was. I had no idea what she was talking about, so I thanked her and went back to the hotel. I found the rest of the group in the lobby gathered around a radio. President Kennedy had been shot, but was still alive as far as anyone knew. The breath went out of me.

Gene Vanderpool decided that there was nothing we could do about it, so we carried on. That night we wound up in the tiny village of Andritzena in the middle of the mountains. As we got off the bus a crowd of villagers gathered around us asking us, "Why? Why? Why did they kill him?" We had no answer. What could we say? We knew as little as they did. It was an awful moment. Still we carried on. The next morning we were up before dawn to hike to the temple at Bassae. It was as good a place as any to be—a sacred place at dawn, surrounded by the timeless mountains of Greece. It took us out of ourselves. As the days passed I would get the papers and try to piece together what had happened. I was reading about Oswald, Cuba, Communists, Jack Ruby, the Mafia, Striptease. I was saying to myself, "This is way over the top. You just can't believe anything you read in these Greek papers." Of course, when we finally got back to Athens, I waded through a stack of *Herald-Tribune*s only to find out that it was all true!

As I took it all in, I felt extremely isolated and far from home, alone and on my own. After a couple of weeks I wrote my parents:

"What has really come home to me here is one of the most fundamental aspects of Greek life, and that is action. They weren't passive. They weren't observers. They participated and applied their minds to the world around them. They took material and worked it into something true and lasting. One has to be true to oneself, and I know when I'm engaged and when I'm not. I'm engaged when I'm in a classroom. I'm engaged when I'm singing. I'm engaged when I'm working with people, trying to solve some problem, the significance of which I can feel is immediate and important—whether it is the lesson for a freshman in Harvard; or the planning of a room that will be suitable for folk music, art displays, and eating."

If I'd stayed the academic course, I could see myself becoming an alcoholic teacher in a small college somewhere. I wasn't brilliant and couldn't write my own ticket in the academic world. I needed to follow my heart, which was leading me more and more into a life of action, involving music and helping to give direction to the new Club 47.

Whatever I did, my years studying Greek culture were not a waste. The Homeric poems were in me; the Socratic dialogues were in me; Thucydides history was in me; the plays of Aeschylus were in me. To say that the study of Classics was good for only one thing and that was to enable you to teach Classics was too limiting. It seemed to me that such a study would inform anything I chose to do. My Dad was well educated and read books all his life. He was in the construction business, and his love of learning didn't make the buildings he built any better, but the people he worked with understood that there was a depth of character in him that set him apart. I wanted to emulate him. Kennedy's death was a vivid reminder that life can be shorter than you think, and if you're not doing what you want to do in your heart, it's just a big mistake. You have to live the life that's truly inside you, not some life that is pleasing to other people, including your parents.

Over Christmas I took the train up to Munich to visit my brother John and his wife Ulli, who were both studying at the Art Academy of Munich. Bill Keith joined me there, having recently finished his stint with Bill Monroe. I bought a little VW bug for $350, and Bill and I journeyed down through Yugoslavia, giving Bill a chance to practice his wheelies on the icy main road through the middle of the country. We made it to Athens in one piece. I took Bill up to Delphi to show him the sights. It was an amazing place, the site of the Delphic oracle, whose power was made visible by the countless temples and votive statues erected by the Greek city-states seeking to stay on the good side of the oracular powers. On our way out of Delphi we spotted a tall girl in an orange coat hitchhiking and gave her a lift. Her name was Anne Waldman. She was going to Bennington College and was a friend of John Hammond's, the intense young blues singer who had been up to the Club a couple of times. She was going to be spending the semester in Athens and was up to do some exploring with me.

Musically, I was on my own. Every so often Bill Keith would send me a tape with all sorts of music on it, including some wild, bluesy, jug band sounding stuff by Koerner, Ray & Glover. Spider John Koerner's brilliantly original versions of "Frankie and Johnny" and "Duncan and Brady" floored me and made me want to get out my guitar and do some singing myself. I had acquired a harmonica with a neck rack like Bob Dylan played, so I could be a bit of a one-man band. A friend of Anne's knew some people at the Hellenic-American Union, and they asked if I'd like to do a concert. I was a little nervous, but everyone seemed to love it. Encouraged by their enthusiasm, I went in to the Fulbright office and asked to meet the man who organized "cultural" events, Darryll Dayton. I think Darryll had been a concert performer himself at one time. He had silver hair swept back perhaps to give a bit of the Toscanini look. He listened to me politely. I just asked if he could organize a few concerts for me around the country. I didn't want any money, just my expenses. When I was finished, Darryll leaned back in his chair and let out a sigh. "Jim, I don't think it's a good time to do this. There's a lot of anti-Americanism out there. There are elections going on. We don't know which way things are going to go. It's just not a good time."

It was news to me—all the anti-Americanism "out there." Against the advice of the Embassy, Anne and I had gone to several political rallies—the Communists, the Socialists, the Conservatives. We definitely stood out in a crowd, and people were always coming up to us and telling us about their relatives in Boston or Queens and asking us how we liked Greece. When we would tell them how much we loved Greece and the Greek food and music, we got nothing back but smiles and wishes for good luck. Whenever I had gotten my guitar out and sung a few songs, people would crowd around and ask for more. Darryll's response had just confirmed me in my belief that the Embassy people were totally out of touch with what was going on in the country. I had occasionally attended parties for Fulbright people, which were always out in the most expensive suburb of Athens where they all lived behind walls in houses with maids and gardeners, where the talk was all about the new Hilton Hotel and how great it was to finally have a place to go where you could get a good burger.

I wasn't totally surprised a few years later when a group of Greek Army colonels ousted the democratically elected Socialist government whose policy was to chart a course more independent of America. So much for all that talk about Greece being "the cradle of democracy." If the cradle didn't rock the way we wanted it to, it would be blown out of the tree.

Anne and I spent several weekends revisiting places I'd been in the fall. She was a good traveling companion, and it was an opportunity to share some of what I had absorbed and dig deeper into what Greece had to offer. All too soon she had to return to Bennington, and I decided to go back to Delphi for Easter. Easter is the major religious holiday in Greece. The whole concept of resurrection is deep in their culture, predating Christian times. The service had already been going for a couple of hours on Saturday night before I arrived. The church was filling up as midnight approached. The combination of the chanting and the incense cast a spell over everyone. Suddenly, all lights were shut off. A single candle was lit, which, in turn, was used to light another and another until the church was filled with candlelight. As each candle was lit, one person would say to another, "Christos anesti!" (Christ is risen!), and the other would reply, "Alethios, Christos anesti!" (Truly, Christ is risen!). Finally the priests and the choir would chant, "Christos anesti!" together with the congregation. The lights came back on. Outside, fireworks were set off. As people streamed out of the church you could see young boys and men hurrying through the darkness, each with a newly slaughtered lamb on their shoulder. By morning each family would have a lamb roasting in front of their house or apartment. The communal ovens were thronged with people bringing their moussaka and various other casseroles to be baked. Up and down the hillsides trees were in blossom. There was no way you could escape the feeling of rebirth and renewal. The feeling brought me back to the conclusion of Aeschylus's great trilogy the Oresteia where the ancient spirits of revenge The Erynys (The Furies) are transformed into the Eumenides (Spirits of Well-being). Over the ages the Greeks had confronted the harshness of life and the darkness in the human soul and had repeatedly affirmed the light and the potential for goodness—even greatness—in each of us. Maybe this is why I needed to come to Greece, to experience this for myself and to learn to trust my heart to lead me toward the light.

IRELAND OF THE WELCOMES

Before leaving Greece, I was visited by Ethan Signer. Ethan had played mandolin in the Charles River Valley Boys and was now studying biochemistry in Cambridge, England. He had just returned from a trip to Ireland with Bill Clifton, an American bluegrass singer who was living in England at the time. A woman named Peggi Jordan had organized some gigs for them in Ireland. Ethan suggested that she could possibly do the same for us later that summer. That sounded good to me, so he said he'd contact her and get something organized.

After leaving Greece I visited John and Ulli in Munich for a few days, and headed for England to meet up with Ethan at the ferry in Holyhead. Once in Dublin, the plan was to meet Peggi Jordan at O'Donoghue's pub near St. Stephen's Green in the center of town. Naturally, while we were waiting for Peggi to arrive, we had to have some pints of Guinness. Two or three hours passed, and still no Peggi. By then we were overhearing a plot being hatched to liberate either the Inner or Outer Hebrides from their Protestant English rulers! These people were going to hire a plane and liberate them! My first hours in Ireland, and I was already in the thick of things!

Peggi finally arrived like a whirlwind. While we had a bite to eat, Peggi said that she had three or four pub gigs lined up. Nothing big, but we'd be able to make a few pounds. Suddenly she jumped up and told us we needed to head over to this hotel because Dominic Behan (Brendan's brother) was having a party there to celebrate the opening of a play of his. There was quite a crowd, but Peggi had no trouble bringing us right into the center of the action. There was Dominic Behan ordering pints by the tabletop! This was the serious heart of Dublin. I'd seen Brendan Behan do a reading at MIT. He was wild enough, but this was the real thing here. It wasn't a stage show. We managed to get out of there after midnight, but Peggi wasn't done. "We're off to a session!" We piled into her VW and wound up in a small hall on one of Dublin's back streets. Although it was one in the morning, the place was jammed, and there was a great session going on—fiddles and flutes. Until then, my only experience with Irish music had been hearing my father sing "The Wearin' of the Green" or the Clancy Brothers and Tommy Makem singing ballads and drinking songs. I knew nothing about tunes. There seemed to be no end to them. One player would start off, and immediately the others would join in. The sound of all those fiddles and flutes playing together had the same mesmerizing effect as some of the old-time fiddling I had heard at Galax. They played set after set of jigs or reels, urged on by the shouts of the people crowded around them, until the session finally wound down. For the first time I heard the expression, "That was mighty! A mighty session!" from a man next to me in the outside toilet. The perfect word to sum it all up—Mighty!

Finally, we were headed back to Peggi's house, when the motor began to splutter. We were out of gas! There was nothing to do but to abandon the car there, take all our stuff and walk the last couple of miles. We climbed the front steps up to the front door of this beautiful old Georgian house and were let in by Peggi's son James, who was about sixteen. He was up and had a big pot of soup on the stove, along with tea, bread, and butter on the table. Everything was ready for us. As I was to find out, this was not an unusual night in this house. I had been welcomed into Peggi Jordan's world. So ended my first day in Ireland!

I stayed with the Jordans for three weeks. Peggi's husband Tom was a civil servant in the post office, as quiet as she was voluble. In addition to James, there was Mary, Louise, and Iseult ("Weeds" and "Thistles"), so it was a full and busy house. Peggi had become very involved in the folk music revival and had organized a series of late night music sessions at a cinema on Grafton Street in Dublin, which eventually gave rise to the formation of The Dubliners. She had also put on Pete Seeger in a concert and was very helpful in setting up little gigs for traveling American musicians like ourselves. She reminded me a bit of Betsy Siggins. She had lots of energy, was not afraid to speak her mind, liked to have fun, and served as a catalyst for this rapidly developing folk music scene. The pub gigs she organized for Ethan and me were full, and people responded immediately to our bluegrass and old-timey music. We were also meeting the local singers and musicians, and after the pub closed we'd fill our pockets with bottles, head for somebody's house, and carry on.

As it happened, my brother John had sold his first painting to an Irishman named Billy O'Sullivan, who was the curator of manuscripts at Trinity College. So John arrived to personally deliver the painting. Billy very generously opened up the Book of Kells for us, turning the pages himself.

FIGURE 4. Peggi Jordan in her element, having a good laugh
with fiddler Denis Murphy and piper Seamus Ennis.
Photograph courtesy of Edai Ni Dhomhnaill.

I had studied manuscripts a bit at Harvard, and to see this book in the flesh, as it were, was very moving. One Sunday Billy also took us out to Newgrange, which was in the process of being excavated. We later looked at some of the gold artifacts from the excavation in the National Museum. They could have been mistaken for Mycenaean. I was beginning to get a feel for the depth of Irish history and was as excited by it as I had been in Greece.

The musical side of things was exciting as well. Peggi took us to a "fleadh ceol" (music festival) at Scarriff in east County Clare. I wound up staying in a farmhouse about a mile out of town and slept in a bed with someone I never saw! He was gone in the morning when I woke up and well asleep by the time I got home, climbing over the gate and sneaking past the dog. Scarriff was basically a one-street village, with a few shops and pubs. There were impromptu sessions in every house, every pub, out in the street, everywhere. Willie Clancy, the great Clare piper was there, sitting on a bench in front of a shop, playing away. I'd heard my neighbor Peter Thompson's parents playing the Scottish pipes in Dedham, but these pipes sounded totally different. There was nothing at all martial about them. The piper sat down, keeping the air flowing to the chanter by pumping a bellows strapped to his arm. It was a bit of a Rube Goldberg contraption, but the tunes coming out of it were soulful, beautiful and dancy. I could tell I was in the presence of a master. Barney

McKenna and Sean Sheehan of The Dubliners had no trouble gathering a crowd wherever they stopped to play a few tunes on fiddle and banjo. I'd never heard anything like Barney's banjo playing. He played a 4-string tenor banjo with a plectrum at a speed that would challenge the best Scruggs-style banjo player. The tunes seemed to pour out of them as they played in total sync.

At one point Ethan and I were in the corner of a good-sized pub in the middle of the afternoon, playing a few songs by ourselves. All of a sudden a big crowd of people came in, following Liam Clancy and the great singer from Connemara, Joe Heaney. Joe would sing a song in Irish while Liam held tight to his hand, urging him on. Then Liam would sing the song in English. It was absolutely electric. People were standing on chairs to get a look in. Seeing Liam like this with Joe gave me an idea of the true depth of the song tradition in Ireland. It seemed to come up out of the earth itself.

Back in Dublin at last, I spent a final Sunday at Peggi's. My brother was heading back to Germany, so we met one last time on Stephen's Green. After he left I hooked up with Barney and Sean, and we took a ride up to a pub in the Wicklow Mountains outside of Dublin. It was here that I first heard the rich deep voice of Ronnie Drew, another member of The Dubliners. This was pure Dublin singing that could almost bruise you with its honesty and humor. It was no easy job getting back to Peggi's that night, but somehow I managed it. I didn't want to wake anyone in the house just yet, so I camped out under a big bush by the stairs with a piece of the Sunday paper I'd been carrying around with me all day long. I used it for a pillow while I dozed away. When it got light enough I sat up and was sitting there reading the paper when a door under the front steps opened and out stepped an old man with a white beard. I'd been sleeping in a room in the basement for three weeks and had never seen him, so I was definitely surprised when he emerged. He said, "Good morning." I said, "Good morning. It's a lovely morning, isn't it?" He then asked, "Are you an American?" I answered, "Yes, I am." Then he said, "Do you know the Song of Hiawatha?" I replied, "By the shores of Gitche Gumee? That one?" "Yes, that's the one," said my friend. "I'm sorry to say that I don't." No problem. He did, and he proceeded to recite the whole poem to me on the spot! I could see past him. There were piles of newspapers and stuff in there. He asked if I'd like to come in, but I got to my feet and said, "I think James will probably be up by now, so I'll go upstairs. Thanks very much, and thanks for saying the poem." I wished him "Good day," and indeed James was up. I got in, and when he had closed the door, I asked, "So who's your man?" "Oh," he says, "the Messiah!" He came with the house. He was somebody's uncle and the condition of sale was that he'd live out his days there. There was no end to the wonders of the Jordan household!

My stay there was a brilliant introduction to my home country and its people and its music. As I was leaving, I thought, "I'll be back here any day now." It took sixteen years!

THE CLUB 47

Bill Keith and John Richardson had kept the apartment on Upland Road, so I had a place to land when I got back. I still had a teaching fellowship and was still taking courses toward a PhD, so it was a bit of a step back in one way, but it gave me some space to figure things out. Right away I had to go down to the Club 47 at its new location. When I left it had been a cellar with a dirt floor. It was now a fine space with stone and brick walls and a brick floor, full of small oak tables with slatted wood chairs from North Carolina. The back wall was white with paintings hung and lit. There was a compact kitchen, a small office, a small dressing room, and two toilets in the back hallway. Byron and Nancy had done a beautiful job creating a functional room using natural materials, perfectly suited to the kind of music we were presenting. Byron was beaming as I looked around. "What do you think? Is it okay?" "Okay? It's fantastic! It's beautiful!"

There were lots of other changes in addition to the new Club. Bill Keith had hooked up with the Jim Kweskin Jug Band, which also included Geoff and Maria Muldaur, Mel Lyman, and Fritz Richmond. Joe Val had gone on to become part of The Charles River Valley Boys, replacing Ethan. Spider John Koerner had moved to Cambridge and seemed to have been adopted by the Siggins's. Seeing and hearing him in person was 100 percent better than hearing him on tape, though that was good enough.

Naturally, I was ready to get back into playing music, and Joe Val suggested that we should try out a kid from Wayland named Peter Rowan who he thought was a pretty good singer. Peter was more than a "pretty good" singer. He was on fire with bluegrass and was eager to join up with Bill and me. In no time at all we had a fine trio and started playing at the Club and at other coffeehouses and colleges in the area. One day Ralph Rinzler called up to say that Bill Monroe would be coming up to Barre, Vermont, to play a show and that he needed to pick up a lead singer/guitar player. Bill Keith suggested that Peter could probably fill the bill and proceeded to give Peter a crash course in Bill Monroe's repertoire, which Peter absolutely gobbled up. On the day, we all traveled up. Monroe was delighted to see Bill Keith again. Before the show, he got together with Peter to run over some songs. Peter surprised him by choosing to sing "Over on the Old Kentucky Shore," not one of Bill's better known songs. That and Peter's singing and solid guitar playing during the show, was all Bill needed to offer him a job. Peter was going to be a Bluegrass Boy!

With Peter gone and Bill Keith focusing more and more on the Kweskin Jug Band, as the end of my academic year approached, I really didn't know what I was going to do. That my academic career was really coming to an end was made clear to me one day by one of my teachers, Zeph Stewart, who taught Latin. By this point in a PhD program I would have been expected to be able to compose in both Greek and Latin. I had been able to squeak by with the Greek, but one day after Latin composition class Professor Stewart came up to me and said, with the kindest of smiles, "You really can't do this, can you?" "No, sir, I'm afraid I really can't." And that was the end of it.

I didn't panic. I knew that leaving the academic path was right, and it was a relief to have it finally decided. My teaching fellowship money went until the end of June. My share of the rent was $50 a month, so I'd be okay to make it through the summer. Then one night Byron asked me to come into his office for a minute. He gave me a look and said, "I think I need to quit doing this." I couldn't have been more surprised, so I asked him what the problem was. It was simple. He was burned out. It wasn't just the move and the setting up of the new place, although that had been a lot. He'd been at it for three years, seven days a week, all day every day. In addition to the nightly schedule, there was now a children's series on Saturday afternoons, classical chamber music on some Sundays, monthly art exhibits. Byron had conceived and designed the monthly calendars, which were mailed to the members. He hired the waitresses and door staff. He was demanding and driven to be the best.

He demanded more of himself than anyone else. It had finally caught up to him, and he knew it. Without any hesitation I said, "Well, I'll do it if you show me how." We shook hands on it. My new life had just begun. Byron spent the next month showing me how to deal with the kitchen, how to make drinks, how to order stuff, how to make out a staff schedule, how to make out a payroll, how to book the performers, how to lay out the calendar, how to do the monthly mailing. I was going to need a lot of luck and every bit of energy I could muster to make this work.

By this time almost every one of the local artists had made a record, thanks in large part to Paul Rothchild, who had already left Prestige records to become A & R Director at Elektra Records. Tom Rush and Jackie Washington were off a lot of the time playing around the country, as was the Kweskin Jug Band, now being managed by Albert Grossman. As a result of this dissipation of the local scene, Byron had already started booking outside artists like Jesse Colin Young and Eric Andersen. There had been a huge change in the whole folk scene, led by the enormous success of Joan Baez, Peter, Paul & Mary, and Bob Dylan. In the Fall of '64 Dylan had come to play Symphony Hall in Boston. I went with Bob and Betsy Siggins, who by now had become friends with Dylan. After the show we followed Bob's car back to Cambridge. Leaving Symphony Hall, his car was surrounded by fans. We all went to somebody's house for a party like every other night, but it was clear that he had become a "star."

When Dylan's first album came out I remember how different it was and how unusual it was. I couldn't put my finger on why I found it so compelling, except that his voice was different; his approach to the songs was his own. Just as I liked what he was doing because it was "different," there were others who didn't like it for the same reason. There was a conservative streak in some people involved in folk music that said "this is the way it's supposed to be." In the end, that is what caused trouble for Bob, because he kept going down his own road. At first there was the "new Woody Guthrie" image, which he helped to create himself with the little dungaree jacket, the living-on-the-street attitude, the social protest songs. That was very popular with the elders of the folk movement.

However, in early 1965 Bob went over to England where the Beatles and the Rolling Stones were in full flight. He came back wearing polka-dot shirts, high-heeled rock and roll boots, and shades. It was like their little boy had gone bad! He had some new songs as well. He had made a big shift. At the Newport Folk Festival he connected with Mike Bloom-field and some of the Butterfield Blues Band and asked them to back him up on three or four of these new songs. The plan was to do those songs first with the band before he played the rest of his set solo, and that's just what he did. But in the audience there was a total uproar—a combination of people cheering and people booing. I was cheering myself. I thought the band suited the songs—especially "Like a Rolling Stone." After Bob finished the set with the band, he left the stage. His acoustic guitar hadn't been put on the stage for him, so he had to go get it. So when Peter Yar-row, who was the emcee, said, "He's gone to get his acoustic guitar," a great cheer went up as if he'd given in to the crowd. It was wild.

There were other things going on as well. Alan Lomax had hosted a blues workshop that afternoon. The Butterfield Blues Band was on it, and Alan gave what Albert Grossman, who had just started to manage the band, thought was a very condescending introduction. I wasn't present myself, but Eric Von Schmidt later played out the scene for me on my white Irish sweater as a shadow show.

> ALBERT: "That introduction was the worst piece of shit!" Boom!
> ALAN: "You can't say that to me!" Bam!

Then both of these round giants of folk music were down, rolling on the ground! So there was tension in the air even before Dylan went on.

I had been asked by Ralph Rinzler if I would be interested in being on the Newport Board of Directors. They picked the talent and programmed the festival. George Wein's staff produced the festival. I told Ralph that I would be interested, so he said, "Why don't you come to the festival and write a critique for the board?" I did, and there was plenty to talk about:

> "Nothing else in the festival caused such controversy. Dylan's appear-ance was the only one that was genuinely disturbing. "The people" so loved by Pete Seeger are "the mob" so hated by Dylan. In the face of violence he has chosen to preserve himself alone. No one else. And he defies everyone else to have the courage to be as alone, as unconnected as he. He screams through organ and drums and electric guitar, "How does it feel to be on your own?" And there is no mistaking the hostil-ity, the defiance, the contempt for all those thousands sitting before him who aren't on their own. Who can't make it. And they seemed to

understand that night for the first time what Dylan had been trying to say for over a year—that he was not theirs or anyone else's—and they didn't like what they heard and booed. They wanted to throw him out. He had fooled them before when they thought he was theirs.

Pete Seeger had begun the night with the sound of a newborn baby crying and asked that everyone sing to that baby and tell it what kind of a world it would be growing up into. But Pete already knew what he wanted others to sing. They were going to sing that it was a world of pollution, bombs, hunger and injustice, but that PEOPLE would OVERCOME. But can there be no songs as violent as the age? Must a folk song be of mountains, valleys and love between my brother and my sister all over this land? Do we allow for despair only in the blues? That's all very comfortable and safe. But is that what we should be saying to that baby? Maybe; maybe not. But we should ask the question. And the only one in the entire festival who questioned our position was Bob Dylan. Maybe he didn't put it in the best way. Maybe he was rude. But he shook us. And that is why we have poets and artists."

There was a group of us who had been performing folk music rooted in tradition. Now there were young people writing their own songs and taking things beyond the tradition. Dylan was leading that group, which by now included Tom Paxton, Tim Hardin, Peter LaFarge, Phil Ochs, and others. When he started, he wrote in the talking blues tradition or the ballad tradition. However, like me, he hadn't come into music through folk music. He came in through rock and roll; I came in through hillbilly music. We hadn't taken any vows of purity regarding folk music. We had grown up listening to whatever we found on the radio. Purity is my idea of a myth in any walk of life. Nothing is pure. Talk to any musician and they'll tell of songs and styles that came from all sorts of places—a music hall song, a dance band song, a blues, a western song. They hear something they like and just start playing it. It's critics, other gatekeepers, and even some in the audience who want to put someone or some music in a box and keep it there.

As I came onto the Newport board, I was finding myself right at the center of these issues. I was definitely coming at things from a different perspective from Alan Lomax, Pete Seeger, and some of the older members. I had enormous respect for what they had achieved, but had some difficulty with some of their attitudes. One time the great guitarist Merle Travis came to play at the Club. He very sheepishly asked, "Would it be alright if I played my electric guitar?" I said, "Sure, you're Merle Travis, you can play anything you want!" It turned out that he'd been told by Alan Lomax at some concert or other that he should play acoustic rather than electric, presumably because the electric wasn't really "folk." Once Doc Watson was sitting on the couch at our apartment playing a great tune. When I asked him what it was, he said it was "You Can't Keep Me from Dreaming," an old Ozzie Nelson song. (Ozzie of "Ozzie & Harriet" who had been a big band singer.) I asked him if he'd play it that night. He laughed and said, "Son, that's not folk music." I guess Doc had gotten the message too. When Elvis Presley had his first hit with a revved up version of Bill Monroe's "Blue Moon of Kentucky," someone asked Monroe what he thought of it, thinking that Monroe might be upset. His comment was, "Them was some powerful checks!" So much for purity!

Right after Newport, the Butterfield Blues Band came to play at the Club for three nights. This was our first experience having an electric band like this. It was Paul Butterfield on amplified harmonica and vocals, Mike Bloomfield and Elvin Bishop on electric guitars, Jerome Arnold on electric bass, and Sammy Lay on drums. The sound in that small room was unlike anything we'd ever had before. We were charging $1 at the door and were paying the band $100/night. They were sleeping on various people's couches. Albert Grossman had just bought them a van, and Paul and I were riding down Mass. Avenue in the van on the way to the Club, and Paul said, "Man, we can't make it on this kind of money." I looked at him and said, "Paul, we're breaking the bank! We've never paid anybody this much!"

Things were beginning to happen that way. Folk music was becoming a business, even for us in Cambridge. Now if I wanted to book the Kweskin Band or Tom Rush I had to call New York. New York had always been a commercial music center, with music publishers, record labels, and managers. In the course of the next year or eighteen months, the level of "stardom," or whatever you want to call it, started clicking in pretty fast. Tom Rush came back from a gig in Detroit excited by a girl he'd heard there named Joni Mitchell. Joni was married to a folk singer named Chuck Mitchell. Chuck was part of the package when you hired Joni, but it was Joni who blew us all away. The next time, she came on her own. Tom Rush then recorded "Circle Game"; Joni got signed by Paul Rothchild at Elektra; Judy Collins recorded "Both Sides Now"; Joni played at Newport and was too big a star to play at the Club again.

The same thing happened with Arlo Guthrie. The first time he came, he played to a smallish but enthusiastic audience for a couple of nights. He was just starting to put together "Alice's Restaurant." People liked him immediately, so I had him back two or three months later. By this time the song had grown and so had his audience. That summer he played at Newport. "Alice's Restaurant" had become a full-fledged epic, and Robert Shelton had him on the front page of the *New York Times*. So he couldn't come back to us.

In order to keep up with the rising prices of artists, after much agonizing, we upped our admission fee to $1.50! Even so, things were moving in a direction we had no control over. The psychedelic dance hall phenomenon was happening out in San Francisco. My friend Charlie Rothschild had started one in New York called The Balloon Farm. I had come to know Charlie first when I was trying to book the Kweskin band through Albert Grossman's office. The first fellow I spoke to there was all agent. He wanted to know what the gross was, how many seats, how many shows. The fact that we were the band's home base, that we were nonprofit, only charging $1.50—none of that meant a thing to him. Fortunately, when I called back, he was out and I got Charlie. He understood our situation. I didn't have to explain anything, and we became friends. Charlie now asked me to help him find a location for a second Balloon Farm in Boston. We found a place, but for various reasons Charlie didn't do it. Someone else did. It was called The Boston Tea Party, and it took off. All of a sudden groups like The Chambers Brothers and the Butterfield Band could make in a night what we could barely pay for a week. The coffeehouse couldn't really compete. I stubbornly tried. I felt that we had got all of this going and that we should be the home of it. In order to pay those groups $1,500–$2,000 for six nights, we'd have to run two or three shows a night, turning the house over. It was not the way the place was supposed to be. It was not the right thing to do. I was doing it out of pride or ego.

However, all of this took time to develop, and there was much wonderful music played in that small place during that time. We prided ourselves on having the best artists in a wide variety of genres: blues bands, country blues, bluegrass, country, old-timey, singer/songwriters, gospel, folk/rock, jazz, Celtic, British, and New England.

We had Muddy Waters, Howlin' Wolf, Junior Wells & Buddy Guy, Willie Dixon & Memphis Slim, Otis Rush, Otis Spann, James Cotton, and The Siegel/Schwall Band.

We had Son House, Skip James, Bukka White, John Hammond Jr., Spider John Koerner, Lightning Hopkins, Sleepy John Estes, Fred McDowell, and Joseph Spence.

We had Bill Monroe, Lester Flatt & Earl Scruggs, Jim & Jesse, and Frank Wakefield & Red Allen.

We had Maybelle Carter, Grandpa Jones, Merle Travis, Mike Seeger, Almeda Riddle, and Clarence Ashley & Tex Isley.

We had Judy Collins, Gordon Lightfoot, Ramblin' Jack Elliott, Pat Sky, Eric Andersen, Jesse Colin Young, David Blue, Guy Carawan, and Richie Havens.

We had The Staples Singers, The Chambers Brothers, The Youngbloods, The Lovin' Spoonful, Earth Opera, and The Blues Project.

We had Mose Allison, George Benson, Gary Burton, Sam Rivers, Ken McIntyre, and Houston Person.

We had Margaret Barry & Michael Gorman, Norman Kennedy, Louis Killen, Dudley Laufman & The Canterbury Contra Band, and Fiddler Beers.

We had a children's series on Saturday afternoons with people like Jackie Washington, The Staples Singers, and Tony & Irene Saletan.

We had a Sunday afternoon classical series, which featured early music by Joel Cohen & The Cambridge Camerata and contemporary classical music featuring future Pulitzer prizewinning composer John Harbison and his wife, Rosemary Harbison, and pianist Ursula Oppens.

John and Rosemary put together some very interesting and challenging programs of contemporary chamber music. Classical musicians had to be paid union scale, so this program, with its small but select audience, couldn't pay for itself. In effect, it was subsidized by the more popular nighttime programs. One Sunday, after one of these concerts, we were standing around, having some sherry, cheese, and crackers—all very genteel—when the door opened and a great big giant of a black man walked in. He was dressed in khaki work clothes. Everybody's head was

FIGURE 5. The Club 47 Calendar by Jim Rooney.

turning, wondering who this person was. I knew who it was right away. It was Howlin' Wolf! He had just driven from Chicago in a van with his band. I'd never met him, so I went over and introduced myself. "We've just finished a little concert here, and we're having a little party," I said. "You're welcome to come in." He stuck out his great big hand and said simply, "Wolf." I brought him over to John Harbison. John was about my age and was into jazz and lots of different kinds of music. I said, "I want to introduce you to your patron." Harbison liked the idea and was very happy to shake Wolf's hand.

Paul Butterfield had told me that I should be getting people like Howlin' Wolf and Muddy Waters. They were total pros. We ourselves were really amateurs, even though some of us were beginning to make a living out of our music. Muddy Waters had established himself in Chicago as a major figure, and here he was coming into our little orbit. Up to this point he hadn't played this kind of a club—a coffeehouse with white college and high school kids as an audience. He called me up when he got to town, asking me where the club was, what time he was supposed to start, and so on. I told him and said, "This is a coffeehouse, but that doesn't mean you have to drink coffee. What kind of 'coffee' do you like?" He picked up on this immediately and said, "Tsivas!" I said, "What?" "Tsivas!" "What?" "TSIVAS! TSIVAS REGAL!" So I had a bottle of Chivas Regal for him when he arrived, and I paid him in cash every single night. That was the beginning of a friendship, because everything was straight.

My friend in New York, Charlie Rothschild, said, "You should get Mose Allison in there." Mose was a very unique artist, who had gotten across to lots of college students like me with his combination of down-home blues, witty lyrics, and unusual piano style. I saw that he was playing at the Jazz Workshop in Boston, so I decided to go talk to him. It was a typical jazz club scene, strictly for older people with money. After his set, I went up to Mose and introduced myself. I told him that I ran this club in Cambridge and that I'd like him to play there. Right away he said, "This is my place to play in Boston." I said, "Our place is different. It's a coffeehouse. It's a different audience." He was probably thinking of a black room with girls sitting around in leotards and guys playing bongos, and he did his best to put me off. I told him I'd pay him what he needed to get and got his phone number. I persisted and called him up a couple of times. He eventually caved in, and we settled on a week.

He arrived in on the Monday afternoon of his first day. He took a quick look at the place, saw the brick and granite, saw the nice oak tables and slatback chairs, saw good paintings on the well-lit walls. Then he went over to the piano. A year or so earlier Judy Collins agreed to come play a couple of nights for free, and we used the money we made to buy a good used Steinway baby grand. This was the piano that Mose Allison sat down at and started to play. Two hours later he got up. Then we went to dinner. That night—a Monday—he played to a full house. Clearly, this was a different experience for him. For the rest of the week he spent mornings at the Harvard music library listening to modern classical music. He'd come over in the afternoons and play the piano for a couple of hours, and then we'd adjourn to the Wurst Haus in Harvard Square for some food and conversation. Mose was telling me all about Marshall McLuhan and the coming Global Village. He'd come back to play to a packed house—a mixture of college kids and older black people who found to their surprise that Mose was white! The experience opened up a whole new world for Mose as it had for Muddy and Wolf.

Agents were always trying to sell you somebody, but I preferred to follow my hunches or the suggestions of people like Charlie Rothschild; Paul Butterfield; or Fritz Richmond, who had turned me on to Richie Havens; or Tom Rush, who had first suggested Joni Mitchell. One day I heard this guitar player on the radio—George Benson. I went out and bought his first album, *It's Uptown*. It was phenomenal—great guitar playing—so I called up Columbia Records and got the name of his booking agent. He was still based in Pittsburgh. I booked him and his trio for a week. I told every guitar player I knew to come and hear him. He was totally unknown. The first couple of nights we probably had thirty or forty people. After that, it was packed. My hunch had proved right.

We also had a concert series, which Byron helped to promote, where we presented such artists as Joan Baez, Ravi Shankar, Buck Owens, Bill Monroe, the Butterfield Blues Band, and the Kweskin Jug Band. I learned about the concert business the hard way. I learned that you could put on a concert that looked sold out. You could have a 2,700-seat hall. If you sold 2,500 tickets everything looked great and everybody was happy—except that your profit was in those 200 seats you hadn't sold.

Presenting such an array of music was exhilarating, but ultimately exhausting. I would come in at eleven in the morning and leave about one in the morning. We were open seven nights a week, plus Saturday and Sunday afternoons. Between the concerts either breaking even or losing a bit and paying artists more than we could really afford, our finances were getting out of hand. The board kept trying to hang in there with me, but I was getting a bit strung out and wasn't thinking that clearly. If I had been, I would have pulled back and regrouped. I was just caught up in the momentum of the time, which was going in this other direction. Our music had become part of the pop music world.

In addition to working night and day, I was a busy boy socially. There were lots of after-hours parties as always. Fritz Richmond had a jukebox at his house with everything on it from Gus Cannon and Dock Boggs to Merle Haggard and Otis Redding. I had discovered soul music and loved to dance to it. There was a black club in Boston called Louie's Lounge, where acts like Joe Tex and Sam & Dave played. I would go there to matinees with Donna Hanly, one of our waitresses. She was blonde, about

5'3" and a great dancer. She'd have on a miniskirt and I'd be wearing bell-bottomed hip-huggers. We were the only white people in the place, so we weren't hard to spot.

Another waitress, Naomi Peskin, told me I needed to upgrade my wardrobe a bit. Through Robert L. Jones, who was now working full-time for George Wein, I had met Charlie Davidson, a great character, who had The Andover Shop off of Harvard Square. He had outfitted jazz artists like Miles Davis, so Naomi and I went in there to see if he could make me a three-piece pinstriped suit. There was one hitch. I wanted the pants to be bell-bottoms so I could wear them over my cowboy boots! This was a first for Charlie, but he did it. I could now go dancing in style. I had also bought a used Mercedes 190 sedan, so I was trying my best to look sharp.

Finally, though, the combination of life in the fast lane, working too much, and the increasing difficulty of making ends meet financially for the Club caught up with me, and toward the end of 1967 I told the board that I was going to have to give it up. At that point our good friend Byron stepped back in and tried to pick up the pieces. I don't feel good about the way I behaved. Byron, Betsy Siggins, Nancy Sweezy, Dan Bump, Manny Greenhill, and the rest of the board tried to make a go of it, but the finances didn't add up, and they finally decided to close the Club in April of 1968.

FESTIVAL TIME

I wasn't there. I was in New Orleans! Ralph Rinzler had been hired to produce a Jazz festival there, but had taken a job at the Smithsonian Institution to start up an American Folklife Division, so he asked me if I'd be interested in taking his place in New Orleans. He also asked me if I would be interested in stepping into his role as talent coordinator of the Newport Folk Festival. I talked to George Wein and the board about it and it was decided that I would start to work full-time that summer for the Folk Festival and would also assist Robert L. Jones with the stage production of the Newport Jazz Festival and the festival touring package shows.

In the meantime, I went to New Orleans. It was an interesting, somewhat strange scene. The head of the festival was an older, fairly conservative man named Durel Black. When Ralph suggested me for the job, Black asked me to come down to New Orleans and meet with him.

Durel was definitely a son of the old South. He was courtly and hospitable and took me to lunch at an all-white businessman's club where all the waiters were black. He liked Dixieland Jazz and had already lined up artists like Pete Fountain and Al Hirt, and it became clear that that was pretty much his idea of Jazz. However, there was a group of people there who had a different point of view. Al Belletto, who ran the Playboy Club, was an alto sax player who'd played with Woody Herman. A TV newscaster named Doug Ramsey was also into contemporary Jazz. Ellis Marsalis, father of Wynton and Branford, was a highly respected teacher and player. There was a band called Willie T. & The Souls, who had been befriended by Cannonball Adderley. So these people wanted a festival that included elements other than Dixieland. After talking to everyone, I thought I could probably figure it all out and become kind of a fifth column for them while satisfying the Durel Black contingent.

Following some of Ralph's leads, I got to know a lot of the local people fairly quickly. Allen Jaffe, who ran Preservation Hall, knew all of the older musicians and was my way in to the four major marching bands. He had sought out all of the musicians from the early era of New Orleans Jazz and created Preservation Hall as a venue for them. Through Allen I met Danny Barker, who was a leader of this group and an extremely knowledgeable historian of New Orleans Jazz. Through him I met a piano player named Armand Hug. He was probably close to eighty and played the entire Jelly Roll Morton repertoire. He had a regular gig at the Royal Sonesta Hotel, and I used to go hear him often. One night we were talking, and I asked him if he'd ever traveled on the road. He smiled and said that he'd had a weekend gig in Biloxi once but had to cut it short because he got homesick! That was the New Orleans attitude. Why go somewhere else when you had everything you could want right there?

I also became friends with Richard Allen, who ran the Jazz Archive at Tulane University. Richard knew everybody and everybody knew him. He knew when and where the marching bands would be playing at a funeral, a baptism, a first communion—every day of the week there was something going on. Richard had an assistant named Eleanor Ellis, who happened to know of an apartment for rent right next door to hers in the French Quarter. I could just catch a glimpse of the Mississippi from my balcony. She took me to an old dance hall called Luthjen's over in a neighborhood the other side of Esplanade. There was a big sign over the dance floor which said, "ABSOLUTELY NO JITTERBUGGING!" We did our best to obey the rules, but sometimes we'd just get carried away! Eleanor's love and affection for the life of the city made my stay a very happy one.

Al Belletto and Doug Ramsey helped me shape the festival up. Through Willie T. they had contacted Cannonball Adderley, who agreed to play the festival, provided Willie T. & The Souls were given a spot on the program. Al Belletto had gotten Woody Herman to agree to come, as well as Carmen MacRae, who would perform with the Herman Herd. I talked to Gary Burton, the brilliant young vibraphone player. He had played at the Club two or three times, and we had become friends. He agreed to come with his quartet. We asked Ellis Marsalis to come with his trio. So the festival was definitely going to have a strong contemporary representation.

Durel Black pulled off a coup of his own and announced to me that he had succeeded in getting Louis Armstrong to come. He hadn't played in New Orleans for many years, so this was going to be a big homecoming for him. Danny Barker put together an all-star Preservation Hall group. At Allen Jaffe's suggestion, we decided that we'd start each night with a different marching band going from Jackson Square in front of the Cathedral to Congo Square outside the Municipal Auditorium. We also planned to have a riverboat cruise one night with three of the local mainstream Dixieland bands playing for dancing. So the roots of New Orleans Jazz were going to be solidly represented as well.

To round things out, I had the idea that we should have some gospel music on the Sunday evening show. We got in touch with a couple of the big gospel choirs in town—each with forty or fifty voices. Mahalia Jackson had come out of this tradition, and I felt that, in addition to having Cannonball Adderley, Willie T. & The Souls and Ellis Marsalis on the bill, this was a real way to insure the involvement of the black community in the Festival. Up until this time the Municipal Auditorium would not have had integrated audiences. They would have had soul shows or country music or rockabilly shows. So this festival was shaping up to be groundbreaking on that score. All sections of the community were to be included.

Come the time of the festival, everything we had planned came together. There was real excitement in the streets each evening as one of the marching bands made its way over to the auditorium. The spirit of celebration continued inside the hall and seemed to bring out the best in all of the performers. Louis Armstrong seemed to be especially moved by the atmosphere and responded to the genuine affection of the audience for him. Carmen MacRae pulled out all the stops as Woody Herman's Herd swung like crazy behind her. Cannonball Adderley gave Willy T. & The Souls an enormous boost. On Sunday night, the two gospel choirs created a mighty, joyful noise, and I felt like the whole festival had been blessed.

After the festival, many of the locals who had been so helpful were delighted with its success musically and financially. Naturally, it made me feel like I had taken on something pretty major and had succeeded. However, I suspect that Durel Black was not all that pleased with the direction the festival had taken, because it was announced not too much later that Willis Conover, the well-established jazz disc jockey for the Voice of America, who had emceed the shows, would be running the festival the following year. However, under Conover's direction, the festival didn't do the business, so they eventually turned to George Wein, who came up with the idea along with local producer Quint Davis for the New Orleans Jazz and Heritage Festival. It became one of the greatest music festivals in America. I would like to think that some of the work I did that spring helped to prepare the way for this to eventually happen.

As soon as the festival was over, I moved out of my apartment, said my goodbyes, got into my Mercedes and hit the road. I was crossing the Chesapeake Bay Bridge when the news came on the radio that Martin Luther King had been shot and killed in Memphis. I was stunned. All the way up to Boston I was listening to replays of his speeches through tears, and it became clear what a void had suddenly opened up. There was no one who could speak out for justice in a voice so clear, so eloquent, so compelling. A day or two after I got back, a soul concert was scheduled for the Boston Arena. The headliner was James Brown. I had never seen him, so I naturally wanted to go. However, because of King's death I was afraid that people would be so upset that they wouldn't welcome a white person coming, so I didn't. It is one of the major regrets of my life. I think of all the times Donna and I went to Louie's Lounge, of the time we went to the Apollo Theater in Harlem on a Saturday night to a Joe Tex "skinny legs" contest, of the day I spent with the Staples Singers backstage at a big gospel show at the Apollo. At no time had I ever experienced a hint of hostility, but on this occasion I caved in to fear and withheld my presence at exactly the time when it was required by King's philosophy of overcoming prejudice by nonviolent witnessing and action. It was a sad lesson.

There was nothing to be gained by keeping myself down in a hole, so I went to work. The office of Festival Productions was in New York, but in May, George Wein shifted his operation up to Newport, where he rented a big house on the water in Middletown, Rhode Island. It was very much a family-style operation. George Wein and his wife Joyce were a very interesting couple. George was full of ideas and enthusiasm. He was deeply passionate about Jazz and had turned his back on his conventional middle class Jewish upbringing in Brookline, Massachusetts, to devote his life to promoting Jazz. Joyce came from a conventional middleclass Negro family in Boston. By marrying each other George and Joyce early on showed that they were as committed to social change as they were to music and to each other. They worked as a team—George pushing full steam ahead and making waves; Joyce calming the waters and keeping things flowing. George's right-hand man was an ex-Vermonter named Charlie Bourgeois. They had been together since George started out in Boston. On the day when I went in to see Duke Ellington at Storyville, Charlie had been the maitre d.' He had long since left the rustic Vermont life behind in favor of the hipper Jazz world. We hit it off immediately, if for no other reason than my name was Rooney. "Rooney O'Vultee!" was one of Slim Gaillard's favorite bebop cries. Thanks to Symphony Sid, I knew immediately what Charlie B. (as everyone called him) was saying when he greeted me with it. I was in. Joyce also had a right-hand girl she had gone through school with, Marie St. Louis. Marie, Charlie, and Joyce worked together to make all of George's dreams and schemes come true.

Robert L. Jones had been part of this family for four years or so. Jones was a born fixer. He wanted to make things work. Back when he was singing at the Club 47, he was also working at the Avis counter in Boston. His monologues between Woody Guthrie songs about all of the various customers whose problems he solved were famous. I had always appreciated his dry humor and his understated approach to dealing with people. We were to become a good team working together. Right away I was put to work writing press releases for the Jazz Festival. I'd done a bunch of that for the Club 47, but now my stuff was going out to a larger audience. Charlie and Bob encouraged me to have fun with it, and I'd slip in baseball metaphors just to see whether they'd get printed. I was surprised when I saw my work verbatim in the *New York Times*! I quickly realized that newspapers have space to fill every day, and they were happy to get something ready-made, complete with a headline—"Brubeck Hits Home Run at Newport." Simple stuff like that made our work fun.

That summer, in addition to producing the Jazz and Folk Festivals, George had a traveling "Schlitz Salute to Jazz" package show touring around the country. Jones and I were to be the tour managers. George liked us to look presentable when we traveled, so I went back to Charlie Davidson and got myself a chocolate-brown summer "jazz suit" along with some Bally slip-on "jazz shoes." It was well worth it, because the artists we were shepherding around were no slouches. Dionne Warwick was the headliner. She was having her great initial success with songs like "Do You Know the Way to San Jose" and "I Say a Little Prayer for You." Cannonball Adderley was also riding high with his keyboard player Joe Zawinul's soulful "Mercy, Mercy, Mercy." Herbie Mann was doing soul/funk influenced Jazz with a hot young band. Gary Burton, who George had taken under his wing, represented a new generation of virtuosic players. Finally, Thelonious Monk brought to the show one of the totally original, iconic figures of modern Jazz. In the presence of such talent, I needed to look and be sharp.

We'd play three cities every weekend during the summer, apart from the festival weekends. We were playing big outdoor and indoor venues—baseball stadiums like Braves Field in Atlanta or indoor arenas that seated ten to twelve thousand people. As had been the case with the Jazz Festival in New Orleans, the audience was totally integrated, which was a first in cities like Charlotte, Nashville and Memphis. The summer of '68 was a tough summer. First there was Dr. King's assassination, then the assassination of Bobby Kennedy in June, and the growing divisions over the Vietnam War. There was a lot of political and racial unrest. These shows proved a point that good-quality positive music could bring people together. George Wein deserves a lot of credit for his firm belief that this music would, indeed, help to overcome and heal the divisions in society.

One of the great personal bonuses for me to come out of these tours was that I got to know Thelonious Monk. I got to know everybody, of course, but Thelonious was special. I had first heard his music on a couple of Blue Note 78s that my brother John had. At Amherst my hip friends at WAMF turned me on to more. I loved the quirky, rhythmic, slightly humorous tunes he came up with that seemed to stick in your head, but I loved even more his ballads—especially "'Round Midnight," one of the very best. The big stadiums and arenas we were playing were confusing and somewhat alien places for someone like Thelonious, and I would always want to make sure that he was looked after. I'd give him plenty of warning before we left the hotel, so he'd have time to get himself together. Then I'd guide him through the labyrinthine bowels of the buildings and get him to the stage when he needed to be there. So we became friends. One additional reason might have been that I might have had a little hash to share sometimes after a show, and we could have a quiet smoke together.

Apart from getting everyone to the gigs, Jones and I would do the stage shifts between acts. It was simple enough. We'd put a drum kit on or off, or a set of vibes, or an electric keyboard, or a guitar amp. Even though we were doing grunt work, we still looked sharp in our suits! Our work was made easy by the attitude of the musicians. They pitched in too. Many's the time Joe Zawinul picked up the other end of his Fender Rhodes as we made our way from a baseball dugout to the stage and back. We were all in it together, and we managed to have fun while we were at it. I especially enjoyed hanging out with Gary Burton and Steve Swallow after the shows. Both of them had fine, wry senses of humor, which took the curse off of the tough traveling schedule. Charlie Rouse and Ben Riley, who were playing with Thelonious, liked to take me to their favorite barbecue places. Occasionally flights would get overbooked, and we'd have to improvise. Dionne came up with a plan once. We got everyone on the plane but her and her mother, who always traveled with her. Then we said to the person at the airline counter, "We've got Dionne Warwick here. If she doesn't get to Denver by tonight, there's going to be a lot of unhappy people. You're going to have to figure out a way to get her there." Somehow another plane materialized. We had it to ourselves. The show went on.

On the weekdays between tours, I would work on the Folk Festival. The board ranged from Alan Lomax to me. I was supposed to be in touch with the younger generation and country music. Allen brought in the raw, unadulterated traditional artists like Bessie Jones and The Georgia Sea Islanders or Ed Young and the Mississippi Fife & Drum Band. Ralph Rinzler and Mike Seeger brought in old-timey and Bluegrass musicians like Clarence Ashley, Dock Boggs, Doc Watson or The Stanley Brothers. Ethel Raim was in touch with Balkan and Middle European music. Bernice Reagon had originally performed at Newport with the Freedom Singers. Currently the leader of Sweet Honey in the Rock, she provided a strong connection to the music coming out of the civil rights movement. Bruce Jackson was an authority on the blues world. Judy Collins, Peter Yarrow, Oscar Brand, and Theo Bikel represented the established, popular artists. Pete Seeger was the spiritual and actual leader of the board, supported every step of the way by his wife Toshi. Everyone brought in music that they thought was strong and deserved to be heard, and we'd weave it all together.

I often didn't get to take it all in because I was working, so, for me, the best parts of both festivals were the parties after the concerts. You might get Duke Ellington and Earl "Fatha" Hines playing four-hands on the piano or Roland Kirk playing three horns at once, backed up by Roy Haynes and Steve Swallow, or George Wein jamming with Barney Kessel, Red Norvo, and Ruby Braff. These people never tired of playing. During the Folk Festival I got my chance to jam at the parties with the fiddler Byron Berline, his dad Lue, Bill Keith, and Bill Monroe. Another time I'd sit in with the Balfa Brothers—Dewey, Rodney and Will. There were blues jams, bluegrass jams, old-timey jams, and jams where all kinds of people just mixed it all up.

In the fall Jones and I headed off to Europe with a couple of packages, which split up and came together in various cities. I spent most of my time with two groups, one featuring the vibists Red Norvo and Gary Burton; the other featuring Horace Silver, Muddy Waters, and the soul singer Joe Simon. Red was a great character, who had started out way back with Paul Whiteman's orchestra. He made some legendary recordings with his wife, the singer Mildred Bailey, and successfully made the transition into the modern era playing in a trio with Charles Mingus and Tal Farlow. He and Gary split a double bill at Ronnie Scott's Jazz Club in London for a week. Gary had his quartet with him, but Red had a pickup rhythm section. After the second night he came up to me and said, "Find me some better players." The club manager came up with a new pair. After a couple more nights, Red came to me again. Same story. He made it through the rest of the gig with the third pair, but a couple of days later we were riding along in the tour bus when Red said, apropos of nothing, "These English drummers think time is a magazine!" We all just broke up.

On this tour I discovered that European audiences were not tolerant of mixing up the genres. The person who suffered most because of this was Joe Simon. He had had one hit, "You Keep Me Hangin' On," and had a beautiful, soulful voice, but he wasn't helped by the fact that he was being backed up by Horace Silver's drummer Billy Cobham, a bebop drummer, who had left the soul groove far behind. Before the first song was over, the whistles and catcalls would start. The audience was there either for Horace Silver's hard-core bebop or Muddy Waters's hard-core blues. It got so he'd just do his hit and leave. He was a lovely person, as nice as he could be, but it was just the wrong place for him. However, for the other artists, Europe was definitely the place to be. Jazz was treated as a real art form. We were playing beautiful concert halls in all the major cities. In the States, most of the Jazz artists spent most of their time in small Jazz clubs playing six nights a week. Europe gave their spirits, as well as their pocketbooks, a big lift.

When we got back from Europe in December, I spent Christmas in Dedham and Cambridge and then headed down to Washington, D.C., where Bob Siggins was doing research at the National Institutes of Health. On New Year's Eve we went to a party, where I met a girl named Sheila Mooney. Sheila was home from San Francisco for the holidays, visiting her family in Alexandria, Virginia. Her spunky spirit appealed to me right away, and the feeling seemed to be mutual, because we went back to Bob's that night and spent as much time as we could together for the next four days until she had to go back to California. The New Year had started with a bang.

After a few weeks of phone calls, I persuaded Sheila to come live with me. I had found a one-room studio apartment in Manhattan on West 45th Street and 10th Avenue—in the heart of what used to be called Hell's Kitchen. However, it was past its rougher days, and I found it a great place to live—not too far from Broadway, not too far from the Hudson River. Even so, it was quite a radical shift for Sheila and her Afghan hound, April, who had been living on the beach in California. It must have been love, although there were times when both Sheila and April were ready to head back. Things began to look up when we started to go up to Newport on weekends in the spring.

One day I was down in the Village hanging out at Izzy Young's Folklore Center. Izzy asked me if Bill Keith and I would do a concert for him at the Washington Square Church. Bill had been playing the pedal steel guitar for two or three years by this time, and I had gotten back into country music through Buck Owens and Merle Haggard. We thought it might be fun to do a split concert—one-half bluegrass and folk and the other half country. Bill suggested that Eric Weissberg could join us. He could play mandolin and he and Bill could do a couple of double banjo things and he could also play electric guitar. On the afternoon of the concert we went to the church to rehearse. The door opened and Richard Greene stuck his head in. Richard had played fiddle with Bill Monroe for nearly two years and was now in New York putting together a rock band called Seatrain with the bass player Andy Kulberg. "Where's your fiddle?" I asked. "Right here," he said. "Why don't you get it out and do this concert with us?" So he did.

I did a couple of Hank Williams songs, "Weary Blues (from Waitin')" and "My Sweet Love Ain't Around" and a Merle Haggard song, "I Must Be Somebody Else You've Known." I also did Bill Monroe's "You'll Find Her Name Written There." From the Sandburg *Songbag* I did "Fond Affection" and "The False Knight upon the Road." We did a version of "Little Sadie," which we had learned from Doc Watson. Eric had a song of his called "Hitchhiker" and we did a jazzed-up version of "Sitting on Top of the World." Richard had an electric viola as well as an electric fiddle, and he gave us a great sound whether we were playing bluegrass or country. People really seemed to like the musical mixture. It was one of those nights when everything jelled.

Afterward, we headed uptown to a club called "Steve Paul's Scene" to hear a new band from the West Coast called The Flying Burrito Brothers. Bill Keith and Richard knew Chris Hillman from the Los Angeles bluegrass scene; Gram Parsons had been in Cambridge a few years earlier in a group called The International Submarine Band, so we were curious to hear them. As I was sitting there listening to them I said, "Gee, that's kind of what we were just doing." The thought popped into my mind that maybe some record label would be interested in us. As a result of working at the Newport Folk Festival I had gotten to know some people who worked for the various record labels, and I called up Andy Wickham at Reprise Records. Andy was English but loved the Everly Brothers and

FIGURE 6. The Blue Velvet Band concert at the Washington Square Methodist Church, 1969 (*l. to r.*: Jim Rooney, Richard Greene, Bill Keith, Eric Weissberg). Photograph © McGuire.

had just signed Doug Kershaw to the label. When I told him my idea, he was enthusiastic but said that their roster was full. However, he went on to say that possibly Joe Smith at Warner Brothers would be interested. I didn't know who Joe Smith was and thought Andy was just putting me off in a nice way. The next day, much to my surprise, I got a call from Joe Smith. It turned out that he was the head of Warner Brothers Records! He said, "We're very excited about this band of yours!" If Joe was excited, I figured I was excited too. "What do you think about Erik Jacobsen producing?" Joe asked. Erik had produced our friend John Sebastian's band, The Lovin' Spoonful, so he was definitely okay with me. "So," Joe went on, "How much do you need?" This was all so unexpected and fast, that I was totally unprepared. Without thinking, I said. "$4,500." "Great," said Joe. It's a deal!" So The Blue Velvet Band came into being.

Bill, Eric, and Richard couldn't believe it. Just like that we had a record deal! Eric, Bill, and I went up to George Wein's house in Newport to rehearse while Sheila kept us fed. Eric remembered a western swing tune called "Sweet Moments" that he had heard at a party out at Tex Logan's house in New Jersey. Bill and Eric worked on a steel guitar instrumental of Bill's, for which Bill came up with the world's longest title: "The Nobody Knows about My Cares and Nobody Cares about My Nose Rag." Eric was getting well established by now as one of the top session musicians in New York, so he lined up a couple of drummers, Buddy Salzman and Gary Chester, and a keyboard player, Pat Rebillot. Richard suggested Andy Kulberg to play bass.

I hadn't done any recording since Bill and I did "Livin' on the Mountain" back in '62. Everyone else had a lot of recording experience under their belts, but if I had any nerves going in, I quickly got over them, and, with Erik Jacobsen's relaxed guidance, things began flowing very easily. The eclectic mix of material made some kind of sense, from the traditional acoustic versions of "Little Sadie" and "The Knight upon the Road" to the country songs of Hank Williams and Merle Haggard and the more modern sounds of "Hitchhiker" and "Sitting on Top of the World" (with John Hammond Jr. sitting in on blues harmonica). It was all over before we knew it.

We came up with what seemed an appropriate title for the album: *Sweet Moments with The Blue Velvet Band*. Eric Von Schmidt and I had a wild time down in Siesta Key inventing and putting together a country music board game for the inside of the foldout album cover (sample move: The Beer That Made Milwaukee Famous Has Made a Fool out of You. Back six spaces). If our approach was lighthearted, we were aware that this was one of those times when we captured something very unique, as I wrote in the liner notes:

> "The Blue Velvet Band has no beginning and has no end. It is composed of many musical minds and traditions, long growing. Today it has an easy, sad, country feel to it; that is the way we wanted it to be. Here we are always together, and we are happy it could happen that way."

Record labels were happy to experiment like this at the time. If it hit, it hit. If it didn't, it didn't. Over time the album acquired its fans, especially in Canada, Japan and Europe. It seemed to speak to people about the great range and depth of this music we had individually all come to love. Over the years I was to discover that it's a big world and that people are out there listening in all sorts of places.

The record done, I went back to work. The Folk Festival had always outdrawn the Jazz Festival, and this irked George Wein a little bit. In early

'69 some booking agent talked George into the idea of putting "Jazz/ Rock" acts on the Jazz Festival to give it a boost. Before we knew it, he had booked several English bands, including Jethro Tull, Ten Years After, and Jeff Beck. George's friends Neshui and Ahmet Ertegun had signed Led Zeppelin to Atlantic Records, so they were invited to make what would be their North American debut. In addition, we had Frank Zappa & The Mothers of Invention, Johnny Winter, B. B. King, Sly and The Family Stone (!!)—plus all the normal jazz artists like Duke Ellington, Dave Brubeck, Count Basie, Roland Kirk, Herbie Mann, and so on. When tickets went on sale in May they flew out the door. At Newport every ticket sold was for a reserved seat—a folding wooden chair—eighteen thousand of them. Soon every single seat was gone, and George was thrilled.

The Jazz Festival was on the 4th of July weekend, and about seventy thousand people showed up. Those without tickets found their way to the fields and hills outside the site, which was enclosed by a wooden board fence. Fortunately the Jazz Festival was one of the first to have really good sound, which meant that we could turn the sound up so that the people outside the fence could hear. There had been a couple of times at earlier festivals when there had been so-called "riots." With that in mind, we did our best to keep the crowd happy so there would be no trouble.

Putting rock music on the stage was a new experience for us. These rock groups were showing up with trucks full of equipment—stacks of big Marshall amps. We were really winging it. We built rolling platforms for the amps and drums. While one group was on, we'd back up a truck to the back of the stage and set the next band up on another set of platforms. We'd roll one set off and another one on. We were used to having pretty fast-paced shows where you'd have three to five minutes between acts. Sly and The Family Stone had never set up in less than two or three hours! We got them down to twenty or twenty-five minutes. They were amazed. So we were stretched to the limit just to keep the show moving.

Because Newport is surrounded by water, a fog would often roll in at night when it got chilly. The people up on the hillside were getting cold and damp. They had nowhere to go and had to stay there all night, so the wooden fence was very inviting. One by one, the boards came out of it to make campfires. By Saturday night the fence was pretty much gone and there were all those wooden chairs! By Sunday the place was just a smoldering ruin. It looked like Beirut on a bad day, but we kept going, because the alternative would have been absolute chaos. After the final show we were absolutely exhausted, but we had put the show on and were proud of that, so we headed for the party, looking forward to a great jam session. When we got there Led Zeppelin were in full swing being drunk, obnoxious, and rude, throwing food around, oblivious of the great artists in the room with them. The jazz artists just couldn't understand what had happened to the Festival. I felt sick and went off to bed.

But there was no rest for the weary. The Folk Festival was coming up in two weeks. The Folk Festival had nothing to do with this debacle, but the town was in a total uproar, and some people wanted to shut the whole thing down. A group of us from the board pleaded with the Town Council, and they finally agreed to let us go ahead, but on the condition that we build a chain link fence around the entire site—in ten days time! That was going to cost $40,000. They also insisted that every off-duty policeman in the State of Rhode Island was going to be on duty that weekend, and we would be paying the overtime. Of course, we were also going to have to rent eighteen thousand more chairs. We decided to go ahead, no matter what. It was important to assert our own identity.

That festival was particularly noteworthy for the lineup on the Sunday afternoon "New Folks" concert, which featured, among others, James Taylor, Jerry Jeff Walker, Van Morrison, Pentangle, John Allen Cameron, and Steve Young. At that show I also announced that a man had landed on the moon. The audience response was basically, "Get on with the music!" That spring, the board decided to invite Johnny Cash to return to the festival. When he had come in 1964, he really connected with people like Bob Dylan, Tim Hardin, and Peter LaFarge and had done a lot since to bring their songs out to a larger audience. Johnny was in New York rehearsing for a television show, so I went over to ask him about coming back to Newport. He immediately said that he would, but he asked if it would be alright with us if he brought along two young songwriters from Nashville, Vince Matthews and Kris Kristofferson. I was familiar with one of Vince's songs, "Love in the Hot Afternoon," country singer Gene Watson's first hit. I was also familiar with Roger Miller's version of Kris's song "Me and Bobby McGee," so I was happy to oblige. On the afternoon of the opening day, as I was sweeping some rainwater off the stage, a young guy with long hair sauntered up to me and asked in a gravelly voice where he could find Jim Rooney. I told him he was looking at him. He looked surprised and introduced himself. "Hi, I'm Kris Kristofferson." Evidently he had expected to find me in an office somewhere, not out there pushing a broom. He'd spent some time in Nashville pushing a broom at the Columbia Studios when he was trying to get in the door, so we had a good laugh about that. That night Johnny and June brought Kris out in the middle of their set to do a song. They were just like parents of a high school kid performing in a talent show—nervous and proud. Afterward I spent some time with Kris at the party and asked him if he'd like to do a short set on the Sunday afternoon concert. He backed up a step and looked at me. "Do you mean it?" "Absolutely!" A door had opened and on Sunday afternoon he walked right through.

Another special moment that year was when the Everly Brothers were reunited with their dad Ike Everly. By this time the Everlys were pretty much playing the Vegas/Atlantic City circuit. However, one of my favorite albums of theirs was their simplest, *Songs Our Daddy Taught Us*. Ike Everly was originally from Central City, Kentucky, the same area that produced Merle Travis and Bill Monroe. Ike was a first-class thumbpicking style guitar player. Like so many from that area he migrated north to Chicago for work. Music was his way out. When the boys were young, he and his wife Margaret started the Everly Family Band. They worked on radio in Shenandoah, Iowa, and Knoxville, Tennessee. With help from Chet Atkins, the boys got signed to a record deal and before anyone knew what hit them, their career took off. With the family band ended, Ike settled in Nashville where he worked as a barber, playing guitar on the side. Over time, with the boys living in California and working constantly, they were seeing little of each other, although it obviously meant a lot to Ike that they had saluted his influence by making that album. At Newport the Everlys did a set on the Friday night show. The singing was great, but it was obviously the same set they would have done in Vegas, complete with lame patter between songs. They didn't seem to have an awareness that this was a different audience. At the party afterward, I was talking to Don about them being scheduled to do a set with Ike the next afternoon on a small workshop stage. He immediately said, "We don't do that kind of thing." I looked at him straight and said, "That's why you're here! That's what this is all about! You and your dad and how the music came from him to you. It's also in your contract that you'll be doing a concert and a

FIGURE 7. Backstage at the Newport Folk Festival, 1969.

workshop. So I'll see you there." Needless to say, that set with Ike was one of the highlights of the weekend. Seeing the smile on their faces as they all played "Ike Everly's Rag" told the whole story. After that the Everlys brought Ike with them to be part of every show, including the Albert Hall in London. It was also the beginning of a long friendship with Don. One of our goals at Newport was to make clear the traditional roots of much of contemporary music. Watching Don and Phil playing and singing with Ike on that small stage that afternoon brought that lesson home, with goosebumps to prove it.

All of us put a lot of thought and effort into that particular festival. Ethel Raim brought up a whole group of Greeks from Stamford, Connecticut, and had it all going in her workshop area: music, dancing, and food. Ralph Rinzler put together a tent with crafts he had collected on his southern trips when he was collecting music for the Newport Folk Foundation. My new partner Sheila organized a group of local kids to paint a big mural about all the music and action they were taking in at the festival. We made a real effort to show that there was more to what we were doing than putting on a great show. It was about the importance of tradition and how it could inform and shape contemporary life. In every way we had made our point, but we were finished financially, because of all of the extra costs as a result of the Jazz Festival debacle. All of our reserves from earlier years were gone. The board had some serious thinking to do.

As for myself, there was no letup in our schedule. In addition to our weekend "Schlitz Salute to Jazz" package shows, George had another "Jazz/Rock" extravaganza booked for the Laurel Racetrack in Laurel, Maryland, between Washington and Baltimore. At Newport we had a big stage and a wonderful facility that George had built with sound, lights, dressing rooms, and so on. When we arrived at the racetrack, we drove to the infield area where the concerts were to be. There we saw a small plywood stage up on metal scaffolding with a post at each corner supporting a tarp for a roof! Every summer afternoon in that part of the world you can count on at least one thunderstorm. During the first storm on the day of the show the tarp first acted as a sail in the wind and then it filled up with rain and acted as a bucket. I needed to get the stage good and dry somehow because of all the electric instruments. I didn't want anyone getting electrocuted. I started looking through some sheds in the middle of the infield and came up with some rolled-up rubber matting. We put that all over the stage and a new layer of plywood over that. No sooner did we have that done when we got hit by another storm! By now it was about four in the afternoon, and people were starting to come in. We were going to have fifty thousand or so and the infield was already getting that muddy quality that festival-goers seem to love. We got the stage built again and were ready to start moving the bands on. By this time Jones and I knew all the roadies after working with them in Newport, so we were all ready to go.

Just as we were about to start loading in Ten Years After, who were opening the show, I looked up and saw this band walking up on the stage. I had no idea who they were. They were some sort of a soul band, with satin shirts and bell-bottoms. I shouted up at them, "Hey! Hey! Wait a minute! Who are you?" "We're the Revells" (or whatever they were called). "We're from Baltimore. Elzie said we could open the show." (Elzie Street was George's local promoter.) I said, "No, no. We're way behind time. Nobody told me. It's not happening." They started giving me the old honky treatment—"motherfucker this and motherfucker that." Elzie himself then showed up and started in with me. I'd had it and let him have it. "Hey! Do you want to put the show on? You want to put the show on? Be my guest!" and I turned to go to my car. Jones and the roadies were standing there with their mouths open. Off I went, only to remember that I'd sent somebody off in my car to get us some pizza, so I was left to fume around the infield for a few minutes talking to myself. Finally, Elzie came over and told me to get on with it. He'd sent his band home. When I got back to the stage, Dick Barber, roadie for the Mothers of Invention, told me that if I'd left, the roadies were ready to go too. All for one; one for all.

By midnight Sly and The Family Stone were singing "Higher and Higher! Higher and Higher!" The crowd was jammed up to the stage, and I could feel it shifting around in the mud. I prayed that it would hold, and it did. We got through the night. The next day was another day. Once again we were building the stage in the afternoon. I was down on my knees hammering away when George Wein showed up and happened to choose that moment to tell me he had a little bad news. His money had run out, so he was going to have to let me go at the end of the tour. I just kept pounding away. I wasn't going to abandon ship.

Of course, that summer really peaked with the Woodstock Festival, sometimes described as the world's biggest "love-in." We were elsewhere at the time, but you couldn't have paid me enough to go. I was "festivaled out." Out in the country there were signs that the "love" message hadn't penetrated some minds. In Memphis we were playing at the brand new Mid-South Coliseum. Dionne Warwick was pregnant and had to miss some shows. On that show we replaced her with the local favorites Carla and Rufus Thomas and added Buddy Guy to satisfy all the local blues hounds. When we arrived, there seemed to be a hefty police presence around the building, complete with dogs. I introduced myself to the sheriff in charge, a large, well-fed representative of the law. I said we were looking forward to a good show in their beautiful new place and went about our business. Everything was smooth. Buddy was on and getting into his music. Buddy has about a 500-foot guitar cord. When he played at the Club 47, he'd gone out the door and all the way down to Harvard Square with his guitar. So here was no different. He jumped off the stage and was up the aisle in a flash, the pied piper of the blues. I was on the side of the stage and was suddenly joined by the sheriff. "Get that motherfuckin' nigger back up here or I'll close you down," he yelled. My well-fed friend was apoplectic. "Hold on! I'll take care of it," I said, and went out on the stage to A.C. Reed, Buddy's sax man. "A.C. we've got to get Buddy back or the sheriff's gonna close us down." So off went A.C. bounding up the aisle, blowing all the way. The audience was going crazy. The sheriff was really popping now. I shouted, "Relax! I've sent him out to get him. Did you expect me to reel him in?" Fortunately, Buddy jumped back on stage in the nick of time, giving me a big wink as he went by.

We finally came to the end of our road in Cincinnati, slightly the worse for wear after our long summer. George's copromoter Dino Santangelo had a party for all of us up on top of the hotel there. Thelonious Monk was talking to Bobby Timmons, another great piano player. Bobby was admiring Monk's suit. It was dark navy blue with a very fine pinstripe, and was very high double-breasted with four sets of buttons. He was a big man, and he looked great in this suit. I was admiring it too, so Monk said to us, "Do you want to see my other suits?" So we went to his suite. He had four or five suits hanging in his closet. They were all identical, except that each had a different color pinstripe. One was green, another blue, another red, and so on. On the inside of the sleeve of each suit was embroidered the name of one of his tunes, like "'Round Midnight," or "Crepescule with Nellie." It was totally hip. The ultimate in hipness. Monk smiled his beautiful smile as Bobby and I looked in each sleeve. That he included me as well made my heart melt. Money didn't matter at such a time.

PART II
FINDING MY OWN VOICE

TIME OUT: *BOSSMEN*

So there I was in the fall of '69, out of work. Even though I was genuinely laid off, for some reason it never entered my head to apply for unemployment. I'd saved up some money over the summer. Sheila and I had decided to get married, but I figured that I'd come up with something. We were young. We weren't worried. At such times you need to get creative, and I did. I woke up in the middle of the night with this thought in my mind that Bill Monroe and Muddy Waters were just alike as people. The more I thought about it, the truer it seemed, and it seemed true about their music too. In the morning I sat down and wrote up the idea in a couple of pages:

> Every field has its "bossman"—the one who sets the style, makes the rules, and defines the field in his own terms. In the world of bluegrass and early country music the man is Bill Monroe. In the world of urban blues and blues bands—Chicago Blues—the man is Muddy Waters.
>
> Bill and Muddy have remarkably similar careers. Both came from rural areas where they grew up listening to the natural music around them. For Monroe it was square dance music, church music, the blues

guitar of a colored man named Arnold Schultz, and, above all, the fiddle playing of his Uncle Pen Vandiver. For Muddy it was string-band music, the sound of the harmonica, church music, preaching, but, above all, the sound of the blues as played and sung by such men as Robert Johnson and Son House—the raw sound of Mississippi Delta blues. Both men brought their music to the city and the structured world of commercial music—Bill to Nashville and Muddy to Chicago. There each man began to work with what he brought with him to give it a new shape, a new style, that would speak to a new time and to new situations. Each man formed a band, and each band became a school to the best musicians in the style. These musicians went on, in turn, to form their own bands, and, in time, the worlds of bluegrass and blues bands took shape.

Armed with this, I called up Ralph Rinzler's cousin Richard Rinzler, who was a book editor. He told me that he'd just signed a writer to write a book about country blues named Peter Guralnick. I knew Peter. He had gotten started writing about music when he came to the Club 47 and wrote his first piece about Howlin' Wolf. However, Richard referred me to an editor at Dial Press named Bob Cornfield, who took me to a nice publisher's lunch in New York, complete with martinis! He read my little piece over lunch and, with no hesitation asked me how much time and money I would need to do it. I figured it would take three or four months to do, so I asked for a $3,500 advance plus some expenses. He said, "Okay, it's a deal." How simple life was then! The record deal with Warner Brothers and this book deal with Dial happened so easily. There were no middle-men involved, no marketing people, no focus groups. If you had an idea someone liked, and it didn't cost the moon, they'd take a chance on it. A lot of good records and books saw the light of day that way. I signed the contract a few weeks later and agreed to deliver the book by May 1. Sheila and I could go ahead and get married. We wouldn't starve.

It also occurred to me that I might look for work as a tour manager and went to see Albert Grossman; I'd come to know him a little bit through the Kweskin Jug Band. The Club had also put on the Dylan documentary "Don't Look Back" in Boston. It lost money, but Albert appreciated that I had taken the risk and gave me a break on the loss. He also appreci-ated that I'd put on The Bauls of Bengal at the Club, which also cost me money. His wife Sally had brought them over from India. One of their main claims to fame would be that they appeared on the cover of Dylan's John Wesley Harding album.

Many people in the folk music community didn't like Albert. They seemed to think that he wasn't honest or was too aggressive as a manager. One person once described him to me as a kind of vulture circling over Greenwich Village picking off innocent young folk singers! One of those singers was Peter Yarrow, one of Albert's first clients as a manager. Another was Noel Paul Stookey, a fledgling stand-up comic with a guitar. Another was Mary Travers, herself a native of Greenwich Village. Albert put these three people together, provided them with songs from Gordon Lightfoot, Ian Tyson and Sylvia Fricker, and Bob Dylan (another innocent he had picked off), hired the vocal arranger Milt Okun, who had worked so successfully with Harry Belafonte, rehearsed them for months before they recorded and got them a deal with Warner Brothers Records at a time when the label needed a boost. Bill Keith and I saw them at the Cape Cod Melody Tent in the summer of '62. Albert had hired a rising young lighting designer named Chip Monck to do the lights and Bill and Terry Hanly, pioneers of rock sound, to do the sound. The great bassist Bill Lee backed the trio up. I had never seen or heard folk music presented this way. The quality of the material, the vocal harmonies, the stage presentation were all absolutely first class. That quality was a hallmark of Albert's work as a manager. There was no doubt that he was tough in his business dealings, but in my limited experience with him I had found him to be fair.

Albert didn't have anything as far as tour managing was concerned, but he told me that he was building a recording studio up in Woodstock and that The Band was involved. He wondered if I'd be interested in coming up there and managing the studio for him. He played me some of the *Big Pink* album. It was right up my alley. They even did "Long Black Veil," which we all used to sing in Cambridge. In the context of what we had done with The Blue Velvet Band it seemed like a natural progression. It didn't take a lot of selling on Albert's part to convince me to jump at the chance, and I told him that I'd go up there as soon as I finished my book.

Sheila and I were back in New York, living in Washington Heights, so the idea of moving to the country appealed to us (and to April, the Afghan hound). Over Christmas we went down to a justice of the peace

FIGURE 8. The happy couple, Sheila and Jim, with nephew
Phillip Driscoll and April, the afghan hound.

in a marriage-mill town called La Plata, Maryland. It was pretty low
key. Sheila's mother was our witness. The justice didn't even put his
cigarette out, but we both said "I do" and went back to Sheila's mother's
for a party with her family, my parents, and Larry and Gloria Casson. We
were together and we were happy.

After the New Year, Sheila started taking some education courses at
Hunter College and I started in on *Bossmen*. I'd taken the title from Jimmy
Reed's "Big Boss Man." It summed up my feeling that both Muddy and
Bill had a certain kind of authority as men, which translated itself into
their music. In December Muddy had been in a bad automobile accident and was laid up in the hospital in Champaign, Illinois. I visited
him in the hospital for a few days, and he was happy for the diversion.
It might have been the first time he had the time to think about his life
and how he had gone about creating his music. In late January I visited
Muddy again, this time at his home on the south side of Chicago. He
couldn't drink Chivas any more—doctor's orders. But the doctor hadn't

said anything about champagne. He smiled a big smile as he offered me a glass—Mumm's—nothing but the best! On the same trip I went to the Chess Studios and interviewed Willie Dixon, who had written so many of Muddy's signature songs like "Hoochie Coochie Man." He had a lot to do with helping Muddy get his personality across in songs that were specifically tailored for Muddy Waters and helped to make him a star. Buddy Guy met me in one of Chicago's countless blues clubs and gave me a glimpse into the way Muddy could spot young talent and bring it into his band. He wanted the best players he could find. He wasn't afraid of competition. Sadly, the great piano man Otis Spann had just died. We had become friends back when he played at the Club 47 with Muddy and then again as leader of his own band, and still later when we had traveled together in Europe. He, too, was a big part of Muddy's sound, and I was very sad to hear of his passing. However, this time spent in Chicago gave me plenty of material to work with. I was off to a good start.

As it happened, Bill Monroe was scheduled to play at the University of Chicago Folk Festival on the next weekend, so I met him there. After Chicago he was heading to Canada for a week or so and invited me to come along. This was my first experience traveling on a bus with Bill. Back when Bill Keith was in the band, I always traveled to gigs in Keith's souped-up Chevy. Monroe and the others were in his road-weary Oldsmobile station wagon. Bill's bus was no less road-weary. The heat wasn't working too well, so everyone stayed bundled up as we journeyed in subzero temperatures from Chicago to Detroit to Windsor to Toronto to Montreal. It didn't seem to matter to Bill. He'd sit there all day in his overcoat strumming his mandolin and watching the frozen fields go by. When we got to a motel, he'd get two rooms—one for him and his companion Virginia Stauffer, and the other one for the band, plus me. This was the true bluegrass life. Every morning was taken up with starting the bus, which was a diesel with a glow plug to start it. The glow plug wasn't working. Every day someone would say, "We've got to get that fixed." That never did get done, so every morning was spent with an industrial strength tow truck towing "The Bluegrass Express" down some snowy street somewhere until it coughed and kicked over, and we'd get on our way.

By the end of the tour everybody had a cold of some sort or another. After Montreal we had one more date at Clark University in Worcester,

Massachusetts. I was looking forward to that, because Bill Keith and I had played there a few times. We left Montreal about two in the morning. Snow was piled up six feet high on each side of the road. We bounced along over the frost heaves—ba-boom, ba-boom, ba-boom—all the way to Worcester. You could not sleep. We arrived at 8 o'clock in the morning and whiled away the hours going to a coffee shop, a music store, a grocery store, and back again—any place with heat! Finally, 6 o'clock rolled around, and we drove over to the campus, which was eerily silent. It was midterm break! There wasn't a student in the place. Whoever had booked the gig had neglected to look at the calendar. The hall probably sat about one thousand people. Scattered around the seats was a meager audience of forty to fifty hardy souls. The consensus of the band was, "Let's get this over with and hit the road and get back to Tennessee where it's warm!" Bill Monroe had other ideas. He gave me a big lesson that night. He played as if his soul was on fire. I heard him play things I had never heard him play. His mandolin breaks were scorching. He gave those people who did show up a show they would never forget. I certainly didn't. He was consumed with whatever had gotten into him. He wanted to play, and he played his heart out.

For all my traveling with Bill that time, I really hadn't gotten much out of him for the book. The few times I did succeed in sitting down with him to talk, it was like pulling teeth. I'd ask a question, and he'd answer, "Yessir" or "Nosir." He was pretty shy. I got off the bus in New York as they passed through on their way back to Nashville, and I was beginning to wonder how this part of the book was going to come to life. A few weeks later I hooked up with him again, and this time I got lucky. The bus, as usual, was giving them trouble, and we went to a garage outside of Roanoke, Virginia. We stayed in the bus all night long waiting for the mechanic to arrive in the morning. Kenny Baker, the great fiddler, was with Bill at the time, and he and Bill wound up sitting in the front of the bus, and they just started talking. I turned on the cassette recorder and did my best to stay out of the way. They knew I was listening, but they didn't let it bother them. Once in a while I'd ask a question to nudge things along. They talked about all kinds of things. Bill talked about when he first left Kentucky to join his brothers Charlie and Birch who were working in Gary, Indiana. He talked about starting out playing music professionally with Charlie; about starting his own band, The Bluegrass Boys. Kenny talked about hearing Bill's music for the first time and how it made him want to play with him. They talked on through the night, and I got the heart of what I needed to get. It had a reality about it that I was never going to get in a formal interview. The setting of the bus in the garage seemed entirely appropriate as a backdrop for the telling of Bill's story.

I wasn't trying to write a full biography of either Bill or Muddy. My main focus was on each man's role in shaping their music and how the two schools of music, Bluegrass and Chicago Blues, came to be. I was interested in them as bandleaders who would attract talented players to them. They would then use that talent to the benefit of their music. For instance, when Bill Monroe heard the banjo playing of Earl Scruggs, he knew that it was a different sound and that it would work in his music. Muddy was the same way. He would recognize the talent of a Little Walter on harmonica or Otis Spann on piano. They had something to bring to his music. As Muddy told me, "They make me look good." I also talked to each man about people leaving the band. Muddy's classic response was, "One monkey don't make no show." Bill wasn't as philosophical about it. He wouldn't speak to Lester Flatt or Earl Scruggs for about twenty years! However, even Bill got over it. Each man came to understand that one of his roles in life was to develop new talent and let it go out into the world.

Armed with these interviews and others, my idea was to use as much as possible of the various people's words, especially Muddy's and Bill's. I would narrate the stories as unobtrusively as possible. Because of my focus on their actual words I believe that the book succeeded in capturing the essence of each man. Each man's language and the way he talked revealed who he was and how he thought about himself and his music. There was music in the way they spoke, and that's what gave the book its energy and validity. Some people thought it was a strange idea. "Bill Monroe and Muddy Waters? What have they got to do with each other?" If you want to put music in little boxes and isolate different kinds of music you can do it, but my experience tells me that all musics are related in some way. I decided to set Bill and Muddy side by side and let the readers find out what the similarities were. As Pete Seeger said very kindly when asked about the book, "Anyone in the world wanting to understand American music could well start right here."

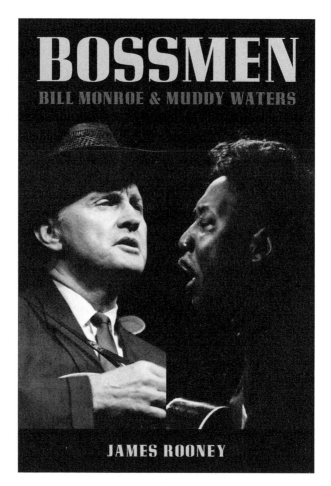

FIGURE 9. *Bossmen* book cover.
Photograph courtesy of JRP Books.

WOODSTOCK

With the book completed and turned in, Sheila and I packed up and headed for Woodstock. I had been in touch with Albert Grossman off and on. He had suggested that, since The Band was to be involved in the studio, I should go out on the road with them a couple of times to see if we would "get along." I had no doubt that we would, so I readily agreed. I drove up to Kingston, New York, one weekend and met them at the airport where we boarded a small, chartered plane to fly to their first gig that weekend. After the concerts, I'd hang out with Levon Helm and Rick Danko and play country and bluegrass songs. So right away we got on great. Robbie Robertson seemed to be more involved in the studio development, so each time we got together I'd ask about it and try to get a picture of how it was coming along. All he'd ever say was, "It's gonna be great, really great."

After moving three times in one year, Sheila and I were ready to settle down. We found a cottage on a side road a few miles out of town in Lake Hill. It was a sweet little place at the base of a small mountain, with a stream and meadow across the road. After we arrived at the house and unpacked everything, I told Sheila I was going to take a look at the studio. I'd never been able to see it because the road wasn't ploughed whenever I went up there, so all I knew was that "it's gonna be great." As I drove up the dirt road leading to the studio I ran into Albert and Sally taking a walk up the hill, so I stopped and we walked up together. Through the trees, which were just starting to bud out, I could see this enormous cinder block shell. The walls were about twenty feet high. The wall facing us was probably eighty feet long. It was huge. I couldn't help but notice that there was no roof on it! Albert turned to me and asked, "What do you think?" I replied, "Well, it's big. It's really big." That was about all I could say. There was no point in asking, "When do we start recording?"

We wandered around as he showed me where things would be. There were going to be two studios in the building—a smaller "B" studio and a large "A" studio, which was going to be as big as a basketball court. After a while, when we were walking back to my car, he said, "Have you got a minute?" (A phrase I came to know well, since it always meant that he was going to show me something that entailed work.) I said, "Sure." He said, "Come down with me to this other place. I want to show you something." We drove down to the village of Bearsville, which consisted of a post office and small grocery at a crossroads. There were a few houses there as well. He took me into one of the houses and said that he was going to turn it into a restaurant. He needed a set of floor plans of the building right away for the liquor board so he could apply for a liquor license. Could I do that? Albert didn't know that my dad was in the construction business and that I'd worked a couple of summers for my Uncle

Jim as a draftsman. So I told him I could do that and asked him when he needed it. "Right away."

When I got home, Sheila said, "Well, how is it?" I said, "I don't know. The place isn't ready to go at all," and then told her about my first task of drawing up plans for the restaurant to be. But I was there to work, and I was going to be paid a weekly salary, so I just plunged in. I measured up the house, drew the floor plan, and brought it up to Albert at his house. He was happy to get it. While I was there I met this great big giant of a man, Paul Cypert, who was running the construction operation. It was quickly established that I would be there to help Paul get whatever he needed. Sally had been writing the checks for the workers and supplies, so that was turned over to me as well. There again, I was the man for the job, since I had done payroll and the books for the Club 47. My past skills, totally unknown to Albert, were coming in handy. As he often did, Albert had got lucky.

Paul Cypert and I hit it off right away. He reminded me of the best men my father had worked with in his construction career. Paul was a master carpenter. He had come to Albert's attention while building a spiral staircase for The Band's producer John Simon. The risers were fitted in a spiral around a central 12" × 12" vertical beam. It was a thing of solid beauty. Albert recognized a master when he saw one and asked Paul, "Have you got a minute?" Paul's "minute" lasted until well after Albert's death. Paul was also my introduction to the native upstate New Yorkers. He liked to work hard and have a couple of drinks at the end of the day. He'd be on the job at seven in the morning, having driven down from his home up in the country in Oliverea. There was a crew of carpenters and blocklayers that he ran. I became Paul's problem solver. Whatever they needed, I would get. I found out about all kinds of stuff—plumbing, heating, electrical. I'd be back and forth to Kingston every day. We were trying to move things along because Albert was already getting antsy about getting the studio up and running. Then there was the restaurant. We were having stainless steel stove hoods made to order. I'd go over to Sullivan County in a pickup to bring them back. I had to go to the Port of Hoboken in a bigger truck to pick up imported chairs. I drove the truck loaded to the brim with oak flooring for the studio over the rainy mountain roads from Messina. I'd go down to the Bowery in the City to pick up a load of used restaurant stoves and coolers. One of Albert's mottos was, "The other side of a bankruptcy is a bargain." So we got all of this equipment at a great price. I'd go with Albert to Simon's hardware, which took up an entire city block, to get brass hinges and doorknobs and locks. In another life Albert had worked for the Chicago Housing Authority. One of his jobs was to buy the hardware—faucets, doorknobs, hinges, etc.—for some of their public housing projects. He was very proud of the fact that his buildings had locks that locked and faucets that didn't drip. Everything worked, and he'd gotten it at the lowest price. He was always looking for a bargain and always looking for quality. He wasn't easy to work for, because he was rarely, if ever satisfied, but I understood his motivation and couldn't argue with it.

So for four months or so this was my life. It had nothing to do with running a studio or music. I was the foreman of the whole operation and was on call at all times. At home, Sheila and I worked on the house every day. Basically, it was a simple little cottage that a hippie couple had been living in, so everything was painted purple and gold. There were barrels filled with used Pampers out back and lots of "stuff" in the house which they had just left behind. I carted truckloads away to the dump. We put in a hot-air oil furnace. I broke out a wall in the kitchen to make one big room with a large window looking out over the valley. Paul Cypert made us a beautiful cherry butcher-block counter. I started the dirty job of taking the asbestos shingles off the outside of the house and replacing them with cedar shingles. Sheila and I painted all the rooms. We dug up and planted a vegetable garden. We got some chickens. I started to grow a beard to get fully into the "back to the earth" mode. We bought everything out of the Whole Earth Catalogue and at local auctions. The auctioneers took a shine to Sheila. Almost as soon as she'd put her hand up for something they'd close the bidding and give it to her. We were busy.

As the work on the studio progressed, there was a lot of specialized construction needed for acoustics and soundproofing. A man from New York named Bob Hansen was the first acoustic consultant. Paul had never done this kind of work before, but he was up to the challenge and was very creative. Hansen would tell him what was required. Paul would think about it, look at the space, and then say, "You could do this, this, and this." That would be it. He'd get it done and get it done right. Rock and roll had opened up the idea of residential studios where a band could come and stay for the duration of the recording, so there was a two-bedroom apartment at one end of the studio. The restaurant was going to have a French chef. Albert had a Japanese gardener who grew organic vegetables. All of this was supposed to be tied together as a feature of the studio. As time passed it became clear to me that this was totally Albert's operation. The Band had nothing to do with it, except that Robbie Robertson would occasionally be asked his opinion about things. But the studio was Albert's all the way. He owned it. He paid for it. The name was the Bearsville Sound Studios.

Amazingly, by mid-September we had the "B" studio ready for a shakedown session. John Simon organized a session with John Hall, later of the band Orleans (and still later a U.S. Congressman from the area). He had a song called "Dancing in the Moonlight," which was the first song recorded at Bearsville. Albert had some kind of a record deal with Ampex at the time, so he got a good deal on the two 16-track Ampex machines. We had a nice big Quad-Eight industrial-strength board. At the time Dolby and DBX had competing noise reduction systems, so we had DBX on the 16-track machines and Dolby on the 2-tracks. We had the latest in limiters, compressors and "gates" which had all been developed to deal with rock and roll volume levels. We also had two real echo chambers as well as two EMT echo plates. The place was well equipped, to say the least.

I, of course, knew nothing about recording technology, but Albert had hired a very good maintenance engineer named John Gardner, assisted by Richard Lubash, who did most of the wiring of the patch bays and so on. He also hired a fine, young, energetic recording engineer named Mark Harman. He had come from California where he'd done a lot of work with Doug Sahm and The Sir Douglas Quintet. Mark was perpetually in a good mood. He never walked when he could run. He was ready, willing, and able to work, which was good, because once we got up and running it was pretty continuous. Usually it was Albert who told me that so and so would be coming in to record. It was always a case of "this person has to get priority." Everybody he talked to had to get priority. That was my job—to juggle all of these people and make sure they didn't get bent out of shape if they couldn't get in right away.

By this time, Van Morrison was living up there with his band. Paul Butterfield was there with his band, too, which now included David Sanborn, Gene Dinwiddie, and Steve Madaio on horns. Dylan was still there when I arrived, but he soon moved his family to New York City and the relationship between Albert and him was going away. Sadly, Janis Joplin had died in October, so Albert had moved the whole Full Tilt Boogie Band from California to some apartments we had just done up. The Band was there, of course, but because the studio wasn't ready that summer they recorded the *Stage Fright* album at the Woodstock Playhouse with Todd Rundgren using a remote truck parked outside. Back when I was visiting Albert in his office to talk about the job, this kid came in to hook up some hi-fi equipment. He was skinny and had long hair and was crawling around under the desk hooking things up. It was Todd Rundgren. After Todd was through making The Band's album, he would take all my studio time from midnight on to work on his own stuff. I'd come in each morning and there would be microphone cables down the hallway, in the toilet, all over the place. He ran the board and the machines himself and played all the instruments. He recorded his huge hit "Hello, It's Me" this way. John Gardner would be tearing his hair out. "This place is a mess! This kid is ruining everything!" I'd say, "Hey! He's good. Let him go. Clean the place up. Let's get going here." Of course, the construction never stopped. After the restaurant ("The Bear") was finished, there was "The Bear Café." A couple of houses were turned into offices and apartments. My day started before eight in the morning and could easily go until midnight or past, depending on what was going on.

Then there was my social life! Sheila and I were happy to be building our nest. In addition, a community was forming around us. Not too long after we arrived, Bill Keith and Geoff and Maria Muldaur moved over from Cambridge. Happy Traum's brother Artie had moved up from New York. John Herald was around. So we all started getting together at each other's places and picking. Some nights brought me back to my early days in Cambridge ten years earlier. There was also a great restaurant in the middle of town called "Deanie's," where everyone would go. It was a well-established place with great old waitresses and a woman named Flo who played the piano. The bar was frequented by a mix of the native Woodstockers, many of them of Dutch descent, and the new musical community, which was taking shape. In time, the Bear bar became another watering hole and a place called the Joyous Lake opened up featuring live music. So there was no shortage of night life. I was definitely burning the candle at all available ends.

There were no festivals in Newport in 1970. The Folk Foundation Board had a couple of meetings to assess the damage. Eventually, the Newport Town Council acceded to our request that we be given a chance to stage a folk festival in the summer of '71, so we began to plan a very modest event, with no big stars. That May Ralph Rinzler had asked me if I could come down and run the music stage at the first Festival of American Folk Life to be put on over the Fourth of July weekend on the Washington Mall. The lineup included Professor Longhair, Utah Phillips, Rosalie Sorrels, Tracy Nelson, John Jackson, and John Hartford with Vassar Clements, Tut Taylor, and Norman Blake. The daylong concert got off to a fine start on a beautiful morning before a relaxed and receptive audience. However, at some point I noticed that there seemed to be a sudden influx of people running into our area. There had been an antiwar demonstration going on near the Washington Monument. The park police charged the crowd with tear gas, driving the people right into our audience. As always, my focus was on keeping the music going, but at a break between acts one of the demonstrators jumped up on stage and started to make a speech. The police were going to cut off the power. I told the cop in charge that, if he did, he'd have a real riot on his hands, so we agreed on a compromise. We'd let a spokesman for the protestors speak for five minutes as part of Utah Phillips's set. We then just junked our schedule and had continuous music for six hours while the whole situation settled down. Folk music had won the day, and the Festival of American Folk Life started its long life.

Heading home to Ralph's that night I was tired, but happy. Then, on the car radio I heard the news—"Riot at Newport Jazz Festival!" Newport had also allowed the Jazz Festival to return, the crowd got out of control, and they closed the festival down. I couldn't believe it. Once again I and several other board members went to plead our case for holding the folk festival, but the Newport Town Council had had enough. It was over.

As it was, I had plenty to do. Every day brought new surprises. One morning a fellow wandered into the studio and said that Albert had told him that I could help him. His name was Darry Wood. He had a truckload of tepee poles he had brought up from Florida. He needed to be shown where to take them and, needless to say, some help in unloading them. It turned out that Albert had ordered a tepee for himself, as had Robbie Robertson, so we unloaded some at Albert's and some at Robbie's. Fortunately, I was not expected to assist in the erecting of the tepees. My job evidently had some limits.

Sometimes it seemed like I was the last to know what was going on. Another morning I noticed a young guy with long curly blond hair wandering around the studio. I asked if I could help him. He introduced himself. He was Nick Jameson, the new second engineer! When I finally caught up to Albert, I said, "Thanks for telling me that we have another engineer. What's he supposed to do? What's he going to get paid? Starting when?" "You can work it out with Mark and John," Albert said. "He's pretty smart." And Albert sailed off, leaving me to figure it out.

Of course, there were some surprises that made my day. Ian and Sylvia's band The Great Speckled Bird, with Amos Garrett on electric guitar, Ben Keith on steel, Jim Colegrove on bass and N.D. Smart on drums, had moved up to Woodstock. One afternoon Colegrove and N.D. showed up at the studio with another fellow in tow. He had on overalls, no shirt, no shoes, long hair, and a beard, a weathered look—a little like Jesus! He turned out to be Bobby Charles. Bobby was originally from Abbeville, Louisiana. While still a teenager he had gotten involved in the music scene in New Orleans. He'd written "See You Later, Alligator" and Fats Domino's "I'm Walkin' to New Orleans." He had a beautiful smile and a lovely soft way of speaking, very laid back. After work that night a few of us wound up over at Bill Keith's with Bobby. In the course of the evening he picked up a guitar and sang me a song:

If I had my way
I'd leave here today
I'd move in a hurry
I'd find me a place
Where I could stay
And not have to worry
Chorus: Some place I'd feel loose
         Some place I could lose
         These Tennessee blues
I'd find me a spot
On some mountain top
With no one around me
With valleys and streams
And birds in the trees

And lakes that surround me
Some place I'd feel loose
Some place I could lose
These Tennessee blues
Chorus:
A place to forget
All my regrets
And keep just the good times
Some place I could sleep
In nothing but peace
And feel free at all times
Some place I'd feel loose
Someplace I could lose
These Tennessee blues
Chorus:

That night the "Tennessee Blues" entered my heart and stayed forever. It affected me just the same way "I'm So Lonesome I Could Cry" had affected me years before. It was a blessing. Bobby had written it that summer when he wound up somehow in the Catskill Mountains. He'd been working in Nashville with the great R&B disc jockey John "R" but had run afoul of the law over some marijuana he was growing. Bobby couldn't stand the thought of jail time, so he found someone to drive him up to the Catskill Mountains to escape the "heat." He heard about the developing music scene in Woodstock and guessed that maybe Albert Grossman might be interested in some songs. He guessed right. Within a short time Albert offered him a publishing deal and a recording contract with his new label Bearsville Records. Albert hired a lawyer to help Bobby settle his legal difficulties. Over the next few months Bobby worked with John Simon and Rick Danko and made one of my favorite albums to come out of Bearsville while I was there.

One day John Gardner told me about a guy he was going to hire to clean up the studio in the mornings. His name was Jon Gershen. He said that he was a good singer, songwriter, and guitar player and that I might enjoy playing music with Jon and his brother David. When Jon came up, we talked and decided to get together. They'd been in a band called The Montgomerys, and they both had interesting voices and wrote interesting songs. David was into pretty hard-core country singers like Johnny

Paycheck, although his own singing was much softer, closer to another of his (and my) favorite singers, Merle Haggard. His songs were pretty straightforward, with a country feel to them. Jon's were jazzier, but still earthy. He had an edge to his electric guitar sound and more of an emotional vocal delivery. My hillbilly/folky style seemed to fit somewhere in between Jon and David. They had already been talking to Stu Greenberg in New York at United Artists Publishing about a publishing deal. We all met with Stu, and he offered us a publishing deal and a recording deal with their own label Avalanche Records. (The name should have warned us off, but it didn't.) We didn't waste any time working up songs and gathering a band, which included Billy Mundi, former drummer with The Mothers of Invention, Ben Keith on dobro and steel, Jim Colegrove on bass, David Sanborn on sax, and John Simon on piano. Nick Jameson was happy to jump into a project on his own and the album came together quickly. It was the first time I had worked in the studio and it was a lovely place to play. It was also a big boost to have such great players available. Before it was over we enlisted both Dick Handle (aka Richard Manuel) and Campo Malaqua (aka Garth Hudson). For a couple of my tunes I wanted to have twin fiddles. I got my friend Kenny Kosek to come up from New York and, as a long shot, called Vassar Clements, who I had met with John Hartford in Washington. To my surprise, Vassar said he'd come up, so he and Kenny played beautiful twin fiddles on a country standard, "Good Woman's Love," and a Cajun version of "Handsome Molly." I was in heaven. Jon and I found ourselves sharing the producing chores during the overdubs and mixing, and we were thrilled with the results. We called ourselves Borderline and the album *Sweet Dreams and Quiet Desires*.

About the same time I got involved with an album Eric Von Schmidt came up to record for Poppy Records, another subsidiary of United Artists. Once again, Nick Jameson was at the controls. Billy Mundi, Jim Colegrove, and the ubiquitous Campo Malaqua played, as did Amos Garrett on guitar and Paul Butterfield on harmonica. Maria Muldaur added her harmonies. The producer was Michael Cuscuna, who was based in New York. Geoff Muldaur had been studying arranging before he left Cambridge, so he was heavily involved in some of the arrangements involving horns. Naturally, as my time allowed, I was dropping by the sessions, and I became aware of a certain amount of friction develop-

FIGURE 10. Borderline, 1973 (*l. to r.*: Jon Gershen,
David Gershen, Jim Rooney).
Photograph by Eric Von Schmidt.

ing between Michael and Geoff. Without any discussion or forethought
I started interposing myself on Eric's behalf between them so that they
wouldn't get hung up and the record could get done. As a result I wound
up being credited as coproducer. It was another step down that road.
Eric called the album *2nd Right, 3rd Row*.

Artie Traum came up with the idea of recording the music we played
when we got together at each other's houses. A bunch of us went up and
spent a weekend at a little 4-track studio north of Albany. It was Happy
and Artie, Bill Keith and me, John Herald, Maria Muldaur, Eric Kaz, Tony
Brown, and Lee Berg. Over the course of two or three days and nights
we recorded fifteen or twenty songs and had a wonderful time doing it.
Happy Traum summed things up well in the liner notes:

> "We had long wanted to put down, for ourselves and anyone else who
> wanted to hear, the kind of songs and instrumentals we play when we
> get together at parties and just pick and sing for fun. We wanted to re-
> cord for a small record company with whom we could work informally,

free from commercial restraints. Artie had come across some Rounder records, liked the way they looked and sounded, and called them up. He then called friends and neighbors and great enthusiasm followed, resulting in this record. I believe we got what we went for—an album of songs that convey the sense of closeness, personally and musically, that we feel, as well as the fun of doing something for its own sake, as opposed to doing it for financial or other ends."

We mixed the album back at Bearsville with Mark Harman. Once again, I was getting involved in the process and enjoying it. We called the album *Mud Acres: Music among Friends*."

Of course, my main focus was on the major artists recording at the studio and keeping everything flowing along smoothly. Paul Rothchild came up to produce an album with the Butterfield Blues Band. He was sporting a full-length fur coat and went around the studio clapping his hands to check the acoustics. Paul had become a major producer on the strength of his work with The Doors and had come a long way since our days in Cambridge. Taj Mahal did an album using the great Howard Johnson along with four other tuba players to play the 12-string guitar bass lines on a Leadbelly song. The sound was amazing. Taj also had come a long way since our early days in Amherst and Cambridge. However, nothing had changed in his energy and positive attitude, and it was a joy to be around him again. At long last, Robbie Robertson called and said that The Band needed to block-book the studio to work on an album. I was looking forward to having them in the studio every day for a while.

However, when they came to the studio to work on their new album, I got the feeling that some of the creative energy had slipped away. One day, I came in and Robbie Robertson was in the control room and Levon was out in the drum booth banging away. For what seemed like an eternity Robbie and Mark Harman were laboring with the EQ knobs and various gadgets to get what they referred to as a "drum sound." It seemed simple enough to me. Put some mikes on Levon's drum kit and let him play. He had a "drum sound." He sounded like Levon Helm! As I watched them on that day and over the course of the next weeks it became clear that the other band members were basically letting Robbie run the show. He wanted to produce the album, and the others were happy to let him. They were busy having a good time. As a result, the album *Cahoots* seemed to me to lack the spark and originality of their previous albums. Something was missing, and I think it was that feeling of joint creativity.

If I had had time to think about it, I might have also noticed that Janis Joplin's death had taken some of the wind out of Albert's sails. He really loved her. He loved her energy. He had been excited about the new album Paul Rothchild was producing with Janis and her new band The Full Tilt Boogie Band. Suddenly, she was gone. There was a hole there that wouldn't be filled. Albert started to let the business side of things slip a bit. He wasn't in his New York office as much. His partner Bennett Glotzer was there, but his focus was on acts he was involved in like Tom Rush and Seatrain. Things came to a head one day when Paul Butterfield came into the office above the Bear Restaurant which I now shared with a bookkeeper. At the time Paul was working every single weekend, going out and playing with his big band—making decent money, so that everyone was getting paid. The band members were all happily living in the area. Paul and his wife Kathy had left behind their life of living in cheap hotels. They had a nice house over the mountain from me. They had a young son, Lee. Paul was as happy as I had ever seen him. That day in the office he was on the phone looking for the plane tickets for that weekend. For some reason they hadn't been sent up from New York. I saw the look on Paul's face as the travel agent told him that he hadn't been paid in weeks and that no tickets would be issued until he was. Paul couldn't believe it. He called the New York office, but Bennett wasn't in and nobody could help him. As it turned out, the plane tickets were the tip of the iceberg. For a good while bills had not been paid for the rental cars, the hotels, the credit cards—everything. Almost overnight, Paul was out of business. The horn players all went to work for Stevie Wonder. Although Paul went on to form a band called "Better Days" with Geoff Muldaur and Amos Garrett, and later worked on his own, he never recovered from that blow.

Very gradually, then, the atmosphere was changing in the world around me. There was the departure of Dylan to New York, Janis's death, the demise of the Butterfield Blues Band, the way The Band seemed to be losing its creative energy. Soon Van Morrison moved to California. As for myself, when I was involved in making music, I was happy, but the work side of things had given me a headache in the back of my head—not a good place for a headache. I went to a doctor, and he told me what I already knew. It was a tension headache. I decided I had better talk to Albert.

When I told Sheila, she asked me what was I thinking about? I certainly wasn't thinking about quitting, was I? I said that I didn't know. All I knew was that I needed things to change if I was going to get rid of this headache. I could sense right away that there was a bit of panic setting in, but I had to do something. Albert stayed calm as he listened to me tell him that I was feeling worn out and needed some sort of break. He said that he realized I had too much to do and said that he'd think about it and try to figure something out. Then he laughed and told me everything would get better, and if it didn't, it would get worse! I had to laugh too. Since I started working at the Club 47, I'd been making things up as I went along. What else was new? Albert was true to his word and told me he was going to hire someone to be my assistant. He turned out to be a former booking agent from New York named Al Schweitzman. He was a nice enough guy, but he was through and through a booking agent. It was all he knew. He didn't know anything about dealing with builders, especially a guy like Paul Cypert. Pretty soon Paul came to me in a state. "I'm not dealing with him! I'll only deal with you!" So, despite Albert's good intentions, my assistant wasn't much use and turned into one more problem I had to deal with. Needless to say, the headache stayed.

In May, our *Mud Acres* group had landed a couple of concerts. One was for Izzy Young at the Washington Square Church where The Blue Velvet Band had its start. We got a great picture that night of all of us with Izzy seated like the grand poobah of folk in the middle. It became the album cover. After that we were scheduled to play at Sanders Theater at Harvard, where I had listened to John Finley and Bill Alfred lecture as a Humanities section man. The day before, I went out to Dedham to visit my parents and my sister Eileen, who was now living with her family in our old house. We had dinner at my parents' house and went to see my nephew Phillip in a school play at Roxbury Latin. My dad was having some kind of indigestion and went to bed. When I came home, my mother told me that the doctor had been there, thought he was having a gall bladder attack and had given him some pills for the pain to get him through the night. However, he was wide awake and in considerable pain, despite the medication, so we decided that we should take him to the hospital. When my brother-in-law Phil Driscoll and I tried to get him up out of bed, he fainted, so we called an ambulance. It turned out that he had had an aneurysm in his aorta. They operated on him all the next day. He came through the surgery, but his kidneys were failing due to the lack of blood caused by his burst aorta. I called my sister Kathleen in Connecticut and my brother John in Illinois and told them the situation. We didn't know how long he might last, but they both decided to come immediately. I rushed back to Woodstock to set things up for as long as I needed to be away. Bonnie Raitt had just arrived to begin her first album, but I figured that Al could cover for me.

As I drove up to my house, Geoff Muldaur was mowing my lawn. There was a blues song about the subject that Big Bill Broonzy used to sing. In his case someone was "digging my potatoes." A tiny thought came into my head at the moment. "What's Geoff Muldaur doing over here mowing my lawn?" But it really wasn't a conscious thought. I was too busy thinking about my dad and what I needed to do. I got some clothes, set things up at the studio, and headed back to Dedham. My dad died a few days later. My brother, my sisters, and I organized a wake in our old house. He was laid out in the front room. Sheila came over from Woodstock to join me. It wasn't easy for her. She'd never really connected with my parents. Her own father had died in a car crash when she was a kid. Her mother had raised four kids on her own. She was an interior decorator and was pretty hip. I guess, in comparison, my folks looked and acted old-fashioned. Sheila showed up wearing a long, brightly colored hippy dress. When she saw my father laid out in the front room I thought she was going to lose it. This Irish wake scene was definitely not for her. It went on for a couple of days. At one point all the men who had worked on the construction jobs—the bricklayers, carpenters, and laborers, most of whom were Irish—were standing outside the fence on the sidewalk. I got my brother John and said, "They look like they could use a drink." We brought some glasses and a couple of bottles of whiskey out to them. We didn't have to be told to do it. We were our father's sons.

Once back in Woodstock, I plunged back into my routine. Bonnie Raitt's album seemed to be going well. However, Sheila and I got another jolt when she got word that her mother had become quite ill. She needed to be with her, and, as it turned out, she was gone for nearly a month. While she was away, I decided to finish off the attic and make it into a nice big bedroom. It was a nice surprise for Sheila when she came home, but the combination of my dad's death, her mother's illness, and my burnout at work was taking its toll. I had also figured out that Geoff Muldaur was indeed sniffing around, so I called him up and told him that we needed to talk. We got together, and I basically told him that as long as I was supporting Sheila and paying the bills, he could stay away. He and Maria were trying to deal with their own relationship, and I think he respected me for being so forthright with him. We continued to be friends.

The momentum of my life kept moving me on. Jon, David, and I finally finished what we thought was a wonderful album. Byron Linardos came and took some pictures for the album cover, and I headed out to L.A. to deliver the album to Nick Venet at United Artists Records. It was a welcome relief from all the other pressures. Outside Nick's office was a staircase leading to the second floor. We put on the album, but he seemed more interested in trying to get a look up the secretaries' skirts as they went up the stairs than listening to our masterpiece, which should have been a tipoff.

When I got home, Sheila and I were talking one night. I was thinking about putting a porch on the side of the house, and asked her what she thought. She just let go: "What are you talking about! We might not even be here next year!" With that, the flood gates opened. After months of not communicating, it all came out. We hadn't been intimate in ages. Both of us were too busy. She had been going to school to get her teaching degree. She'd gone to interview for a job, but the interview hadn't gone well, so she abruptly abandoned that career path and had started working with her friend Norma Cross at a little restaurant in town called The Squash Blossom. I said, "I think I'm going to have to stop working like this. Albert's not going to change. I know that. Too much is never enough as far as he's concerned. It will never end. I've got to stop." Sheila looked at me and said, "Well, what will we do?" I said, "I don't know what we'll do. All I know is what I won't do." We looked at each other, and I said, "I don't know. Maybe we should separate for a while and see what we can sort out. Let's think about it." The next day I went to Albert and told him. "I've really got to quit now. This is it." He was fine about it and said that if that's what I really needed to do, I should do it. I told him I'd stay on for a month to help make some sort of transition work. Driving home that night I felt such a sense of relief. Whatever had been building up inside me over the past year was being let out. After a few days I asked Sheila if she had figured out any place she could go. She said that she hadn't and that she thought she should stay on to sort of look after me and make sure I'd be okay. I said, "Separation means separation. You're going to have to find some other place to live." That was a shock. It wasn't just her either. She still had her dog April and I had bought her a nice little Morgan horse, which we stabled in the garage and pastured across the street. I had paid for everything, and I couldn't just give the house to her. That was the hard reality. However, once that reality was clear, she did make a move to a carriage house over at John Court's, Albert's former partner. His wife Wendy and Sheila had become good friends, so that worked out. When the news got out that Sheila and I were splitting up, it came as quite a shock to everybody, but we were the only ones who really knew what we needed to do, so we did it.

RAMBLIN' MAN

With Sheila gone and no job to go to every day, my life was suddenly my own to do with as I pleased. It was a strange feeling. I'd worked for the Club for two and a half years, the Newport Festivals for two years and I'd been working for Albert for two and a half years. It seemed to be a pattern. All of the jobs were seven days a week, all kinds of hours. Whatever had to be done, I'd do it. Sheila and I had spent all of our spare time together working on the house. In two years we had transformed it into a very sweet little spot, and we'd done it together. I had chosen to change all that. There was a part of me inside that needed to be dug out and satisfied. Right away I started playing more with Jon and David. We acquired a sound system and started playing every weekend at a place called The Log Cabin up on Route 28 in Phoenicia. It really was made out of logs. There was a bar with pool tables downstairs. Upstairs was a good-sized room with a small stage and a dance floor. Soon we were getting a good crowd to come out to listen and dance.

In the daytime I continued to finish the attic for something to do, but I also just started getting my guitar out. Along with the sunflowers out back I had grown a few pot plants, so I'd have a few tokes while I was strumming in the kitchen. It wasn't too long before a song emerged:

If I'd known then what I know now
I could stay not have to go now
And have her love to keep me from the cold
If I'd played my high cards different
She'd have wrapped me up in cement
And told me that I didn't look so old
If I told her that I loved her
And showed her that I meant it
She might have called me "Baby" all her own
But that's all past and gone now
I'm just stumbling on and on now
And this fever's just some interest on the loan
Bridge: Don't try to think about it
Get some rest, go hunt some rabbit
Take your time, don't move away too soon
These problems you've been having
They're only temporary
Why don't you wait until we shoot the moon
I've got to laugh to keep from crying
It's no fun, I'm always dying
And waking up again alone
I guess I'll have to grin and bear it
Can't seem to find no one to share it
And pay off this interest on the loan

All my time spent listening to the songs of Hank Williams, Harlan Howard, and Merle Haggard was time well spent. What I went for was the irony and dark humor they all put in their songs—the "laugh to keep from crying" bit. It was the way to get through, and it perfectly suited my mood. I was going out most nights. Suddenly I seemed to be quite popular with a lot of my soon-to-be former wife's girlfriends, as well as a few others. It seemed that the chase was what got me going. I hadn't a clue about marriage and the kind of communication you needed to do to make marriage work. I wasn't ready for that, as it turned out. It scared me. I did my best to cover up my fears by going out and blowing off quite a lot of steam.

I needed to get away. I made a start by heading for New York every week or two. Albert had agreed that I could be officially laid off so I could collect unemployment. I'd go to the employment office in Kingston every week. To no one's surprise, there were no jobs around for a studio manager, so I'd collect my $75 and get on the bus to the city, where I'd hook up with Bob Neuwirth and Sandy Bull. Neuwirth had come to Boston to go to the Museum School to study painting. He fell into the folk scene and was part of the gang around the Club. We shared a love of Hank Williams and country music. From Cambridge he moved to New York and became one of the crowd around Andy Warhol. Memorably, he showed up at a birthday party of mine in Cambridge with Nico on his arm. He also started traveling with Bob Dylan and working some for Albert Grossman. He was fast and funny and smart. If a band was out on the road getting weary, Albert would send him out to cheer up the troops. I needed some cheering up and stimulation now, so I turned to him. He was sharing an apartment with Sandy, who was a true instrumental virtuoso. He played guitar, banjo, oud, pedal steel guitar, and dobro and had played a couple of times at the Club.

Sandy wasn't much for going out but loved to sit in his apartment and pick. Neuwirth and I would hit the streets. He always knew what was happening. Max's Kansas City was the current hot spot. We lucked out one night and caught an incredible night with Willie Nelson and Waylon Jennings. You never knew what might develop, though many nights we were happy enough to get back to the peace and quiet of Sandy's and pick some songs. Neuwirth also told me about a film I should see—"The Harder They Come"—a reggae movie starring Jimmy Cliff. It hit me right between the eyes, with its story of a struggling singer trying to find his way in music. I immediately bought the sound track album. The song that jumped out at me was "Sitting in Limbo." I think I understood that I too was going to have to wait for the tide to come and take me wherever I was headed.

Christmas came, and I decided to go home to the family in Dedham. My mother had had a rough year, first losing my father and then seeing the state I was in. When I had broken the news about Sheila and me, she wasn't totally surprised. Although she had been enthusiastic enough when she first met Sheila, she had not felt her enthusiasm reciprocated. She was much more observant than I was and sensed that we weren't totally in sync. That feeling had been reinforced at the time of my dad's wake and funeral. I also don't think that she was that upset about me stopping working for Albert. She and my father had found him rather an odd duck. She was supportive of my desire to focus more on my music. So home was a good place for me to go. It was solid ground. I felt loved no matter what.

On Christmas Day we went to my sister Eileen's. Her oldest daughter Kate mentioned that she'd just heard "One Morning in May" on the radio. I said something about how nice it was that someone was still playing our old record. She said, "Oh, no. It wasn't you. It was James Taylor!" The next morning I went out and bought a copy of the *One Man Dog* album and played the cut of "One Morning in May." Indeed, it was our melody, but the credit on the album read, "traditional, arranged by James Taylor." I'd have to call Harold Leventhal at Sanga Music, who had agreed to publish the song back when we recorded "Living on the Mountain" and see if we could get the correct credit (and the money!). Maybe there would be hope in the New Year after all.

Almost immediately, Geoff Muldaur, Amos Garrett, and I flew down to Siesta Key to get together with Eric Von Schmidt to work on a new album. This time I was the official producer. We spent our time playing bocce on the beach in the afternoon and playing Eric's songs at night. Proceedings were well lubricated with rum, and inspiration was assisted by a certain amount of grass—even a bit of opium! (not a good idea) With our preproduction work successfully completed, we went up to Bearsville to record. We gathered in Maria Muldaur, Garth Hudson, Billy Mundi, and Jim Colegrove and some horn players headed by the trumpeter Peter Eklund. One of the highlights of the album was a version of "Joshua Gone Barbados," Eric's great song about his time in St Vincent's. We also did a wild version of the racehorse song "Stewball," featuring Garth Hudson playing a pump organ recorded in the huge "A" studio. We all sang on our unofficial theme song "Stick to Rum." Eric had a Brechtian piece called "Fat, the Water Rat," which allowed Geoff to show off his horn arranging skills. We closed out the album with a wild preaching piece called "Fast Acne." Eric was a fan of a preacher he'd heard on the Library of Congress recordings named "Sin Killer" Griffin. This was his homage to him and was appropriately over the top. I really enjoyed pulling the whole album together. I felt comfortable in the role of producer, working with lots of different personalities and seeing an album take shape. When we were done, Eric and I went down to Brooklyn to deliver the album to Kevin Eggars, who owned Poppy Records. While there we met another artist on the label, Townes Van Zandt, who knew who Eric was and was glad to meet him. I'd never heard his music, but I was intrigued by the title of his new album, *The Late, Great Townes Van Zandt*, which reminded me of the way disc jockeys for a long time always referred to Hank Williams. I'd say that's the connection Townes had in mind.

Back in Woodstock, I resumed my routine of going out at night. One night I was sitting at the bar in the Joyous Lake when this girl came in and sat down. I hadn't seen her before, and we started talking. Something about her clicked with me. Her eyes, her smile, her laugh. I don't know: something just clicked. Her name was Judy Ghen. She had lived in Woodstock before and was now living up in Canada—a place called Magog in Eastern Quebec. The next day I telephoned her and asked her if she wanted to go for a ride with me over to Poughkeepsie to visit this band I liked, Dan Delsanto and The Arm Brothers. We stopped for dinner on the way back, and I dropped her back where she was staying. She was the first girl I hadn't gone to bed with in months. She was different. I liked her. She headed back to Canada where she was living with a boyfriend, but we agreed to stay in touch.

It wasn't too long before I had a reason to call her. I was going to New York to play a television show with Eric Weissberg. His recording of "Dueling Banjos," from the movie "Deliverance" was zooming up the charts, and Eric suddenly needed to pull a band together to seize the moment. One of the first shows was a big TV show for the promoter Don Kirschner. Lots of people were going to be on it, including Taj Mahal, Mahavishnu John McLaughlin, and Al Green. Judy came down from Canada, and we went down to New York and checked into the Chelsea Hotel. During the rehearsal Taj Mahal stuck around and we decided on the spot to do "Salty Dog Blues" together. We didn't go on until nearly one in the morning, by which time we'd been drinking and smoking for hours. When the time came, I was ready. Our country blues-meets-bluegrass version of "Salty Dog" had a great energy to it, and Eric and Steve Mandel brought the house down with "Dueling Banjos." As it happened, I was visiting my mother in Dedham when the show aired. She turned to me after our spot and said, "You're really happy doing this, aren't you, Jimmy." Jimmy was possibly a bit too happy that night, judging from my eyes, but she was right. The headache in the back of my head had gone away.

Soon another piece of my puzzle fell into place. I went to see Bill Monroe play in New York. After the show Bill's son James mentioned that he had a motor home he was going to sell for $5,000. I told him I'd take it, and when I got home I went into the bank. I don't think that Mr. Gibbs at the bank realized that I had stopped working for Albert, but I'd been making the house payments, and they gave me the money to buy the motor home. I was beginning to see a way out. Judy came down once again, and as we drove out of Woodstock headed for Nashville to get the motor home, a great sense of freedom and relief came over me. I was moving into the unknown, and it felt great. As we drove through the night though, that feeling was replaced by some serious indigestion, which turned out to be appendicitis! I was lucky to make it into St. Thomas hospital in Nashville before it burst.

I was in there for three or four days. Judy would come and visit. She was wearing Levis, cowboy boots, and a T-shirt (no bra), which said "Bertha Has Balls." She turned a few heads. The farmer in the bed next to me who was in for a hemorroidectomy forgot about his troubles when she came in, shot him a big smile, and asked him how he was doing. She even got a smile out of one of the nuns. She definitely wasn't consumed by loneliness while I was in there. She was out every night and had already made friends with a couple of guys who were looking after her. Eventually I checked into the Holiday Inn near the hospital on West End Avenue. Judy was out rambling most of the time, so I called a few people up to say hello. One night, Vassar Clements showed up and said, "Wanna go pick?" I said, "I don't know. I can hardly button my pants. Why not!" So I put my pants on as best as I could and we went down to the Pickin' Parlor on 2nd Avenue and sat in with the band. I found out later that he really appreciated the fact that I had called him and got him up to Woodstock to play on our record at a time when his phone wasn't ringing a lot, and I think he understood that I needed a lift that night.

As soon as I had my stitches out, I went out to James Monroe's and got the motor home, found Judy, and drove the big beast down to Eric Von Schmidt's. I figured that swimming in the Gulf of Mexico would help me heal in a hurry. Needless to say, we had a ball at Eric's—drinking rum, cooking over a fire, and singing songs. It was the best medicine. I had an idea for a song that seemed to sum up my relationship with Judy. We were "Partners in Crime." Like so many of my songs, it was a waltz:

Since I can never make you all mine
I'd like to ask for some of your time
Time to go crazy and time to have fun
Time to lay sleeping out under the sun
I know you need to ramble and you need to roam
You need to spend some time alone
But when you are looking for a partner in crime
Don't ever fail to drop me a line
'Cause I will be waiting and ready to go
Ready to rock and ready to roll
Yes, we'll roll together down that highway of life
Me not a husband and you not a wife
But partners and friends we always will be
And that's what I'd like for eternity
Yes, partners and friends we always will be

Eric loved it and volunteered to paint me some signs to go on the side of the motor home. He came up with two desperadoes with kerchiefs over their faces, pistols drawn, facing in opposite directions, with the logo "PIC: Partners in Crime."

When we got back to Nashville, Judy decided to hang out there with her newfound friends. As I wrote in the song, I knew already that there was no point in tying her down. I left the motor home there with her, so she had a place to stay, and drove the Mercedes back to Woodstock by myself. On the way, my radio went out, so I had some time to think about things for a change. By the time I got to Woodstock I had figured it all out and called up Sheila. She was a bit frosty on the phone at first: "What do you want?" I said, "You might want to talk to me because I think I've figured out a way to give you the house." Sheila came over, and I laid it all out for her. "We'll refinance the house jointly, get a $30,000 mortgage for twenty years and pay off the old mortgage. I'll get my money out. Then we'll get divorced, and I'll give you the house in the settlement. The payments will be about the same. All you'll have to do is make them until you want to sell it. You'll have established your own credit. Then you can get your money out, and we'll both live happily ever after!" Which is what we did after we gave each other a real heartfelt hug.

I flew back to Nashville to get Judy and the motor home. I bought her a Norton 750 Commando motorcycle, had a rack for it put on the back, and drove back to Woodstock. She decided to ride the bike back up to Magog via Bangor, Maine. After she called to say that she'd safely made it to Bangor, I promptly got out my guitar and wrote a swinging little number called "Alive and Well and Hangin' Out in Bangor, Maine." I cleared my stuff out of the house and parked the motor home over at Bill Keith's while he was away in France. Paul Cypert gave me some oak flooring left over from the studio, which I used in place of the shag carpeting. I took out a sort of dining booth and replaced it with a new bed and storage area up front. I also put in a cassette deck and a couple of good speakers. My new home was taking shape. I then headed out to a few bluegrass festivals. I was the life of the party wherever I went. One night I had John Hartford, Doug Dillard, Norman Blake, Vassar Clements, and John McCuen all jammed in there. It was a jam session in every sense.

A couple of times I drove up to Magog. We'd go dancing in a joint where Judy's boyfriend, Bruno, was drumming in a band. At the end of the night they'd go to bed in his cottage by the lake, and I'd go to my camper. Needless to say, it was a strange arrangement, but I was happy to just let things play out as they would. On one of our excursions I decided to head over to Saratoga Springs. I remembered a bar Rosalie Sorrels had told me about that had the best Bloody Marys and the best juke box in town. She wasn't kidding. The Bloody Marys were delicious, and the jukebox had both Billie Holliday and Hank Williams on it, along with Duke Ellington, Dinah Washington, and Count Basie. About twelve Bloody Marys later it was closing time, and we had to go. Of course, the beauty of a motor home is that you're always home, and there is no need to drive if you've had too much to drink or are too tired. But I was feeling fine and headed down the Northway to Woodstock. Some time later I was awakened by the bouncing of the motor home. We were in some sort of a dirt road going fifty miles an hour! I jammed on the brakes. The motorcycle rack jumped so high that the bike cracked the rear window. Judy fell out on the floor. We hadn't hit anything. Needless to say, I was wide awake now. Adrenalin was pouring out of my ears! After having a look around, I saw that we had turned off the Northway, crossed a four-lane highway and were lucky that this dirt road was directly in our path. I slowly backed out and got back on the highway. I was sober now, and we made it back to Woodstock in one piece. We could have been killed or, worse yet, killed someone else. I was taking risks and pushing my luck, but that's what I wanted to do.

From the very beginning, Judy had tried to tell me that she didn't think our relationship was good for me. I think she worried that I was going to get hurt. When we went back up to Magog, and it was time for me to go, she broke the news to me that she had decided to stay with Bruno. Even though it came as no real surprise, it was not what I wanted to hear. That night I parked the camper in a lay-by off the highway. The place was a mess, as was I, but when I woke up in the morning I proceeded to write a song:

> *Chorus:* She was only the best
> No need to sit here and cry
> Why don't you give your heart a rest
> Why don't you learn how to say goodbye
> She never lied, she told you the truth
> She never told you that she loved you
> So now you're feeling like a fool
> You're going down slow in your blues
> *Chorus:*
> It's just her eyes, her laugh, and her body
> That keep her on your mind
> It's just her soul you see in the morning
> Dancing like a dream in your eyes
> *Chorus:*
> She's got to go, she can't stay with you
> She's finally found her home at last
> You ought to know, you helped her find it
> And soon you'll be part of her past
> *Chorus:*

It was a waltz with a bit of a Cajun feel to it. As I sat there strumming and writing, I began to feel happy. As sad as I was, the song was lifting me out of my hole. It was good. I knew it was good. I got up off the bed, put my yellow pad and guitar away, cleaned the place up, and hit the road, heading back to Woodstock.

Right away I got together with Jon and David. The people at United Artists wanted another album! The first one had disappeared without a trace, but Stu Greenberg told us that things would be different now. They'd reorganized, and a guy named Murray Deutsch had taken over. Murray was a classic music business veteran, with a permanent tan and a big smile. He assured us that everything would be run by him in New York, and those people in L.A. would have nothing to do with it. So we said okay. It didn't hurt that we'd be getting another advance and a good recording budget, so the wolf would be kept from the door.

I played Jon and David "Only the Best" and another one I had written about Sheila called "Beginning of the End." They both had some good new ones as well, so we got going on the new album. Jon wanted to take on the role of producer, and I was in a mood to let him. Since I wasn't working at Bearsville any more, Jon looked at other studios and found the CRS Studio in Bridgeport, Connecticut, where Harry Chapin had recorded "Cat's in the Cradle." Jon also found us a house to rent for a month right on Long Island Sound. This was the rock-and-roll approach to recording. We could all stay there and rehearse and drive into Bridgeport to record. We had Ben Keith, Amos Garrett, and David Sanborn again, plus a great young drummer named Christopher Parker and a fine young New York bass player, Will Lee. For horns, Jon got Randy and Michael Brecker, Barry Rogers, and Stan Free. Everything was first class. Eric Von Schmidt agreed to do the artwork. This was going to be good.

Just before leaving for Bridgeport I got a call from Judy. She had three kids who lived with their father out in California. He had agreed that she could come out before school started for a visit. She wanted to know if I'd take her out there in the motor home. I suggested that she might enjoy joining me at the beach house while we were recording, and then we could head out to California. Everything felt good as we rehearsed at the house. Being at the beach was wonderfully relaxing. Musically, things were shaping up. After a few days, we headed into the studio in Bridgeport to begin recording. The studio was right in the middle of downtown Bridgeport. Compared to Bearsville, the studio was small and a bit cramped. We were all situated in small spaces enclosed by movable soundproofing panels called gobos. Partly because I wasn't a seasoned studio player, I felt confined and was finding it hard to get a groove going. Eric showed up to take some pictures and show us some ideas for the album cover. He had gathered a lot of illustrations out of an old magician's catalogue. One of them showed a man seated at a table in an open-sided box up on sawhorses. His hands were manacled to the table, and a hand was reaching down from a cloud suspended above the box holding a violin. I immediately said, "That's it! That's how I feel in the studio when I'm in my little space with the earphones on and I can't move around." David had a song called "Heaven's So Hard to Find." Somehow it all seemed to make sense. However, Jon was doing his best to overcome any difficulties, and we were getting some wonderful tracks.

One day the 16-track machine was down for some reason. Jon suggested that if we wanted to kill some time, there was a motel a couple of blocks away with a bar in it. So Judy and I went over there and walked into the bar, past a sign saying "No Jeans Allowed." Naturally, we had jeans on, but paid it no mind. A security guard decided to make an issue of it and before it was all over we were arrested, maced, and I got a broken nose courtesy of a Bridgeport cop. To add insult to injury, we were both charged with assaulting a police officer! The bail was going to be $7,500 apiece! That meant that I'd need to come up with $1,500 to bail us both out. Fortunately, I had just received my first royalty check from "One Morning in May," which James Taylor had graciously credited to Bill and me when it was brought to his attention. So now I had the money to get us out of jail. God moves in mysterious ways! When we got back to the studio the next day, Jon was pretty spooked. Violence of any kind upset him. I felt bad that we had disrupted his work and decided that, since I was finished recording what I had to do, it would be best if we left him to finish mixing and mastering without any further distractions.

We bid a fond farewell to Bridgeport and didn't look back as we set out in the motor home for the long trip across the country. Along the way, we would get off the interstate in some of the smaller towns and find an interesting place to check out. We'd have a few drinks and start talking to people. Sometimes I'd get my guitar out and play a few songs. In the camper we'd listen endlessly to Merle Haggard's tribute album to Jimmy Rodgers, *Same Train, Different Time*, or Waylon Jennings's *Honky Tonk Heroes* album of Billy Joe Shaver songs or Willie Nelson's incredible *Live at Panther Hall*. If we wanted to rock we listened to Steve Winwood and

Traffic or the Rolling Stones. Bobby Charles was for when we wanted to be quiet and close.

Being with Judy's kids was definitely a good influence on us. We became an instant family, going to Disneyland, camping at campgrounds down the coast. I really liked the kids. Bobby, the oldest, was responsible, helpful, and curious. Briar, the middle one, was thoughtful and quietly observant. Brooke, the youngest, was a spark plug, full of fun and energy. I could see bits of Judy in all of them. They gave me a deeper insight into who she really was. For all the unconventionality of her life, she had taught them honesty, openness, and resourcefulness.

On our way back, as we came into Texas, I gave Jerry Jeff Walker a call. I had first met Jerry Jeff at the Newport Folk Festival in 1969 just after "Mr. Bojangles" came out, and we'd hit it off. He'd recently moved to Austin from New York, but he wasn't home, so we just kept driving on I-40 until we got to Nashville. I saw that Norman Blake was playing at a music club called the Exit/In. The previous year John Hartford had come up to Bearsville to record the brilliant album *Morning Bugle* with Norman and the great bassist Dave Holland. One day John and Norman were out at my house listening to Bill Monroe's new album of fiddle tunes he had learned from his Uncle Pen, and I gave Norman a copy of *Bossmen*. So, this night at the Exit/In Norman sang a song he'd written called "My Uncle." He mentioned that he'd gotten some of the words for the song from a quote of Bill Monroe's in *Bossmen*. He then mentioned that I was in the audience. A few minutes later I felt a tap on my shoulder. I turned around and there was Greg Thomas, a drummer who used to be my neighbor in Lake Hill. I said, "Greg! What are you doing here?" He said, "I've just moved here." We spent the night out at his house, and the next day he mentioned that he was looking for someone to share the house. I thought for a minute and said, "I might be interested." I thought for another minute and said, "Let's do it!" If Jerry Jeff had been home, it might have been Austin, but he wasn't, so it was Nashville.

I drove back to Woodstock to get some stuff and took Judy back up to Magog. We said goodbye once more and parted company. I came back down through Vermont and stopped in to see my old friend Carol Langstaff. I had visited her once before right after I stopped running the Club 47. She had moved to Vermont from New York, where she had been a model for a time and had studied dance with Martha Graham.

That time I had helped her paper the bathroom in the old farmhouse she had bought, but she hadn't shown any signs of being interested in a romantic involvement, even though we both really enjoyed each other's company. Since that visit, we had both changed. One look at my motor home and the look in my eyes and she could tell that I was in a wild and wooly phase. She, on the other hand, had a little girl named Sarah and was happy being a hippie mom (with no husband yet).

From there I went to New York City to see Stu and Murray at the record label. I went up to the floor in the building where I remembered their office had been. It wasn't there! I found a janitor in the hall and asked him where the United Artists office was. He gave me a look and said, "They're gone. They closed up." And that, as it turned out, was really that. There had been a corporate upheaval, and the label was finished. The record never came out (until 2001 in Japan and, miracle of miracles, in 2013, along with the first album, on the Real Gone/Razor & Tie label). To add to my woes, Poppy Records was also part of the United Artists collapse, so I lost Eric's album as well. (*Livin' on the Trail* finally surfaced on Kevin Eggars's Tomato records in 2002). I saw four months' work go down the drain just like that. The only consolation was that we'd been paid.

It seemed clear to me now that there was no reason to stay around Woodstock and that Nashville was as good a place as any for me to hang my hat. Greg had already connected with some musicians, including a bass player named Steve Mendell and a singer/songwriter from Oklahoma named James Talley, and we had some good jam sessions at the house swapping songs. In town, Elliston Place seemed to be the center of action with its triangle of bars—the Exit/In, which always had good music; T.G.I. Friday's, which featured a happy hour with cheap drinks and free hors d'oeuvres; and The Gold Rush, which was open until 3 o'clock in the morning. Nashville had only gotten liquor by the drink in restaurants in 1969, but they were making up for lost time. If you gave the bartender a $2 tip at the beginning of the night, you could drink all night long, no problem. My other source of sustenance, other than the free hors d'oeuvres at Friday's, was the special at Krystal where you could get a Krystalburger, fries, and a Coke for 39¢. I wasn't going to starve.

Some time in November I got a call from Judy. She was pregnant. It wasn't my baby. The father, Bruno, wanted no part of it, so she needed to leave Canada. I didn't hesitate. I said, "You'd better come down here then." It was just one of those relationships you couldn't get out of. Nowadays I think they call this a "codependent relationship," but I wouldn't have known anything about that. Coming up to Christmas I agreed to drive her out to California again to see her kids. As before, we had a good time with them, and it was a good way to spend the holidays. On the way back the engine blew in Gurdon, Arkansas—a dry county. We got out of there as fast as we could but only made it as far as Memphis. The engine was dying fast when I spotted a huge RV sales lot off the highway. I literally rolled in. They were telling me how much it was going to cost to fix it when I asked, "How much would a new one cost?" They said that they'd allow me $4,500 (!) on the old one. The new one cost $9,000. They'd finance the difference. I told them that I was a record producer from Nashville. No problem. I rolled out of there in a brand new eighteen-foot cab-over Dodge motor home!

People looking at me at the time might have been shaking their heads. I was out every night drinking, apparently doing nothing productive—not a pretty picture. But there was some method in my madness. I was beginning to find other singers, songwriters, and musicians. There was a tavern on West End Avenue called Bishop's Pub. It was just a beer joint with a pool table, but it had become home for a group of songwriters from the Houston area. Guy and Susannah Clark, Rodney Crowell, and Richard Dobson would sing songs and pass the hat. I met Townes Van Zandt again. He seemed to be at the center of this group. He and his girlfriend Cindy lived outside of town in sort of a country shack with a front porch just right for making music. Jack Clement was doing a record with Townes at the time, so one day Guy and Susannah and I went over to Jack's Tracks Recording Studio to hang out. Jack was busy working, so I didn't really connect with him. We hung around and played darts for a while and eventually left, but at least I had finally set foot in a Nashville recording studio.

During the course of the year I became good friends with James Talley. James was steeped in the music and folklore of Oklahoma and the Southwest. He had put together a beautiful book of songs and photographs by a photographer named Cavalier Ketchum called "The Road to Torreon." It really captured the beauty and dignity of the poorest people of New Mexico. It reminded me of "Let Us Now Praise Famous Men" by James Agee and Walker Evans.

Talley had been signed as an artist to Capitol records by an A & R man named Bill Williams, who was trying to bring some new blood into mainstream country music. Although slick artists like Barbara Mandrell were on the rise and line dancing was about to become a craze, Bill Williams had also signed the quietly soulful country singer, Stoney Edwards, perhaps encouraged by the success of Don Williams. I first heard about Don Williams from Albert Grossman, who had managed the Pozo-Seco Singers and thought I would like him. He was right. His first solo album had a different, more acoustic sound. Some of the songs, like "I Recall a Gypsy Woman" had a folk feel to them. The producer was Allen Reynolds, who also wrote several of the songs. The album was on JMI Records, which was owned by Jack Clement. The publicist for JMI was John Lomax III, one of the famous Lomax family. We had met often at Bishop's and at various picking parties. My natural instincts were steering me to the folky side of the Nashville music scene, although I hadn't personally connected yet with either Allen or Jack. It wasn't time.

A lot of the time I was busy drinking over on Elliston Place. There was a character I met in the bars named Bobby Jameson. Bobby had a gimpy leg and a cocky attitude. We hit it off and became sort of a duo. We called ourselves "The Berry Brothers" ("He's Huckle, I'm Dingle, we're a double, not a single, and together we're the Very Berry Brothers!"). We played at Friday's for drinks and tips. He had a tall blonde girlfriend named Amy. Bobby kept body and soul together with care packages of Indian jewelry sent to him periodically by his mother out west. Amy would deck herself out in as much jewelry as she could handle; Bobby and I would put on rings and bracelets, and we'd set out to the bars, where we cut a large swath. Inevitably some one would comment on a piece of jewelry. It was all for sale, so that was a pretty good source of cash.

Another hot spot was kind of an upscale bar called Jock's. Judy had taken up with one of the bartenders there named John Annas, so the bar tab was taken care of. There was a small stage and the regular act was a great girl named Arizona Star. Star was totally outrageous—platinum blonde, lots of makeup, feather boas, very camp. This was definitely not the honky-tonk Nashville scene. For that I could make my way downtown to Tootsie's Orchid Lounge on Broadway. Judy had got herself a job waitressing there. Tootsie was famous for helping down-and-out songwriters. Willie Nelson and Roger Miller both gave her credit for helping them through their thin times, and there was no shortage of people trying to follow in their footsteps. One of Tootsie's trademarks was her hatpin which she wore stuck into her big beehive hairdo. If someone at the bar was getting out of line she'd say, "It's time for you to take a walk." If he didn't take the hint, she'd repeat, "I said it's time for you to take a walk!" If it still wasn't sinking in, she'd calmly walk around the end of the bar, come up behind the offending party and give him a big jab in the ass with her hatpin, saying, "I told you twice! It's time for you to take a walk!" And out the door he'd fly, with the hoots and howls of laughter following him. Tootsie ran a good place. Judy loved her.

A guitar player from Mississippi named Steve Blaylock introduced me to what was left of what had once been a thriving black jazz scene. There were three or four lounges, which had jazz on weekends in North Nashville near Fisk and Tennessee State University. The place I really loved was called Deborah's. It would get going about midnight. They had fabulous ribs and always a great organ trio.

Blaylock was responsible for getting me my first paying Nashville recording session. He called me up and asked me if I'd play rhythm guitar on a session he was organizing for a white girl gospel singer. The pay was $10/song. Greg was the drummer, so our household income was going to take a big jump. The studio was just at the foot of Music Row, and I was excited. The singer arrived with her mother, who was also the producer. Blaylock ran the session. He gave us all Nashville number charts, which he had taught me how to read. The songs were pretty straightforward country gospel songs, and we got six good sounding tracks together in short order. Blaylock had the engineer throw some extra echo on the girl's voice, and she and her mother were delighted with the results. The mother gave us our checks for $60, saying, "God love you," to each one in turn, and said that she'd be calling us real soon to do some more. I was on cloud nine and headed to Jock's to reward myself with a drink. I asked John Annas if I could cash the check at the bar. He obliged, and I was happy with my first Nashville session money in my pocket. I was the lucky one. Everyone else's check bounced. The Lord giveth and the Lord bounceth away. Needless to say, we never got called for that next session.

Toward the end of May, Ralph Rinzler called me up from the Smithsonian. The Festival of American Folklife was now in its fourth year and was going to stretch to ten days over the Fourth of July week. Part of the program had unexpectedly fallen through and he needed to put some shows together in a hurry. Could I help? I was more than ready for something constructive to do and flew up to Washington. Ralph had also asked Mike Seeger and Ethel Raim to join in the effort, and it was good to have a resurgence of the energy we all had shared at Newport. I was to be in charge of ten days of concerts on the main stage on the Mall. There would be four kinds of music represented from different parts of the country: Cajun and Zydeco from Louisiana; Mexican American from Texas; Country from Nashville and Texas; and Latin from New York City. We quickly came up with a strong lineup of musicians. I was already familiar with some of them, like the Balfa Brothers, Wilma Lee and Stoney Cooper, "Uncle" Josh Graves, Tex Logan, James Talley, and Steve Young.

In all we were going to have nearly one hundred and twenty-five individual musicians, so I had to make their travel arrangements, arrange for them to get paid, plan their accommodation at a local college, and figure out their performance schedule. In Washington nothing is simple, and I had my hands full dealing with all of the paperwork and various bureaucratic hurdles, but I got it done one way or another. Every night at the college there were jam sessions. I couldn't get enough of playing with the Balfa Brothers—Dewey, Will, and Rodney. They loved to play "Only the Best," and we talked about getting together to record it some day. In another room, a Chicano showband from Brownsville, Texas, teamed up with the Bob Wills Alumni Band from Austin. It was wild. In still another room, Josh Graves and Tex Logan revived old days on the WWVA Wheeling Jamboree with Wilma Lee and Stoney Cooper. My bureaucratic woes evaporated. All indications were that the festival was a big success. Many thousands of people came and heard all kinds of folk music from various parts of the country. The music from my stage was broadcast all over the world by the Voice of America. I had succeeded in getting all of the musicians paid, and they were proud to have been asked to perform by the Smithsonian. Bill Keith and I spent the rest of July playing a few dates in France and Switzerland with a young French musician, Pierre Bensusan, who played mandolin with us. I soon discovered that his real instrument was guitar, which he was already playing in different tunings. Pierre was a lovely person with a fine, quiet sense of humor. He was definitely a special talent, as subsequent years have shown. Bill and I then crossed over to England, where we played some pub and folk club gigs arranged by a bluegrass/old-timey enthusiast named John Atkins. The highlight of this trip was a visit to the Cambridge Folk Festival, where we heard and met some of the new generation of folk-based musicians—Martin Carthy, Bert Jansch, Dave Swarbrick, and John Renbourn. We also became friends with a group there who played bluegrass led by Pete Sayers, who had spent time in Nashville and had his own version of the Grand Ole Opry in Newmarket. Also in the group was John Holder, who, with his wife Gaye Lockwood, was involved in organizing the festival and also did beautiful posters for it. As it happened, Arlo Guthrie was appearing at the festival that year with his excellent guitarist John Pilla. Arlo asked if we'd like to join them on their sets, which we did. Everything seemed to click for us at Cambridge. It would remain a favorite place for us to return to over the years.

After Cambridge, I headed back to Nashville to do some gigs with Josh Graves and Steve Young. Steve and I had become friends at Newport in '69 and had renewed that friendship in Nashville. The intensity of his singing and his songs like "Seven Bridges Road," later a hit for The Eagles, never failed to move me. Josh had stayed with us while Flatt & Scruggs were playing at the Club. He was fascinated with my upside-down guitar-playing and we actually worked up a little blues instrumental together at the time. Josh was inclined to revert to being a sideman, but Steve and I decided to help him put a set together that really focused on him. His dobro had belonged to Bradley Kincaid, whose big hit was "The Prisoner's Song" ("If I had the wings of an angel, over these prison walls I would fly"), so we put that in. Then we did some blues and then some songs he had done with Flatt & Scruggs. I had been inspired to learn "Reuben's Train" back in 1960 when I heard Josh and Earl play it on the *Foggy Mountain Banjo* album. By the end of the set people would have an idea of what an extraordinary musician he was. It was a privilege to play with him.

Not long after, Bill Keith called to say that he had lined up some gigs for us in Holland, Belgium, and England, so it looked like I'd be heading up to Woodstock to rehearse. Judy had been living happily with John Annas, and one afternoon they went down to the courthouse and got married. On August 18, she had her baby—Johanna. James was her middle name—named after me. When I told Judy of my plans, she asked if I would take her up to Magog so that she could at least show Johanna to her father, Bruno. I couldn't refuse, so at the age of one month Johanna

FIGURE II. Judy and Johanna, September 1974.

took her first trip. Sadly, when we got up there, Bruno refused to see her and missed out on the life of a wonderful, positive, generous, big-hearted person—Johanna James.

When we got back to Woodstock, Judy left with Johanna to continue on in Nashville. I needed some money by now, so I asked Paul Cypert if he'd hire me on as a $4/hour carpenter. Albert Grossman was having him remodel yet another house, so I was put to work Sheetrocking. I'm sure Paul was wondering how I had managed to get in this position. I'd had a good woman, a nice house, a good paying job, and now I was sleeping in my motor home pretending to be a carpenter! Whatever he thought, he kept it to himself. One morning, after a night in the Bear Bar with Paul, I found a hundred dollar bill in my jacket pocket. Paul knew nothing about it. In November Bill and I went to Europe. Audiences there seemed to like our mixed-bag repertoire—some bluegrass standards and fiddle tunes, some country, a bit of jazz, and even some Bach! We made enough money on that tour to keep me solvent for a while, but I was uncertain about whether to go back to Nashville. Something told me that the time wasn't yet right. I needed to cool my jets and regroup.

SITTING IN LIMBO

I headed back to Dedham for the holidays. Without my saying anything, I think my mother understood that I could use some space to settle in. She was planning to sell the house in Green Harbor, but it was available for me to stay in for the time being. Green Harbor in the winter was pretty quiet, so I entered into sort of a forced retreat, with lots of time to think, to strum my guitar and write the occasional song, to go for walks on the beach, to learn to live with myself. To earn my keep I put a new roof on the house and painted the trim. It wasn't the most fun I'd ever had in my life, but it seemed to be what I needed at the time. I wrote a song ironically called "Lonesome in Paradise":

> Don't get me wrong, I'm not complaining
> There's not too many can afford to live like me
> About a mile from the beach, hid back in the trees
> Near a pond where I used to play
> Where the evenings are so sweet
> And the swallows ride the breeze
> And the moonshine on the water makes you weep
> But it gets lonesome in paradise
> And I know I'll always miss your eyes
> I'm tired of the trees and I'm bored with the breeze
> Yes, it gets lonesome in paradise

Eventually, I drove up to Cambridge to see Joe Val & The New England Bluegrass Boys at the Passim, which was where the old Club 47 had been. That night I ran into Everett Lilly's son, Everett Alan Lilly, and another friend from the Club 47 days, John Nagy. John had gotten into producing records for Rounder and suggested that it might be a good idea to record a live album at Passim. I got Bill Keith, Jim Colegrove, and guitarist Steven Bruton to come over from Woodstock and asked Everett Alan Lilly to join us as well. I did a mixture of material similar to The Blue Velvet Band album—some folk, some bluegrass, some traditional country. Like a lot of live recordings, it had its good moments, but not enough for an album. The night of the gig, I met Everett Alan's brother Tennis, who played bass and sang. He invited me and his brother to his house to jam some night, and as soon as we got together, we immediately fell into some three-part harmony singing. After a couple of get-togethers it became clear to me that we had something special. I called up John Nagy and suggested that maybe we should complete the album with some tracks by the three of us plus Joe Val. We went to a little 4-track studio run by an engineer named Peter Troisi and recorded James Talley's "Calico Gypsy," Dolly Parton's "My Blue Tears," Flatt & Scruggs's "Rough and Rocky Road," one of mine called "Do You Think It Will Ever Go Away," and Willie Nelson's "One Day at a Time." We were very happy with the results, so we combined these new tracks with the "live" ones. Byron Linardos came down to Green Harbor to take some pictures for the cover, and Rounder put it out. I called it *One Day at a Time*, which had definitely become my theme song.

One night I went into a place called Jonathan Swift's in Harvard Square to hear a country singer named John Lincoln Wright. John had a strong, rich voice and fronted a really good band with fiddle, steel, and electric guitar. He did a mixture of classic country songs by Ernest Tubb, Bob Wills, and Merle Haggard plus his own songs, which were quite good. I was really impressed by the quality of the music. At the end of the night I introduced myself, and, without any hesitation, he invited me to come up and sit in with them the next time he played. John wouldn't have known it, but this invitation meant a lot to me. I hadn't been around since 1968, so it gave me a way in to the current Cambridge scene. Through John I found another music bar in Inman Square in Somerville called "The Inn Square Men's Bar." In the window they had a neon sign that said "Ladies Invited." By day it was a hard-core social security drinkers' bar, which featured "the world's longest happy hour"—8 A.M. to 8 P.M. After 8 P.M. they'd have gone home to bed, and it was time for the hip people to come

FIGURE 12. *One Day at a Time* Rounder album, 1975.

in for some music. It was a great place to play and became a regular gig for me with Everett and Tennis—my new "Partners in Crime."

I found out that an old friend of Bill Keith's, Elizabeth Rush, and her husband Dave Marsden were living nearby in Plymouth and had opened an East Coast branch of the Athena Booking Agency. They booked Jerry Jeff Walker, John Hartford, the New Riders of the Purple Sage, and a new singer named Emmylou Harris. I played them what was going to be my new Rounder album, so I became their opening act. I could go out and make between $500 and $1,000 for a gig. Everett and Tennis and I would travel in the motor home, so it worked out. When I wasn't up in Cambridge or opening a show somewhere, I was down in Green Harbor, reading, writing songs, walking on the beach, watching "Candlepins for Cash" on a little black-and-white TV. Mulching.

Bill Keith was going to make an album for Rounder Records and asked me to come down to Washington to sing on it. Bill had assembled a fantastic group of musicians—David Grisman, Vassar Clements, Kenny Kosek, Tony Rice, and Tom Gray. He gave them plenty to chew on, from traditional material like "Rickett's Hornpipe" to Duke Ellington's "Caravan" and Duke Jordan's "Jordu." I did a bluegrassy version of the Rolling Stones song "No Expectations," which I had learned from Clay Jackson, a Texan who was in the original Charles River Valley Boys. I also did the old hillbilly classic "Detour," made popular by Tex Williams and one of Flatt & Scruggs chestnuts "I'll Stay Around." Bill closed the album with a tune that was to become his trademark, "Auld Lang Syne," played entirely on the Keith Tuners, which he and our good friend Dan Bump had invented. Bill titled the album *Something Auld, Something Newgrass, Something Borrowed, Something Bluegrass*, displaying his wonderful penchant for wordplay. This album firmly established Bill as the foremost of a new generation of banjo players. It was one of the highlights of my musical life to be a part of it.

It wasn't long before another recording opportunity presented itself. David Gessner, known as "Durg" to his friends, had worked for me at the Club 47. He had some family money and was trying to help musicians. He asked me if I'd be willing to help John Lincoln Wright produce a record, which he would put out on his own ESCA label. I jumped at the chance. I got together with John and the band and went to work. John's songs were varied and well written, and, as a result of many nights of playing together, the band arrangements were tight. John had paid a lot of attention to the music of Bob Wills, Ernest Tubb, and Merle Haggard, and it showed. I worked again with Peter Troisi at the Great Northern Recording Studio in Maynard. John's voice recorded beautifully. My role was to oversee the sessions, to help Peter and John decide when we had what we needed, and to keep things moving in a positive direction. We all worked on the mixing together, and everything fell into place effortlessly. The album successfully captured the energy and depth of John's music.

As a result, perhaps sensing that I was on a roll, Durg said that he'd be willing to pay for some recording sessions for me. I decided that it was time to record some of the songs I had been writing since I went off the rails up in Woodstock. Judy had become an inspiring agent and our life together with all of its ups and downs gave me plenty to write about. A song called "In It for the Long Run" summed it all up:

We've had our ups
We've had our downs
We've had our ins
We've had our outs,
But we still love each other and we're free
We're in it for the long run
The minutes and the years
We're in it for the long run
The hours and the days
We're in it for the long run
Today, tomorrow and all our yesterdays.

I rerecorded "Only the Best" because the version with Borderline had never come out. Then I did a couple of my honky-tonk numbers that I'd been doing when I sat in with the Sour Mash Boys, "Cruisin' Town" and "Alive and Well and Hangin' Out in Bangor, Maine." In addition to Everett, Tennis, and Joe Val, I had an excellent dobro player named Roger Williams, a drummer named Rick Nelson (the other Rick Nelson), Bill Elliot on piano, and Kenny Kosek and Larry Feldman on fiddles. By now Peter Troisi and I had a good rapport. Durg left us alone, and I felt confident running the sessions and mixing with Peter. I was happy with the results, as was Durg. The demos were my idea of the way I wanted country music to sound.

ENTER: "COWBOY"

In early April I screwed up my courage and decided to take my tapes and drive down to Nashville to try my luck, like so many had before me. One of the people I called when I got there was John Lomax III, who was still working for Jack Clement. John was based at Jack's Tracks and invited me to drop by. His office was finished in rough-sawn lumber, and Lomax explained that it had once been part of a tree house Jack had built in his apartment! I'd heard lots of stories about Jack. This just added to the intrigue. As we listened, "Only the Best" came on, and Lomax said,

"I bet Cowboy would like this." (Everybody called Jack "Cowboy.") I said, "Well, where is he?" "He's in the next room." The next thing I knew, Jack came in and started to waltz around the room, balancing a glass of water on his head, not spilling a drop, while he sang along with the chorus of my song! He then sat down and called a couple of people up. "Hey, come over here! I heard this great song. You ought to come over." There I was sitting there with my mouth open thinking, "Oh my God! This is it! This is it!" Jack Clement, who had written "Ballad of a Teenage Queen" and "I Don't Like It but I Guess Things Happen That Way" for Johnny Cash and "Just a Girl I Used to Know" for George Jones, liked my song!

He even liked me. I didn't have to explain myself to him. From his time up in Boston on the *Hayloft Jamboree* he knew about the Lilly Brothers; he knew about Joe Val. He asked me who was playing on "Only the Best." I said, "Everett Lilly's sons, Everett Alan and Tennis, and Joe Val." "Oh yeah. Those guys. Are they still around up there?" So he wasn't surprised to find someone from Boston playing hillbilly music. Then, as he got to know that I'd gone to Harvard, that I had a master's degree in Classics, that I played the guitar backward and upside down, he really took a shine to me. I was obviously odd. He liked odd people.

As I floated down the stairs to go out, Jack introduced me to a quiet, soft-spoken fellow, Allen Reynolds, who had produced the Don Williams record I liked so much. He smiled warmly, shook my hand, and said, "Welcome." The simple beginning of a long friendship. Behind Allen in an office there was another fellow. I just remember a slight man with black-rimmed glasses and a slightly shifty manner. Jack introduced him as "Webster. He takes care of me," he said, and then he laughed. They all laughed. It was evidently a private joke. As I climbed back into my motor home I was in shock. My big day had arrived at last. A red-letter day, if there ever was one.

The next day was a Saturday. Every Saturday Jack had a jam session at the Tracks, and he invited me to come along. Musicians started showing up—drummer Kenny Malone; piano player Charles Cochran; bass player, Joe Allen; guitar player, Jim Colvard. I recognized their names from the credits on my Don Williams album. They all piled into the studio and snapped to attention when Cowboy shouted that it was time to "Strike up the band!" Just then this great-looking, lanky blonde burst through the door to be greeted by various expressions of approval. She

introduced herself to me with a nice low, silky smooth, southern accent, "Hi, I'm Marshall." This was Marshall Chapman. She seemed to
be in the same phase as I was—rockin' away—so we immediately went
out and brought back some beer from the "hurry-back market" down
the street. We spent the whole afternoon at the studio. There was lots
of music, lots of laughter. I don't remember playing, but I might have. I
think I was just in awe.

That night I stayed in my motor home parked on the street outside of
Jack's Tracks. Sunday morning I got up and rang the bell. Jack let me in.
Sitting there in his office, I asked him what I should do. He said, "Why
don't you go back up there and make some more tapes with those guys?
Send me the 16-track master of 'Only the Best' and I'll fool with it." So
I did. Jack told me to send any songs I cut to Bob Webster, who, I now
found out, ran Jack's publishing company. I'd call every so often, trying
not to be a pest but looking for some reaction. Webster was always very
straightforward. If he liked something, he'd say so. He was always cor-
dial, never dismissive. He didn't blow me off. I never forgot that. One day
Webster put me on hold, and Jack came on the line. He'd got the master
of "Only the Best" and had put Buddy Spicher and Jimmy Buchanan on
the track—two of the top fiddlers in Nashville. Jack also added himself on
mandolin and singing harmony and remixed the whole song. He never
said anything about money. Not a word. I stood there holding the phone,
hardly believing my ears. That did it. I decided to go down there and see
what would happen. I had about three hundred bucks. I found an apartment in a place called "The Americana." It was a six-story building with
a pool on the roof right near Music Row. They didn't require a deposit
and only wanted the balance of the month's rent in advance—$100. So I
gave them the hundred, and there I was. I had an apartment in Nashville!
I had some gigs booked that summer back in New England so I knew I
could make the rent through the summer.

My time in Green Harbor had been time well spent. Because of my
isolation I had been forced inward. That house and the land around it
had been a very nourishing place for me growing up. My best friend Jim
Reagan and I had spent hours and countless days exploring, playing pi-
rate, running on the beach, making drip castles. The woods and fields and
marshes and the pond were my own private world. I now knew that that
time was coming to an end for me, and I was ready to move on. Before

I left, though, I had to let my mother know how much this place meant to me, so I wrote "The House" and sent it to her:

> Those honeysuckle summers have flowered and gone,
> The warm summer evenings down by the pond.
> The marshgrass is windswept and turning to gold,
> The house will be shuttered, soon to be sold.
> The house has its memories of feet tracking sand,
> Of surf in the distance and flowers in the hand.
> It remembers the children sunburned and small,
> It remembers the pictures hung on the wall.
> There are memories of birthdays with lobster and corn,
> Root beer and raspberries fresh from the farm.
> It remembers the laughter from out on the lawn,
> The silence of deer just before dawn.
> A woman and man had brought it to life,
> Shaping their dreams as husband and wife.
> Brothers and cousins and friends lent a hand.
> Soon there was the house sitting close to the land.
> It had room for more children, room for their friends,
> A forty foot porch brought the outdoors in;
> A fireplace to take the chill from the night,
> And old fashioned lamps that cast a warm light.
> As the family grew older, the house did too.
> It weathered and mellowed in the salt air dew.
> Gardens bordered with granite blossomed and bloomed,
> And a towering linden stood tall through the storms.
> But time has its way of pushing us on.
> The house is no different; its day has gone.
> And we have gone too, out in the world, out on our own,
> But the house still lives in us, deep in our bones.
> So we'll carry its spirit wherever we roam,
> And the house will forever be our true home.

It was mid-June when I arrived in Nashville and the annual D.J. Convention was on, so I decided to check it out. I got out of my motor home downtown, and the first person I saw walking toward me was Don Everly! Right behind him was Bob Neuwirth! Talk about serendipity!

Don was headed to the Municipal Auditorium to play on a Hickory Records showcase, so I came right along. Don and Phil had split up quite dramatically three years before, and Don had moved back to Nashville when his publisher Wesley Rose had given him a record deal with the Acuff-Rose company label Hickory Records. He seemed genuinely happy to see me, and after he was finished playing, we went across the river to the Gerst Haus to get some beer and bratwurst. Don talked about how Newport had made such a deep impression on him and how good it had been to be reunited with Ike. Running into Don seemed like as a good omen. I had the feeling that this time in Nashville was going to be different from the last time.

The next day I went over to Jack Clement's house on Belmont Boulevard to announce my arrival. Jack welcomed me back. To my surprise, I ran into Richard Lubash, the fellow who had wired the Bearsville Studio. Jack had him wiring in an Ampex 4-track machine to a tiny board in one of the bedrooms. As it turned out, that was it for Jack. For the first time in years he had no studio. It took me a while to fully realize it, but I had arrived at what must have been the lowest ebb in his career. When I had seen him at Jack's Tracks in April, he was in the process of selling it to Allen Reynolds, who had started producing Crystal Gayle. He had also sold the Jack Clement Recording Studios on Belmont. When Jack had introduced me to Webster with the wry comment, "He takes care of me," this was what he had in mind. Webster's job was to worry Jack's financial worries. The biggest worries of all came when Jack decided to fulfill his lifelong dream of making a movie. The movie was called "Dear Dead Delilah," the final and biggest nail in Jack's financial coffin. Soon Jack's publishing partner, Bill Hall, left, taking Don Williams, Dickey Lee, and Bob McDill with him. Don Williams had made a record deal with ABC Records, so JMI was effectively finished. Jack was down to zero, with his little 4-track recording setup in the bedroom, and here I was arriving, thinking, "This guy's going to really do something for me."

Through the summer I kept going back up north to play clubs, coffeehouses, and festivals with Everett and Tennis. When I came back to town I'd drop by Cowboy's, but it was pretty quiet over there. A fellow named Rick Sanjek was in the front office purporting to be Jack's "manager." Webster seemed to be there in the morning, but once he went to lunch he seldom returned. I had plenty of time to spend at the pool on the Americana roof. The apartment itself was pretty much like living in a motel. It had yellow shag carpeting. I had snagged some furniture from Jack's basement, had a little black-and-white TV, and a radio/cassette player. By the end of the summer, things were looking thin. I had one final gig booked up in Ohio, but I couldn't see how I was going to make it through the winter.

One day in early October I went over to Jack's and walked in the door to find a band set up with a sound system in the living room. They turned out to be Crystal Gayle's road band, Peace and Quiet: Chris Leuzinger, guitar; Spady Brannan, bass; Dwight Scott, keyboard; and T'ner Craw-czyn, drums. Jack was with them, and they were all playing away. After a while Jack told me to go get my guitar, so I did. He asked me to play something, so just out of my head I picked "No Expectations." Right away we got a good groove going on it, and Jack just loved it. In the course of the afternoon I sang two or three other songs and had a great time. Finally, the session wound down, and Jack called me into his office. He said, "Well, you're going to be my rhythm guitar player. We rehearse every day, Monday through Friday. Be here at 10 o'clock, in tune and ready to play. We'll work from 10 until 4, and I'll provide lunch. I'll pay you $250 a week." That was it. To myself I said, "Hallelujah! Thank you, Jesus!" I was going to be able to make it through the winter. I could stay in Nashville.

It seems that Rick Sanjek had been doing some "managing." Elektra/Asylum Records had decided to open an office in Nashville and the man running the operation was none other than Jim Malloy who had been Jack's engineer at RCA when he was producing hit records for Charlie Pride, Bobby Bare, and lots of others. The first thing Malloy did was to sign Jack as an artist, giving him a signing bonus, plus a two-album record deal. (Maybe the "Asylum" part of the label had some appeal to Cowboy.) As soon as the signing check cleared, Jack went out and bought a better board to go with the 4-track Ampex and hired the band. He was back in business! And I was the beneficiary.

People in the outside world think of Jack as a flamboyant, extravagant, over-the-top person—which he certainly can be—but he was also in the Marines as a young man. So, underneath his flamboyant exterior he had a thing about discipline. When he said, "In tune and ready to play at 10 o'clock." He meant it. He didn't mean 10:01. We would all show up in the morning, have a cup of coffee in the kitchen, chat, tell a few jokes,

FIGURE 13. "Cowboy" Jack Clement. Photograph: © McGuire.

tune up, get ready, and exactly at the stroke of 10 Jack would appear in the doorway, sometimes in a bathrobe, sometimes fully clothed, usually with a baton in his hand. When he would let go with "Strike up the band!" we'd hit the downbeat on whatever song he called out, and we would spend the day rehearsing songs. Naturally, we did many of the songs he had written like "I Don't Like It, but I Guess Things Happen That Way" or "Gone Girl." We did other people's songs like Waylon Jennings and Billy Joe Shaver's "You Ask Me To," Billy Ray Reynolds's "It'll Be Her," or Sandy Mason's "When I Dream." It was inspiring to be playing on such good songs. I picked a couple from the Jack Music catalogue to sing—Vince Matthews's "This Is My Year for Mexico" and "Laid Back Country Picker"—and, of course, Jack's favorite, "No Expectations."

We went along for two or three weeks like this and had worked up forty or fifty songs. Then one Monday morning I walked in to find that three horn players had been added to the band—Irv Kane on trombone, Denis Solee on saxophones and piccolo, and Bob Thomas on trumpet. With the horns we added another element to the repertoire—dance music. At some point in his past Jack had been a ballroom dance instructor for the Arthur Murray dance schools and was a firm believer that music should be danceable, so we worked up arrangements of "Brazil," "Undecided Now," "San Antonio Rose," and any number of waltzes. Jack then added two more singers to the mix, Rick Shulman and Richie Jarvis. Rick was a great big flamboyant guy with a rich deep voice. Richie was as little as Rick was big—barely five feet tall. He was a lovely singer, with a high, clear voice. Rick and Richie could do songs like "Soul Man," "Hold On I'm Coming," "Desperado," or even "Rocky Top." The whole aggregation was called "Cowboy's Ragtime Band." Before it was over we had well over one hundred songs we could play at the drop of a baton. Cowboy would call the song, and off we would go. We were expected to snap to attention, play the arrangement, get everything right—and have fun besides. Jack himself helped by issuing us his

"COWBOY'S RAGTIME BAND BAND MEMBER RULES:"

1. Be alert
2. Be on time
3. Don't bring or invite anyone
4. Don't talk about your troubles
5. Don't mention the words "earphones," "headphones," "cans," "earmuffs," or the like
6. Be quiet when the cowboy is speaking
7. Don't be timid or shy with your playing
8. Have a good day
9. Listen
10. Remember that it only takes 3 minutes to cut a hit record

This was a new experience for me. Other bands I had been in had been more laid-back affairs—especially in Woodstock. Rehearsals there were always pretty casual. If you knew that one fellow was going to come late, you'd come late. The next thing you knew, an 8 o'clock rehearsal would gradually come together after nine. The wind goes out of your sails, and it's hard to get much done. With Jack, we got a lot of work done, and it was totally exhilarating. I was learning a lot as I focused on playing rhythm guitar many hours a day. I'd ask Chris Leuzinger to show me some of the chords and I got so I could play or fake most all of it. Most importantly, I could keep the rhythm going strong even if I was dampening the chord.

Finally, we were ready to spring the band on the world. We played shows at the Exit/In and downtown at the Old Time Pickin' Parlor. However, both those places were listening rooms; there was no place to dance. That problem was solved by getting us a gig at George Jones's Possum Holler. It was a good-sized place downtown with a dance floor, surrounded by tables and chairs on a couple of levels, a big bar in the back of the room, and a stage big enough for all of us. This was what Jack had been looking for. He was dying to play for people to dance. We'd start at 9 o'clock and go until 3 in the morning. We did it three nights a week until Christmas. Word quickly got around, and all kinds of people started showing up—Mel Tillis, Merle Kilgore, Bobby Bare, Webb Pierce. Jack would get them up, and we'd do their hits. With the horns, Rick and Richie, Jack and me, it was a full show, and people kept coming back for more.

After the New Year, Jack began to focus on his album, which had started out being the point of all that rehearsing, before Jack's desire to put on a show took over. He booked some time at Woodland Sound Studio in East Nashville. On the first day, after we got set up with Jack, me, and Peace and Quiet, we recorded four songs in a row in about twenty minutes: "You Ask Me To," "It'll Be Her," "The Last Thing on My Mind," and "When I Dream." We cut one right after the other. Just like that. No playbacks. All but "Last Thing on My Mind" made it onto the album, so all that rehearsing really paid off and proved the truth of Jack's saying that "It only takes three minutes to cut a hit record." Then, in true Jack Clement fashion, he took about a year to finish the album!

That session was a big step up for me. When I came to Jack, I had been playing in bars a lot and had a tendency to play too hard. Jack taught me to play to the microphone. Less was more. For me, "When I Dream" was a magic cut. To have played on something that was that good and had such a beautiful feel to it was a revelation. We never disturbed the feel. That's what I loved about playing with Jack. We could crank it up and rock with the best of them, but the band had wonderful dynamics, and we could bring it down to a whisper and let it float like a feather if we had to. I was starting to learn a lot about playing in the studio and was more focused on the process. I got to know where I should be sitting in relation to the microphone and was more comfortable in a studio situation.

There was always more to learn with Cowboy. One day Jack and I and Rachel Peer, who had played bass with Richie Jarvis and was now becoming one of Jack's group of players, went over to The Creative Workshop to record "We Must Believe in Magic," which had been written about Jack by Allen Reynolds and Bob McDill. I was honored that Jack asked me to play with him on it. As we got into it, I was putting a lot of emotion into my playing, trying to sell the song, playing soft here and strong there. I thought I was doing a really good job of it, when Jack suddenly stopped and snapped at me, "Will you please stop doing that! Just play steady!" I thought to myself, "I'll play steady alright, you asshole!" So I did. I was steady as a rock. That was the track. The song didn't need me to sell it. It sold itself. All I needed to do was to truly believe in magic. That was the real Cowboy way.

Early in January I went up to Woodstock. It had been a couple of years since I'd been up there, and I was feeling much better about myself than when I left. My experience with Jack had given my confidence a big boost. Artie Traum gathered us all together to make another *Mud Acres* album at the Bearsville Studio. It was nice to be there when I didn't have to run it, and the music flowed effortlessly for a few days. Happy led us all in a rousing old-timey version of "Sally Ann." Bill Keith did a beautiful version of the old tune "My Love Is but a Lassie Yet." Bill and I did a Flatt & Scruggs chestnut "Sleep with One Eye Open." John Herald's "Bluegrass Boy" and "Woodstock Mountains" seemed to capture what our music was all about. Our new bass player Roly Salley knocked us out with "Killing the Blues." I was sure that song would have a rich long life, which it has. Artie livened things up with his jazzy songs, "Cold Front" and "Barbed Wire." Paul Siebel sat in with us and did a heartfelt version of Hank Williams's "Weary Blues from Waiting." Paul Butterfield and John Sebastian closed the sessions with a stunning rendition of "Amazing Grace" on two harmonicas that sent us all out into the clear winter Woodstock night feeling that something very special had happened. Simple music among friends was strong medicine.

One of the big bonuses of this get together was that I met Pat Alger. Pat was originally from Georgia and was part of the small folk scene in

Atlanta before he met John Herald at a concert and was talked into moving to Woodstock. The week after Pat moved there, John moved to San Francisco! So there Pat was with his wife Chris left to deal with the cold and the snow. However, Artie Traum took them under his wing, bringing them firewood and helping them stay fed. Soon he and Pat teamed up and had become an opening act for college concerts in the area. For this album Pat sang one of his songs called "Mason Dixon's on the Line." I was impressed. He was a lovely singer and an excellent acoustic guitarist. He would also drink a beer with you. We hit it off.

Later in the Spring a few of us went to Japan for a *Mud Acres* tour. We were there for three weeks and were treated like kings. An amazing cartoonist named Mitch Ashura put together a takeoff on *Mad* magazine called, of course, *Mud* magazine, in which we each had our own comic strip! I was "Left Hand Jim," Bill Keith was "Bill, The Mechanism Freak." (no doubt inspired by the Keith Tuners). This trip made a lasting impression on me. In Japan I found all these people who knew everything I had done up to that point, especially my work with Bill Keith and The Blue Velvet Band. The thought occurred to me that if my music meant so much to them, why was I treating it so casually? When I played at that time very often I would have smoked a joint and maybe had a few beers. So it registered with me that since these Japanese people were so respectful, *I* needed to pay a bit of respect.

Due to the success of the Japanese tour and the pending release of the new album called *Woodstock Mountains: More Music from Mud Acres* we decided to become a group, and someone came up with the name "Woodstock Mountains Revue." We played in New York at The Other End, The Mainpoint outside of Philadelphia, and Jonathan Swift's in Cambridge. There were a lot of us, so it wasn't a big moneymaker, but we really enjoyed doing it which was the important thing. If I could make a few dollars at everything I did, I could keep my head above water. I had bought a Plymouth Valiant from James Talley for $400, so the motor home was parked most of the time, and it wasn't gobbling up gas. When I was in Nashville, I was picking up a few sessions at Cowboy's, so, one way or another, I was making a living and paying my bills.

Another boost to my finances came from an unexpected source. One day Allen Reynolds invited me over to Jack's Tracks to listen to a cut of "Only the Best," which he had just recorded with George Hamilton IV.

FIGURE 14. Woodstock Mountains Revue outside the Other End, NYC, 1978
(*l. to r.*: Paul Colby, owner Other End, Roly Salley, Bill Keith, Eric Valdina[?],
Pat Alger, Rory Block, Artie Traum, Jane Traum, Happy Traum,
John Herald, Jim Rooney. Photograph © Estate of David Gahr.

I'd known George since we had invited him to play at the Newport Folk Festival in the late sixties. George had been one of the country artists who had made the connection with the folk revival with hits like "Abilene," "Early Morning Rain," and "The Last Thing on My Mind." When I had sent him a letter inviting him to the festival and explaining how we paid $50/day, I received a very nice, handwritten letter back from him saying how honored he was to be asked and here was his $50! I set him straight on that, but he was a genuinely humble, self-effacing man. So my song brought us back together. I was doubly honored that Allen, who was such an accomplished songwriter himself and a serious judge of songs, had thought enough of "Only the Best" to record it. After we had listened, he told me that they were going to recommend to the label that it be released as a single. What a thrill it was to be in that control room listening to that mix! I'd been in Nashville less than a year. Two or three months later I was driving somewhere up in the Northeast. It was a Saturday night, so I made a stab at tuning in The Grand Ole Opry. Almost immediately through the static I heard George Hamilton IV singing, "She was only the best, No need to sit here and cry." I couldn't help it. My eyes filled up and I had to pull over. A dream had come true. I had turned that rough morning-after up in Magog a few years back into a song that was now going out in the world. Judy had given me that. In addition, I could now ask ASCAP for an advance, so that also helped ease the financial pressure.

BABY, LET ME
FOLLOW YOU DOWN

Late in the summer I went up to Eric Von Schmidt's place in Henniker, New Hampshire, to help him celebrate the sale of a big painting of Custer's Last Stand to the Western Museum at Wichita State University. It was a great reunion of the old Cambridge crowd. Geoff Muldaur was there with Sheila. Fritz Richmond had come from California where he was working as Paul Rothchild's recording engineer. There were a couple of new additions to Eric's circle of friends, Darlene Wilson and Chance Browne, members of "The Cruel Family," in which Eric, of course was Father Cruel, who coined the family motto, "We Do Not Compromise with Reality." Chance had played guitar with me along with Everett Alan and Tennis, on a torture tour of the Northeast the previous winter. We were all sick at one time or another. To add insult to injury, the money wasn't very good either. Although Chance loved to play guitar, he was really a cartoonist. After the final gig he presented me with a cartoon showing the motor home being beset by three figures like they used to be drawn in the corner of old maps. Chance explained them to me. "This one is the North Wind; this one is Pestilence and Disease; and this one," pointing to the central figure who had bushy pointed eyebrows and a satyr's leer, "is the Winds of Sarcasm!" I had evidently cut Chance, who was a sweet, sweet person, with my rapier wit. It told me that I needed to be nicer to nice people.

However, that winter was far behind us. There was a full August moon overhead. Eric had a big side of beef, and we made a pit and set about roasting it all night long. Of course, we had to stay up and baste the beef.

By the end of the night Eric and I were well basted ourselves and had hatched the idea to put together a book about our former life and the folk scene back in Cambridge. Even in the light of day, hung over as we were, the idea stuck, so I decided to stay around for another day or two, and Eric and I put our heads together.

Eric had done a lot of illustrating of children's books in addition to his work on the Joan Baez songbooks, so he was experienced in what it takes to put a book together. I had my own experience doing *Bossmen*, so we both felt like this was something we were equipped to do. The very first thing we did was to make an outline of the history of the scene, which would have been from 1958 to 1968. Between us, one or the other of us had been present throughout the whole ten years, so we had the advantage of being eyewitnesses. Eric rummaged around and immediately came up with some photographs and fliers and posters he had designed for Manny Greenhill's various concert series and the Newport Folk Festival. Right from the start we had the idea that this would be an illustrated story and that the visual material would play an important part. We each set out to write something about our own recollections, and we wrote to a number of the people who had been part of the scene asking them what they thought of the idea, inviting them to contribute by writing something or sending us pictures or anything else. The response was favorable, and we got the go-ahead to appoint ourselves "class historians."

Shortly before Halloween Eric was awakened in the middle of the night by someone banging on the front door. He thought it was some kids getting an early start on Halloween, but when he opened the door a man shouted, "Is there anyone else in the house?" Eric was half asleep and befuddled at first and couldn't figure out why he'd be asking this question, until he noticed a strange orange backlight behind the man. The new studio was on fire. The volunteer fire department arrived, sprayed the back wall of the house and managed to save it, but the big barn on the other side of the studio had a lot of old hay in it and went up like a torch. The whole studio was gone, but fortunately Eric had not yet moved into it. He still had all of his artwork, all of his historical artifacts, all of his music and records, which was a blessing. I knew nothing about this until I got an invitation in the mail to come to "Charcoal City" for a cleanup party! I couldn't believe it. Leave it to Eric to turn a disaster into an excuse for a party! I immediately called him and suggested we put off getting together, but he wanted to get out of his "charcoal pit" and get to work. That settled it, and I went up to join him. We blew up some pictures of Joan Baez, Bob Dylan, Tom Rush, Maria Muldaur, and others; assembled collages from Eric's graphic work; and made up simulated chapters with a brief outline of each covering various elements of the scene—bluegrass, blues, songwriters, and so on. We put it all together in a big folder and set about contacting publishers. Through my old editor at Dial Press, Bob Cornfield, we got in touch with Bill Strachan at Doubleday/Anchor Books in New York. He had edited the Foxfire books and when we walked into his office, we saw a picture of Bob Dylan up on his wall, so we thought we might be in the right place. He liked our idea of an illustrated story, though he thought it might take some selling to the production department. He asked us to make up a budget and told us he'd see what he could do.

On the morning of New Year's Eve, Eric got up to find that his pipes had frozen. He put on some clothes, grabbed an axe and a bucket, and made his way through the snow to a small stream near the house. He chopped a hole in the ice and filled the bucket. As he turned to go back to the house he slipped and fell, spilling the bucket of ice water all over himself. He was not amused—he was furious! After he'd gotten some dry clothes on and a hot rum in him, he came up with a plan for New Year's Eve. He went into town and bought a lobster and a bottle of champagne. Once back at the house, he proceeded to light a fire in every fireplace in every room, all eight of them. As midnight approached he boiled a big pot of water on the wood stove and plunged the lobster in it. He opened the champagne and proceeded to drink it and eat the lobster with relish as the year came to a close. He then grabbed a shotgun, loaded it up, stepped out into the yard, which, even in the snow, still smelled of charcoal. At the stroke of midnight he aimed the gun up at the sky, pulled the trigger and, as he put it to me, "shot God in the asshole!" shouting, "I've had enough! Now lay off!" The next week we heard from Bill Strachan. We had a deal. God had evidently got the message.

We signed our contract in New York toward the end of January and immediately headed to Cambridge to begin interviewing people. From there we went to Woodstock and then headed out to Berkeley, finally winding up in Los Angeles. We then went down to Siesta Key. Eric's place had been built as an artist's studio. There were two adjoining rooms with a window wall running the length of the building, so there was lots of light. Each room had drawing boards and lots of shelves. There was a little galley kitchen and bathroom in the middle. We set up shop. Eric was in one room. I was in the other. We'd get up every morning, have some breakfast, and go to work. We'd assigned each other different parts of the story to tell depending on who had been there at the time. We had transcribed all of the interviews by hand—about seventy in all—and had them typed up. Then we would literally cut and paste the quotes into the narrative as we wrote, so by the end of the day there would be cut-up paper all over the place. Neither Joan Baez nor Bob Dylan was among those we interviewed. Joan opted out for reasons of her own, and Bob wasn't really part of the Cambridge scene. In the end it might have been just as well that other people had a chance to tell their stories and say what this was all about.

As we went along we would also begin to think of which photos to put where. We'd collected some good ones from photographers who were part of the scene—Rick Stafford, John Cooke, Rick Sullo, and Charlie Frizzell. We'd also selected a handful of photographs from Dave Gahr, the foremost photographer of the folk era. Late in the proceedings we also connected with another Cambridge photographer, Steve Fenerjian, who sent us a box of about thirty contact sheets that were a treasure trove—a whole document of the scene as it really was at parties and in people's apartments. It was total "fly on the wall" stuff. No one was looking at the camera. One photograph showed Bob Dylan in the middle of a room of people gathered at the Indian Neck Folk Festival. No one was looking at him. One of the last times in his life that could happen. These photographs gave us that extra something to make this book a real document of the time.

We now turned to the task of putting it all together. It was our job to deliver the book "camera-ready." With all of his experience illustrating and making collages, Eric really shone. He had the idea to do a photographic collage for the cover of people from earlier generations and people from our generation, all flowing together in a kind of river. We also came up with a title for the book. Initially we were calling it *Where Do You Come From, Where Do You Go?* That came out of my approach when interviewing people to always start off at the beginning. "Where do you come from, and how did you start getting involved with music?" Suddenly, one day as we were working, it just dawned on me. I said, "Eric,

FIGURE 15. Eric and me—still standing.
Photograph: © 1979 J.B. McCourtney.

the title of this book is *Baby, Let Me Follow You Down*," recalling Dylan's credit to Eric on his first album. It was so simple. It described what we were talking about in terms of all of us following our hearts, following a tradition down some road, not knowing where it would take us. The idea just snapped into place like that, and there it was.

Another wonderful idea of Eric's was to make the book echo the medieval manuscripts with their calligraphy and large illustrated capitals starting off sections of the narrative. Each chapter heading was the title of a song with a verse under it, all done in a beautiful calligraphic script by Paul Fowler, using, as Eric put it, "a little Elizabethan Zen." The illustrated capitals were photos, old engravings, or woodcuts. Of course, all of this meant more work for us as we laid each page out. We thought we were under a firm deadline to deliver the book by the 1st of July, so we went at it hammer and tongs. The photographs had to be copied, reduced, enlarged—whatever it took. We had been supplied with a book of layout rules from the production people at Doubleday. We probably broke every one of them, but we got the job done and shipped it off by the second week of July. Not a moment too soon. Since April we had been literally working from the time we got up until the time we went to bed. Eric would have a cup of rum at hand from morning to night. Toward the end he was showing some signs of alcohol poisoning, and I wasn't far behind. For the next couple of years, any time I sat down at a typewriter my back would go into a total spasm. "PLEASE! DON'T DO THAT AGAIN!" When it was done, we were almost too tired to celebrate, but we did. What had started as a crazy, full-moon, rum-inspired idea nearly a year earlier, was now a reality that would prove to be the defining telling of the story of one of America's most creative and important musical times. Happily, we had lived to tell the tale!

TOONTOWN

After a couple of days on the beach swimming and playing bocce, I headed back to Nashville and picked up where I had left off. Judy and Johanna had been in and out of my life since I moved to Nashville. She was no longer with John Annas. Sometimes they had stayed with me, which I loved because Johanna was such a bright spark, but Judy just had to be on her own and, after a stint living in the basement of the Kountry Korner bar a few blocks from me, had moved down to Winchester, Tennessee, so they weren't around now. Over at Jack's there had been some changes. A while back Rick Sanjek had hired a receptionist named Terrell Tye, who eventually had married Jack's new engineer, Curt Allen. The attic had been converted into a studio with a 24-track machine and new control board, and Jack had been busy most of the summer working on an album with John Prine. I had met John at a festival in Maine the previous summer. We were there for three or four days and had some quality time in the bar where we got acquainted. Much later he told me that after meeting me he went and told his guitar player that he thought he had just met Huckleberry Finn! I had a motor home instead of a raft, but I was certainly floating freely down the river of life, and I had red hair and freckles, so maybe he was partly right. I was happy to run into John again. He and Jack had piled up quite a few 2-inch tapes, and John and Rachel had struck up a relationship. Love was in the air at the Cowboy Arms and Recording Spa—Jack's new name for the place.

I got a chance to check out the new studio almost immediately. One morning I came in the back door, as usual, into the kitchen. There was an English fellow with curly hair and a round, smiling face standing there. He turned out to be a drummer named Tony Newman. He was a real English rocker, who had played with Jeff Beck and David Bowie! Tony and I poured ourselves a cup of coffee and went back to find Jack in his office. Pretty soon Rachel Peer came in. Then Phillip Donnelly showed up. Phillip was from Dublin and had come to California with the British folk singer Donovan. Out in California Phillip crossed paths with Lee Clayton, who wrote the hit song "Ladies Love Outlaws." When Lee came back to Nashville he brought Phillip with him, and I'd heard Phillip play with Lee a couple of times and immediately loved his play-ing. It was all in his fingers. He had the touch. As we all gathered in Cowboy's office, Jack and I got out the guitars and started strumming a few songs—a good way to start the day. After a few minutes he turned to me and said, "Why don't you all go upstairs and do something?" Curt was already up there plugging things in, so up we went. I pulled out "I Recall a Gypsy Woman," sang it a couple of times, and Curt recorded it. Even though I had just met Tony and had never played with Phillip, it just fell into place. Then I decided to do "No Expectations." Tony and Rachel got an instant groove going. Phillip's playing took off as the song picked up steam, and we were rocking over the top by the end. We all looked at each other when we were done. We were all laughing. I had just walked into this wonderful musical group.

I soon got another chance to record. Jack had hired Tony Newman's former bandmate with David Bowie, Herbie Flowers—one of the top bass players in the world—to come over for a month and play on whatever Jack wanted to record. One morning we were gathered in Cowboy's office, strumming as usual, when he turned to me and said, "Why don't you go upstairs and warm up the band?" Up we all trooped. This time I pulled out "South in New Orleans," which had been a hit for Johnny & Jack, a great hillbilly duo, back in the fifties. With Herbie and Tony laying down a rocking rumba feel, we cut the song in no time at all. When Jack heard it, he was up and dancing around the room, and he quickly decided to finish both "No Expectations" and "South in New Orleans" to be my first (and last) JMI single.

In the Fall, the Woodstock Mountains Revue got together for a month-long tour of the Northeast supporting our new album *Pretty Lucky*, which we had recorded in January just before Eric and I submerged to write *Baby, Let Me Follow You Down*. When I got back to Nashville in December, Curt Allen took me up to the studio and sat me down at the control board in front of the speakers. "No Expectations" came on first. Jack and Curt had been busy. They had added Rick Shulman's rocking acoustic guitar to the track. The first instrumental break was the fine electric guitar of Jerry McKuen. The second instrumental section hammered you with the horn section of Irv Kane, Dennis Solee, and Wayne Jackson (of the Memphis Horns) blaring out the melody followed by Phillip Donnelly taking off, augmented by the wild fiddling of Buddy Spicher. Curt, Rachel, and Kathy Johnson joined in with me on the final verse ("Take me to the airport and pour me on a plane"). Then the whole thing rocked off into the distance with guitars, fiddle, and horns going full tilt. The phrase "I couldn't believe my ears" comes to mind here. I really couldn't. This was a RECORD! It was MY RECORD! Then Curt said, "How about this?" and played me "South in New Orleans." This featured the great Lloyd Green on dobro and Dennis Solee on piccolo, giving it just a hint of Mardi Gras. What really floored me was that Jack and Curt had put so much thought and effort into taking the basic tracks, both cut on the spur of the moment with my live vocals, and turning them into complete productions. I felt very lucky to be in such good hands.

When I had nothing to do, Bob Webster put me to work making a digital copy of the entire Jack Music Catalogue. This was a real eye-opener. It gave me an insight into how many songs never see the light of day after they are demoed. I got a chance to listen to the hundred songs by Bob

McDill or Allen Reynolds or Jack, which had never been recorded by any artists, some deservedly so, but others hidden gems still waiting to be discovered. I was talking to Jack about this one morning when he opened his desk drawer and fished out a sheet of paper, which he handed to me.

PINEAPPLE JACK CLEMENT'S
TEN TIPS FOR SONGWRITERS

1. Remember that experts are often wrong.
2. Experts tend to be narrow and overly opinionated.
3. Experts don't buy records.
4. There's nothing wrong with waltzes if they're played right.
5. A good song gets better with age.
6. Reveal some of yourself with most of your songs.
7. Don't get stuck on one song too long. Work on other songs as you go.
8. Learn to grow from setbacks, delays, and getting your feelings hurt.
9. Write the worst song you can think of.
10. Write the best song you can think of.

While I was looking over the list Jack mentioned with a smile that he'd written his first million-seller while taking a crap one morning! The song was "It'll Be Me (and I'll Be Looking for You)," the song on the flip side of "Whole Lot of Shakin' Goin' On" which Jack had recorded with Jerry Lee Lewis at Sun Records. The implied message was: Don't take yourself too seriously, but always do a good job.

I began to think of some songs of mine that I'd like to demo. Jack had agreed to publish "Interest on the Loan." I had started to write with a keyboard player named Lamar Hill, and we had a song called "The Girl at the End of the Hall" that Jack also liked. Lamar had played in Doc and Merle Watson's band "Frosty Morn" and was a fun-loving guy. He had come over to the pool at the Americana where we ran into Marshall Chapman. He asked who that was, and I mentioned that she lived at the end of the hall on the sixth floor. From then on Lamar would always ask me if I'd seen the "girl at the end of the hall" lately. The song almost wrote itself. ("The girl at the end of the hall / Is always out having a ball / I guess that's why she never answers my call / This mysterious girl at the end of the hall.") While we were at it we also came up with a whimsical number called "The Boy in Me." ("You bring out the Christmas toy in me / You bring out the boy in me.") I was getting beyond writing about me and my broken heart. I was having fun with it. I got a session together with Peace and Quiet and we demoed the songs. We weren't trying to do a full-fledged production. The purpose of a demo was to show the essential structure and feel of a song so that it could be played for an artist or producer who was looking for songs—hopefully hit songs—to record. I was learning the publishing process.

When I first moved to Nashville, my Uncle Jim Flaherty had sent me a card with a hundred bucks in it saying, "Good luck in Toontown." Every so often I'd send the family a "Note from Toontown" to give them a bit of the flavor of the life I was leading. About this time I wrote:

> "It has been many months since most of you have heard from me. Don't worry. I do exist. I've just been trying to keep all the balls in the air. Every so often one gets away from me, but I hope I'm getting better.
>
> I continue to be a member of Jack Clement's recording family and have continued to learn and grow here. We have seen the studio in the attic become a reality over the last few months, thanks to revenues from some songs which Jack publishes. This is the ninth studio Jack has designed and built (from Memphis to Beaumont to Nashville) and I have learned and relearned a lot about recording in the process of putting this one together.
>
> One nice thing about Jack's is that there is no lack of stimulation. If there isn't recording to do, I can go out in the garden with my friend Peck Chandler and tie up tomato plants or pick beans or just croon to the plants. Peck is a wonderful writer as well as a gardener, and I have been helping him record some of his songs.
>
> I also spend a lot of time with Bob Webster. Bob is the "professional manager" of Jack Music, Inc. He has been with Jack Clement for over eighteen years—since Beaumont, Texas—and he knows the complete history of every song in the Jack Music catalogue. Recently he has had three top ten single records working—"Lay Down beside Me" by Don Williams, "When I Dream" by Crystal Gayle, and "Amanda" by Waylon Jennings. Just by hanging out with Bob I have begun to get a

good working knowledge of the publishing business. All over burgers and beer, a ballgame and beer, or just beer. Bob likes a good cold beer now and then. Mostly now.

That's about it. The Woodstock Mtns. Revue heads for Geneva, Cambridge, Brussels, and Denmark for three weeks of festivals and shows. After that I'll be back here to get involved in more playing, recording and gardening."

The Woodstock Mountains Revue European tour was a big success. One afternoon after a midday concert at the Nyon Folk Festival in Switzerland, a group of young Italian enthusiasts came up to me and introduced themselves. They seemed to know a lot about what I had done, including The Blue Velvet Band and even Borderline. They told me that there were some people at a record label in Milan, Appaloosa Records, who wanted to put out a record album by me. My first reaction was, "I don't think so." I couldn't imagine that there would be any demand for me in Italy! However, they were so nice and so sincere that I told them that if the label people wanted to get in touch with me they could. When I got back to Nashville there was indeed a letter—a very businesslike letter—from a man named Giovanni Bonandrini in Milan inviting me to make a record. He sent me a catalogue. I was impressed. One of their labels called "Soul Note" had people like Sonny Rollins and Miles Davis. They were a real record company. Suddenly it seemed that another door was opening for me.

Over the past two or three years I'd been accumulating tapes, starting with Durg's sessions and subsequently what I had been doing at Jack's. Appaloosa was going to give me $5,000 to make an album, so I organized a session with the addition of Ben Keith, who had recently moved back to Nashville from Woodstock. We cut John Prine's *Bruised Orange* and Allen Reynolds's *Ready for the Times to Get Better*. Finally, I did Bobby Charles's *Tennessee Blues*. Curt Allen and I mixed all the tracks and sent a package off to Giovanni and Franco Ratti, who was the man actually running the Appaloosa label. A month or so later I got a letter in the mail—kind of a fat letter. There were fifty $100 bills in it. My kind of mail! So I paid everybody and put what was left in my desk drawer. Any time I needed some money I'd pull out a hundred.

THE DEAD COWBOYS

Since I had first run into him when I arrived in June of '76, Don Everly and I had become pretty good eating and drinking buddies. Many Sundays I'd join Don and his wife Karen at their apartment while Don whipped up a gourmet meal and we talked about music, books, and art. Our major hangout was the Sutler Saloon, run by a Nashville character named Johnny Potts. I had talked Don into getting together with Phillip, Tony, Rachel, and Lamar, and we somehow came up with a name for the band—The Dead Cowboys! Johnny Potts was adding another room so he could have music on a regular basis, and we volunteered to open it with a series of four Monday nights in January of 1980—"Nights of The Dead Cowboys" (riffing on "Night of the Living Dead"). They were quite the nights. My compadre from the Woodstock Mountains Revue, Pat Alger, had recently moved to town, so we invited him to open with a few of his songs before The Dead Cowboys hit the stage. Our standard of success was that Phillip Donnelly needed to be levitating at the end of the evening. He'd get excited and start hopping a little bit until finally both feet were off the ground. When that happened we'd all look at each other and give him another goose. Don would start off with Jimmie Rodgers classic "T for Texas, T for Tennessee." We'd do some of the Everly Brothers standards like "Wake Up Little Susie," "Cathy's Clown," or "So Sad (to See Good Love Go Bad)," with Rachel taking Phil's part. I'd do "South in New Orleans," "Tennessee Blues," or "Sitting on Top of the World." By the end of the night Don would be rocking with "Lucille" or a scorching version of Blondie's "Dreaming," which made people aware that he was still listening, still a true rock-and-roller.

Don took us to Holland, France, and England that summer. We were in France for a month, splitting the bill with Wanda Jackson; I remembered her from when she was singing with Hank Thompson's band back in 1954. When Rockabilly music came in she had some hits like "Fujiama Mama" and "Let's Have a Party," which made her famous in France. Now, however, Wanda had been "born again" and was primarily singing gospel music. When we climbed aboard the bus the first morning, Wanda and her husband Wendell had staked out the two "shotgun" seats across from the driver and already had their Bibles out. She was happy to see Don again. They'd worked together some on shows in the late fifties. I

FIGURE 16. With Don Everly (*c.*) and Phillip Donnelly.
The Dead Cowboys French tour, 1980.

introduced myself to her and reminded her of the show in Boston. They were both very nice. She had a pickup band from England working with her. They were in the middle of the bus, so The Dead Cowboys naturally gravitated to the back of the bus, because we instinctively understood that was where we probably needed to be.

Off we went, headed for the Atlantic coast and our first gig. We were working every other day. The shows were sponsored by Marlboro cigarettes, and they had engaged the services of four gorgeous models from Paris to basically shill a crowd, even though the shows were free. They would go around wherever we were going to be playing, dressed in their lovely short shorts and Marlboro T-shirts, and hand out little free packs of Marlboro cigarettes. They were also staying at the various hotels along the way, so we all got to be friendly. Lamar, of course, fell in love—and who could blame him?

On one of our nights off we decided to set up in the hotel bar and have a jam session. Until then Wanda had never heard us play. She would go out and do the first half of the show and get right back on the bus while we played the second half. This night she and Wendell happened to be in the hotel lobby and heard music coming out of the bar, so they stuck their heads in and decided to come in and listen. Wanda was just blown away by Phillip's guitar playing and by the sound of the whole band. All the next day she kept telling us how impressed she had been and how much she had enjoyed our music. A couple of days later we were in another place with nothing to do. Tony and I took a couple of the girls to dinner in the hotel restaurant. As we passed the bar on the way into the dining room we noticed Wanda and Wendell standing in the bar with Don and Phillip. When we came out after our meal they were still there. As we came into the bar the conversation was going like this: Phillip Donnelly was saying to Wanda, "You know, from outer space you can't see any boundaries. We're all together on this planet!" Don was talking to Wendell about "taking coup." Wendell liked to shoot elk up in Alaska. Don was saying, "I've hunted ever since I was a kid shooting squirrels to eat. Now I just walk up to them and tell them, 'I could shoot you, but I'm not going to.'" The conversation was definitely deep and philosophical. Wanda and Wendell were drinking Belgian beer, enjoying themselves. They even bought their band some wine. They had totally loosened up since hearing us play, and we were becoming friends. The next morning, however, when I came down to breakfast, I felt sorry for them because they thought they had sinned by letting down their guard and having too much fun. They were still friendly with us, but they weren't going to let that happen again. Hanging out with the Dead Cowboys could be dangerous for your soul!

After France we went to London for a couple more gigs to wind up the tour. The first one was at a club where everyone was dressed up like they did in the fifties. The guys had leather jackets and D.A. haircuts. The girls had ponytails and cute dresses. Everyone was dressed like they were in "Blackboard Jungle" or "Happy Days"—everyone except us, of course. They were expecting a totally retro show from Don. The Dead Cowboys weren't their idea of a great sock-hop band. The next night was a different story. We were at a big club called The Venue, and the place was packed with people who were really into music. They were with us from the opening notes of "T for Texas" right through the final scorching performance of "Dreaming." After we left the stage the audience kept standing and shouting for nearly half an hour. We were downstairs getting changed when the manager came and told Don he'd have to go back on before they started a riot. It was a great way to end the tour. The Dead Cowboys lived for that short period of time and what a sweet time it was.

The next day Phillip, Don, Karen, and I got on a plane to Dublin. Before we had left Nashville, Phillip had told Don about a big folk festival at Ballysadare up in Sligo on the west coast of Ireland. Recalling his experience at Newport, Don told Phillip that he'd be up for going. It was just the three of us—Don, Phillip, and me—The Dead Cowboy Campfire Trio. We were to do one night at a small club also called The Venue, in the village of Strandhill and one set the next afternoon at the festival a few miles away. The setting for The Venue was amazing. We were within walking distance of the sea and some gigantic sand dunes. Back of the hotel on the top of a mountain was Queen Maeve's prehistoric grave mound, which could be seen for miles. This was the country Yeats had grown up in. We couldn't help but feel that we were in a very special place.

Before the first night's show at The Venue Don was a bit edgy. He hadn't played without drums since he was eighteen. We worked up a set. I sang some songs, Phillip sang a few, and Don did some including a couple from "Songs Our Daddy Taught Us." We did enough Everly Brothers material to keep the audience happy, and it all went like we'd been doing it for years. The following afternoon we made our way to the festival grounds, where we did our set on the main stage. Don was over his nervousness, and his vocals were clear and strong. We had become a good little acoustic trio, with Don and me giving Phillip a solid rhythm to work off of. As they say over there, "It went down a storm."

Fortunately for us, we had caught this festival at its height. The group Planxty absolutely ruled. They were different from The Clancys and Tommy Makem; different from The Dubliners. They had two outstanding singers—the intense, emotional Christy Moore and the gentler, sweeter Andy Irvine. Andy had also introduced the Balkan sound of the bouzouki to Irish music. Donal Lunny, also on bouzouki, gave the group a strong rhythmic underpinning, which laid the foundation for the soaring sound of Liam O'Flynn on uillean pipes and whistle. The energy of their music was thrilling. There were lots of other people there as well, including Ralph McTell (whose best known songs were "Streets of London" and "From Clare to Here"), Phillip's former boss, Donovan, and my great old friend Ramblin' Jack Elliott. We'd wind up every night back at the Venue jamming and singing songs.

We were asked if we'd be willing to play the night after the festival ended at The Venue for the festival staff. By that time we almost felt like staff, so, of course, we did it. That was the magic night. The music just poured out of us. By the end people were almost in tears, they were so happy. The Dead Cowboy Campfire Trio finally packed it in just before dawn. It had been quite a reintroduction back into Ireland after a sixteen-year hiatus, and I could feel myself being irresistibly drawn back.

PART III
FOLLOWING MY OWN
PATH

AT HOME IN THE STUDIO

My life at this time was nothing if not full. Judy and Johanna had been back with me for a few months after a stint living over in East Tennessee, and we were making a stab at being a family, which gave me the opportunity to share in Johanna's life, taking her to school and gymnastics classes, helping her learn to ride a two-wheeler, taking her to Disney World and then to the beach at Eric Von Schmidt's in Siesta Key, reading stories to her at night. She was nothing but a positive presence in my life. Our life together was not going to last, however, because Judy decided to move back to her mother's in California in September in the hope that she could connect Johanna with her other kids. My role in Judy's life seemed to be trying to get her to the place where she could be on her own, so I had to let them go and wish them well.

My work life now was almost entirely taken up in studio sessions. I offered to help both Bill Keith and Peter Rowan when they started to work on new albums. My growing facility in the studio made it possible for me to bring their vision to fruition quickly and easily. Curt Allen and I got together to produce an album for Franco Ratti at Appaloosa on a new member of Cowboy's musical family, Pat McLaughlin. I first heard him at a funky little joint called Springwater. He was very unique, hunched over a telecaster, bobbing and weaving, almost like a boxer, with a singing style that reminded me of Van Morrison. His band included my former Ragtime Band mate, Dwight Scott on Hammond B-3 organ, a fine sax player named Jay Patten, Larry Paxton on bass, and Tony Newman on drums. Pat wrote songs that made sense even if you didn't totally understand the lyrics. The groove carried everything before it, and the little joint would be rocking about midnight. In the studio we just set the band up and let them go. Pat called it "Wind It On Up." It was live as it could be.

Franco said he could help organize some gigs in Italy, so I got in touch with Bill Keith and Peter Rowan to see if we could reconstitute our old trio. Over the course of eighteen months in 1980 and '81 Peter, Bill, and I did three tours. Bluegrass was a natural for the Italians. Mandolins, guitars, and violins were their instruments. They loved emotional singing. The country was full of mountains. Peter, Bill, and I were a good combination. We could do hard-core, Bill Monroe–style Bluegrass, some Jazz, and some original and contemporary songs featuring emotional vocals from Peter and me. We played from Naples to Turin and a lot of places in between. One of the highlights was when we brought Tex Logan with us to Naples. We played in a large tent called Theatrotenta Parthenope, which probably held fifteen hundred people. They went absolutely wild when they saw and heard Tex. I couldn't help but think back to when Dick Curley and I first laid eyes on Tex at WCOP and how excited we were to see and hear him in action. The Neapolitans had exactly the same reaction, and they really let it show.

Franco continued to be a big supporter of my music and asked me to do a second album. In the aftermath of the Dead Cowboys tour Phillip, Lamar, Rachel, Tony, and I had become what they call in Nashville a "section." We were basically a rhythm section you could use to cut basic tracks. We were playing on demos for John Prine, Roger Cook (who wrote "I'd Like to Teach the World to Sing in Perfect Harmony" and "You've Got Your Troubles, I've Got Mine"), and Richard Leigh (who wrote "Don't It Make My Brown Eyes Blue"). I decided for this album to do three or four sessions with us all playing live up in Cowboy's studio.

We did three of John Prine's songs, including "Fish and Whistle," which seems to me to sum up the mystery of man's relationship with God:

FIGURE 17. Tex Logan, Peter Rowan, and Bill Keith tearing it up in Naples.
Photograph courtesy of Dino Luglio.

Father, forgive us for what we must do
You forgive us, we'll forgive you
We'll forgive each other 'til we both turn blue
Then we'll go fish and whistle in Heaven.

I had been helping Peck Chandler demo some of his songs. Peck's songs
had some kind of spiritual level to them even when they were talking
about the world of the flesh. That's why I was drawn to do "Heaven Come
a Woman":

Heaven come a woman, comin' like a waterfall
Set her lover hummin,' hummin' like a pay phone call
Heaven come a woman and I'll serve you most of all.

Other songs I chose were in the air around Jack's: Bob McDill's "Amanda,"
Allen Reynolds and Bob McDill's "We Must Believe in Magic" and Allen
Reynolds's beautiful "Dreaming My Dreams." I also did my own versions
of Bill Monroe's "Six White Horses," which gave Phillip Donnelly a chance
to stretch his blues chops, and "Satisfied Mind," the song that launched
Porter Wagoner's career and which I clearly remembered hearing him

sing on the radio back in 1954 on the WWVA *Wheeling Jamboree*. The song I chose to be the title song of the album was "Brand New Tennessee Waltz" by Jesse Winchester. I had met Jesse up in Montreal a few years earlier when I was playing a coffeehouse there. He was a lovely, quietly strong person, who had the courage of his convictions. He had left the United States for Canada during the Vietnam War. He had, indeed, "left Tennessee in a hurry," and he continued on his own path. Something about the song resonated in me when I thought of my own musical journey in the last few years;

> At the Brand New Tennessee Waltz
> You're literally waltzing on air
> At The Brand New Tennessee Waltz
> There's no telling who will be there.

I was happy with the finished album. Everything came together effortlessly. I'd been playing and singing almost continuously since Eric and I finished *Baby, Let Me Follow You Down*. I had passed beyond imitating Hank Williams or Lester Flatt or some singer from the mountains and had finally found my own voice as a singer. This was me. I was hitting on all cylinders, and I could hear it on this album.

It was not lost on Jack that I was very happy working in the studio. One day we were sitting in his office and he said, "You know, you need to learn how to run the board." I said, "I don't know about that, Jack. I'm not very technically oriented." He gave me a look and said, "You don't have to be a mechanic to drive a car do you? You've got good ears. You know what music's supposed to sound like. It's not that hard. Do it." He told me to get Curt Allen and Jack "Stack-a-Track" Grochmal, who had recently joined Cowboy's crew, to show me where everything plugged in and where the on/off switches were. Basic stuff. Jack himself came up and gave me some tips. "Keep the needles in the middle. Don't mess with the signal with limiters or compressors or other gadgets unless you absolutely have to. If something doesn't sound right, move the microphone or try another one. Get the signal on tape as clean as possible." This was exactly what I needed to hear. Up at Bearsville I had watched some big name producers at work—David Rubinson, Paul Rothchild, and Robbie Robertson, among others. They immediately plugged in gates and limiters and compressors on just about everything both when recording and later when mixing. I thought that this was a complicated process that was way beyond the likes of me. Jack swept all that away. Suddenly I thought to myself, "Oh, maybe I'm not so stupid after all." It wasn't as if I was a total novice. I'd been recording and around studios since 1962 and a lot in the past few years. I'd seen what kind of mics were used for vocals, on drums, on guitars. I had a pretty good idea of how things went and what things should sound like. Jack was right. It was time for me to just do it.

One Saturday morning Cowboy called me up. "What are you doing?" "I don't know. What am I doing?" "Come over here. I've got Vic Damone over here, and I need you to record him." So over I went. I knew who Vic Damone was. He'd been up there in the pop world with Tony Bennett and Frank Sinatra. When I arrived, Jack had Kenny Malone, Joe Allen, and Charles Cochran there to accompany Vic on some songs that Jack had picked for him to sing. Everyone was relaxed and in a good mood. Vic himself seemed very nice, very professional. I'm sure he felt he was in good hands. He had no idea that I'd never recorded anyone in my life! I went upstairs and busied myself getting everything set up, putting the mics where I thought they should be, checking everyone's headphones, and finally went downstairs to tell them I was ready. They all came up and started running the first song. I adjusted the mics and asked them if they were all okay. They were. Everything was fine. So I pressed the red "record" button. After they finished, they came in to listen back. I was sweating bullets, fully convinced that it wouldn't play back. I had no confidence whatsoever. I hit "playback"—and it played back!!! It sounded just the way it did when it went in. They were all happy and went in to do another one. So there I was. I was an engineer!

Shortly thereafter, Carl "Blue Suede Shoes" Perkins showed up with his band. He wanted to put some songs down, so he was the second person I recorded! Jack had thrown me into the deep end of the pool, and fortunately it turned out to be not as deep as I had thought. True enough, recording had changed a lot since my first experience in 1962. Then we had 2 tracks—basic stereo. What you recorded was what you got. The Blue Velvet Band recorded to 8 tracks, which meant that we could overdub harmonies and additional instruments, which would subsequently be mixed down to 2 tracks. At Bearsville we were up to 16 tracks, and now Jack had a new 24-track machine, which meant that every instrument could have at least 1 track, up to 6 or 8 for drums—all of which had to be mixed together, which was where the real craft came in. Each instrument had to be placed or "panned" in a field from left to right. You had to figure out volume levels for all the different elements in relation to the vocal, which was the focus of everything. There were EQ settings to adjust for high, middle, and low frequencies, as well as different levels and kinds of echo to use. It was a bit daunting at first—all of these possibilities—but I learned to trust my own instincts, my own ears.

I knew what I wanted in an engineer as far as the rhythm of a recording session went. What I didn't want was somebody who wasn't ready to record when I was ready to play. I'd had that experience. I'd had experience with bad headphones. I'd had experience where I couldn't see the other players, where I felt like I was in a box or a prison, where I couldn't move freely, where communication was difficult. As a result, when I started doing this, I would show up early. I'd check everything myself—the earphones, the microphones—so I knew for sure that everything was working before anyone ever came into the room. My main focus was on insuring that the musicians would be comfortable. I was there to help them play music and to forget about recording. Bill Keith had once compared going into a recording session to a visit to the dentist! I didn't see why it had to be that way.

Johnny Cash's daughter Cathy was organizing demo sessions for his publishing company. Once a week she'd show up with five musicians and a singer or two. We'd demo about eight songs in two three-hour sessions, doing overdubs as we went along. I'd mix the eight songs the next day and send them off. Doing that every week for a few months was invaluable experience. I had to move fast and work quickly, making lots of little decisions on the fly. It was a great journeyman's apprenticeship—recording, overdubbing, mixing, editing. With each passing week I was gaining confidence that I understood the process. I was becoming a pretty good seat-of-the-pants engineer.

One benefit of adding another arrow to my quiver was that it was another way for me to make some money. Somehow or other Jack and I agreed to a figure of $12/hour for my services. Curt was branching out into his own production work, so suddenly there was an opening for me. Bob Webster put me to work engineering demo sessions for Jack Music. In addition to Carl Perkins, I recorded Billy Lee Riley, who Jack had worked with back at Sun Records; Merv Shiner, who had the original hit on "Here Comes Peter Cottontail"; Jimmie Rodgers of "Honeycomb" fame; and Johnny Western, who'd written the theme for "Palladin" and several other TV Western theme songs. On Johnny's album, the guitar player was Billy Strange, who had played on all the big-time Hollywood Western sound tracks. So there I was, recording Johnny Western and Billy Strange! I was having a ball.

An incredible bonus of learning to be an engineer was that if the studio wasn't booked, I was free to use it for my own purposes. This is stuff you pray for! Pat Alger had moved back to Atlanta from Woodstock. There wasn't much of a music scene happening there for him so he had started coming over to visit me and spend the weekend on my couch. We'd go out and hear music, and he started getting a feel for the place. He was feeling good about his songwriting and had a single coming out by Livingston Taylor—a song called "First Time Love" that he'd written in New York with his friend Peter Kaminsky. He'd accumulated some songs, so I offered to demo them for him. I got the studio for a day and asked Charles Cochran, Kenny Malone, and Joe Allen if they'd play. They were happy to do it, and, since it was for me, refused any pay. This kind of generosity was the norm at Cowboy's. We cut four or five songs, and while we were working I got a call from John Allen Cameron, who was in town recording with Randy Scruggs. John was the most popular singer in Nova Scotia and had been on the famous "New Folks" concert at Newport in 1969. I invited him to come by, and he came in just as we were mixing a song called "Overnight Success," about a singer who beats his brains out playing honky-tonks for years and then finally has a hit, becoming an "overnight success." John Allen loved it and asked Pat if he could record it. So Pat got a cut off of his very first Nashville demo session! It probably made it look too easy, because he and Chris finally decided to take the plunge and move to Nashville. Pat's own "overnight success" was still a few years down the road, but at least he was on the road.

To show my appreciation for Jack's generosity, I wanted to bring some paying business into the studio. One night I ran into Bela Fleck at the Station Inn, my favorite bluegrass music club. He said he was going to produce an album with an outstanding young fiddle player named Blaine Sprouse. I asked him where he was going to do it, and he said he was looking for a studio. I said, "Why don't you do it over at Jack Clement's?" He asked, "Who's the engineer there?" I said, "I am." I could see that this might not be exactly what he was hoping to hear. I'd say that Bela's impression of me was someone he always saw out at night, sort of a genial drunk—which maybe I was! However, perhaps because of my connection with Bill Keith, whom he greatly admired, he came over and took a look at the place. I gave him a good deal, and the result was a beautiful album titled *Brilliancy*.

I was definitely still learning while I was earning, because at one point Bela asked me if I could edit the 24-track tape. "You could just edit this section here right out, couldn't you?" I think he might have been testing me, but I said, "Yeah, I could do that." I was used to editing with a razor blade on 2-track tape before, but never on the two-inch 24-track tape. I had enough confidence in myself by now, so I did it. I was sweating, but I did it.

I was soon given another opportunity to develop my skills. Jack's Canadian publisher, Jury Krytiuk started sending people down to record at Jack's. The first group was a bluegrass band, Denis LePage & Station Road. There was no producer involved, and, as is the case with many democratic bands, the boys seemed to be having trouble making decisions about whether a take or a particular solo was good or not. Ordinarily, it was not the engineer's place to be making those decisions. However, they had a limited budget and didn't have all the time in the world, so I took it upon myself to stick my oar in and help them along by saying, "That's good. Why don't you move on," or "You're almost there. Why don't you give it one more shot?" They seemed to be happy to be relieved of some of that responsibility and left me to mix it, which also would have normally been overseen by the producer. I called Jury up to tell him that I had the job done, but that it seemed that I was also taking on the responsibilities of a producer and how would he feel about paying me for that. He had no problem with it. From then on, in addition to my hourly engineering fee I would get $750 as a producer's fee. This was a big step forward for me.

The next group he sent was a folk trio called The Garrison Brothers. They had good songs, some of them written by one of the guys, Kevin Evans. I put a band together to play with them—Phillip Donnelly on electric guitar, Marty Stuart on mandolin and fiddle, and Lamar Hill on piano. I was moving in the direction of a mixture of acoustic and electric instruments similar to what we'd done with the Blue Velvet Band album or what I had done with the Gershen brothers in Borderline. This was a natural way for me to go, mixing bluegrass musicians, folk musicians, and country musicians. I'd gone through hillbilly and country music; I'd gone through folk music; I'd gone through bluegrass, so I had a feel for all of these different styles and had no trouble combining them. This approach worked for The Garrison Brothers, and they had a hit up in Canada with one of the songs.

I further developed my producer skills working with another Canadian artist named Keith Barrie. This gave me an opportunity to match him up with some good songs from some of the Nashville writers I had come to know. I was also interested in trying my hand at hiring an arranger to write parts for a string quartet to add strings to some tracks. I also got to work with a real Nashville background vocal group (including a rising young singer named Kathy Mattea), which brought my bluegrass harmony training into play. Each new project was an opportunity to learn and grow. The studio was my new classroom, my workshop, my new home.

COMING INTO MY OWN

I went out one night in early '83 to hear Richard Dobson, my old friend from the Bishop's Pub days. His drummer Leland Waddell asked me whether I could help Richard make a record. I could easily have blown him off (since there was little or no money involved), but Richard was a good friend, and I liked what I was hearing that night, so I found a time when the studio was free. I had a hunch that Phillip Donnelly's style would work with him, so I had him come in and listen to the songs, which were a combination of the romantic and the political. Phillip was instantly enthusiastic. I hired "Stack-a-Track" to engineer, which left me free to play some rhythm guitar and produce. We recorded the entire album in a weekend and mixed it in another couple of days. It had a great live feel to it and jumped out of the speakers. It really suited Richard's style, and it didn't cost him a lot. He called it *Save the World*.

Opportunities in life are not always apparent. If I hadn't said "yes" to Richard, a subsequent chain of events might never have happened. One of the songs we recorded was called "The Ballad of Robin Wintersmith," which Richard had written about an English daredevil motorcycle rider. The chords were a bit like "No Expectations," and Phillip had burned it up. This was the song that opened a door for me. Richard called me one fine summer day and invited me out to his place in the country for a barbecue. At the party I met a friend of his from Texas named Nanci Griffith. I'd never heard of her, but Richard told me she was a good writer and singer. After a while we got the guitars out and started swapping songs. Richard was right, and she was a good guitar player to boot. She told me how much she liked Richard's album, especially "The Ballad of Robin Wintersmith," and asked me if I'd be interested in helping her make an album. I said that I'd be happy to. She sent me two albums she'd made in Texas with a guitarist and producer named Brian Wood. I thought they sounded fine—lovely acoustic folk albums. After I'd listened, I quizzed her a bit. "What's wrong with what you're doing? What do you need me for?" She wanted a fuller sound. She wanted drums. She wanted Phillip Donnelly. She wanted Lloyd Green to play steel and dobro. (He was a favorite of her aunt's!) There was nothing vague about Nanci. She had definite ideas and thought I was the one to help her fulfill them, so we started working toward that goal.

During the course of the year I'd have her come up to Nashville every two or three months and do a gig. Pat Alger, Pat McLaughlin, and me—"Pat, Pat & Jim"—would open up for her and insure that she got a crowd. I got Roy Huskey Jr. to play bass with her, and Pat Alger and Mark Howard to play guitars. Mark was a fine guitarist; John Hartford had brought him over from Chattanooga to play with him. In the course of doing these gigs Mark, Roy, and Pat got familiar with Nanci's songs, and she also got to hear a song Pat had written with Bill Dale and Fred Koller called "Once in a Very Blue Moon," which she liked well enough to learn.

By June of '84 we were ready to record. I hired "Stack-a-Track" to be the engineer and gathered an interesting group of musicians together. There were veterans such as Kenny Malone and Lloyd Green, who had played on countless thousands of sessions. (Lloyd once told me that he'd played on more than twelve thousand sessions that he kept track of—and then he stopped counting!) Roy Huskey Jr. came out of that tradition. His dad, Junior Huskey had been one of Nashville's top session players until his untimely death at the age of forty-three. Roy (known as Junior Huskey Junior) had followed right along in his dad's footsteps. They might have done all that work, but they hadn't lost their enthusiasm and sense of commitment. They gave the sessions real depth. Then there were some relative newcomers such as Ralph Vitello on keyboards, Pat Alger, Mark Howard, and Phillip Donnelly. I also brought in Bela Fleck and Mark O'Connor, new arrivals from the bluegrass world. Nanci brought up some friends from Austin—a good guitar player named Stephen Doster and two backup singers—Denise Franke and Lyle Lovett. As more and more people came up the stairs, Stack was beginning to wonder where to put them all, but we figured it out, filling up all the nooks and crannies of the studio. Nanci was snug in one corner where she could see everyone and I could get what isolation I needed to get her vocals live. She cut thirteen songs in two days. She was a trouper. She was prepared.

The chemistry between the musicians flowed beautifully. Arrangements came together quickly once everyone had listened to Nanci sing and play the song. Her guitar playing was important in setting the tempos, and Kenny and Roy would lock right in with her, as did Mark and Pat and Stephen, since they already knew the songs. Lloyd Green liked Phillip's sound and his energy. Phillip, in turn, was very deferential to Lloyd and created some subtle backing for Lloyd's solos. Bela Fleck and Mark O'Connor were sitting together and often came up with little riffs. They had amazing ability and there was great freshness in their playing. I was a novice producer, but my instincts were to let the musicians figure out as much as they could with Nanci, without interference from me. When things seemed to be jelling, I'd get them to pull it all together, and we'd cut it. We might listen back once and do it again, or just do it again while we had the groove. There seemed to be a natural feeling of cooperation in the room. Everyone responded to Nanci's singing, her guitar playing, her professionalism—her willingness to hang in there and do all the vocals live. Another thing that helped was the quality of the material. She was a good listener and was paying attention to other songwriters around her. So we did Lyle Lovett's "The Woman I Am" and Bill Staines's "Roseville Fair," as well as "Once in a Very Blue Moon" and "The Ballad of Robin Wintersmith." Each of Nanci's songs seemed to call for a distinctive musical setting, which gave the musicians something to work with and develop.

As we moved along through the course of the two days we were all increasingly aware that we were involved in creating something very special, and were putting everything we had into it. I remember going into the studio as we were working on the last song. I just happened to look over at Roy Huskey and saw that his fretting fingers were absolutely black, because he'd been playing continuously for two days. I wouldn't have known about it if I hadn't seen it, because there was never a flaw, never a hint of the time wavering. Like Roy, Nanci never faltered, never wavered, and we had achieved our goal.

For the next two days we did some overdubs, mostly harmonies with Lyle, Denise, and Nanci. She had a great ear for harmonies and harmony arrangements, which made my job easy. After finishing the overdubs, we mixed for two days. Stack really made it sing. As a result of my engineering experience I was now able to communicate what I wanted to Stack with confidence, and he could respond. Finally, on Sunday we went over to Masterfonics and mastered with Jim Lloyd. Mastering an album involved paying attention to the very high and very low frequencies, as well as the overall volume levels from track to track, so that nothing would jump out at you when you were listening. It was sort of like polishing wood with very fine sandpaper to bring out its depth and sheen. When this was done, Nanci went home with the whole album finished in a week. It turned out to be a big step in her career, but it was a big step for me as well. When I listened to it, I could see that it all fit together and was really good. In addition to being an architect, my Uncle Jim was an excellent watercolorist. To work in watercolors you had to work fast, and I liked to work the same way. Successfully completing Nanci's album so quickly and efficiently confirmed to me that this was something I could do and do well.

While I was working toward recording Nanci's album, I was also working with John Prine. One day John and I were riding around and he mentioned that he was thinking of starting his own record label. With a tip of the hat toward Buddy Holly, John decided to call it Oh Boy! Records, and he asked me if I would help with the producing. The first thing we did was a Christmas single on red vinyl of "I Saw Mama Kissing Santa Claus" and "Silver Bells." Naturally, we recorded in July, when all Christmas music is recorded. We had a big time. We had sleigh bells, and Rachel and her brother tap-danced to the "cathouse" piano playing of Opry veteran Del Wood. Oh Boy! Records was going to be fun, if nothing else!

Every so often John had been getting a bunch of us together to demo some of his new songs, so we now turned our attention to those. We had recorded some of the tracks at Cowboy's, some at the former Jack Clem-

FIGURE 18. The Jim Rooney Once in a Very Blue Moon Olympic Sink or Swim Team:
(*l. to r.*: Bela Fleck, Lloyd Green, Richard Dobson, John Catchings, Pat Alger,
Ralph Vitello, Jim Rooney, Nanci Griffith, Stephen Doster, Denice Franke,
Lyle Lovett, Roy Huskey Jr., Jack "Stack-A-Track" Grochmal).
Photograph courtesy of Nanci Griffith.

ent Recording Studio (now called The Sound Emporium), and some at
Jack's Tracks. Rachel, Phillip, Tony, and I had played on most songs, but
occasionally John had used other musicians. The one unifying element
was John's unique delivery and the quality of the songs, like "Unwed
Fathers" and John, Roger Cook, and Sandy Mason's "Only Love." Then
there were a couple of typically goofy songs like "The Bottomless Lake"
and "The Oldest Baby in the World." I absolutely love how John can look
at our experience from all sides, from the inside out, and the outside in.
John and I got together with Stack, mixed everything and came up with
a sequence. John called the album *Aimless Love*. Oh Boy! Records was in
business. My work and play together with John Prine was becoming one
of the real blessings in my life.

I continued engineering as well. Ken Irwin from Rounder Records brought in The Whitstein Brothers, a duo from Louisiana who sounded a lot like the Louvin Brothers. Ken then brought in a young girl who sang and played fiddle. Her name was Alison Krauss. She was barely sixteen. I was very impressed with her, not only for her playing and singing, but for her strength of character. She was obviously excited to be recording her first album, but she remained in control of things. One day Ken wanted her to do one more song, but she simply told him that she was tired and that they'd done enough for one day. I thought to myself, "This girl is no pushover!" At one point Jack Clement brought Johnny Cash upstairs. They'd been listening downstairs in Jack's office. Johnny volunteered to put a bass harmony on one song (which Ken Irwin chose not to use). Alison was young enough that her parents were still with her, and you wouldn't have blamed her if she'd let all of this throw her, but it didn't. She kept her focus. You could tell she was going somewhere.

There was no shortage of talented people coming my way. An amazing string bass player, Edgar Meyer, had come to town. I met him at one of John Hartford's weeklong Christmas parties. Bela Fleck asked me if I would engineer a session with Edgar on spec. As a rule, I didn't do things on spec. I wasn't getting paid that much, and I could definitely use the money, but I was happy to make an exception for Bela. Mark O'Connor, Sam Bush, and Jerry Douglas had all agreed to do it as well, so I knew it would be a great session. To add insult to injury, the only day they could all do it was on St. Patrick's Day, so I would be missing a big party at Phillip Donnelly's. As it turned out, it was well worth the sacrifice. We recorded five pieces in the course of the day. It was very advanced acoustic music, and I remember thinking, "Who are they going to get to put this out?" It was definitely not Bluegrass and was even more advanced than "Newgrass." Who knew exactly what it was? Bela took what we had recorded to MCA, who were launching a "Masters Series" to showcase the range of musical talent in Nashville, and they gave him the go-ahead to do a whole album. It was very challenging work for me as an engineer. Edgar and I worked together to get the best mic placement to capture the full sound of the bass. One of the pieces involved about six or seven overdubbed basses. Edgar had all the parts arranged—all bowed. The piece was several minutes long. We recorded a track of Kenny Malone playing conga and Edgar playing piano and put the basses on top of that one at a time. Edgar had perfect pitch, and everything had to be right on the money. I was punching in and punching out on the 24-track machine because he would go over a section repeatedly until he was satisfied. I was getting tendonitis with all the punches, but I thought to myself, "If I'm getting tendonitis, what is he getting?" In the end it was an amazing piece, which I jokingly called, "The Killer Bees Meet the Killer Whales!" That was Edgar's first album in a long and distinguished career. It is one of the honors of my life that I was involved.

Edgar was extremely open to the new acoustic music that was blossoming in Nashville. It was grounded in Bluegrass, but there was a new level of virtuosity in the playing of Sam Bush, Jerry Douglas, Bela Fleck, and Mark O'Connor that was taking the music in new directions. That was one of the great reasons to be in Nashville. I was living in the same town with Bill Monroe and Sam Bush, with Earl Scruggs and Bela Fleck, with Josh Graves and Jerry Douglas, with Kenny Baker and Mark O'Connor, with Roy Huskey and Edgar Meyer. There was a depth there that I really valued. Basically, when I came to Nashville in 1976, I was starting over. I had been welcomed in by Jack Clement and his circle of friends and had worked my way in from the ground up. I was now starting to find a place for myself in the big scheme of things and had become part of this extraordinary community of creative people. It was very satisfying be able to contribute to it by helping artists like Nanci, Alison, and Edgar when they were just starting out.

COMPLETIONS

At the end of '84 I got a chance to reconnect with my old Cambridge community when Tom Rush put on three nights of concerts at Symphony Hall in Boston as a reunion of the Club 47 gang, including Joan Baez, Mimi Farina, Eric Von Schmidt, the Charles River Valley Boys, Spider John Koerner, Joe Val, Peter Rowan, Bill Keith, me, and lots more. Every night Eric would hold court after the concerts, and the music would never end. Some of us stayed around for a couple of days and on New Year's Eve, Joan, Mimi, John Cooke, Fritz Richmond and I decided to go over and surprise Joe Val at the Old South Meeting House where he was playing a First Night concert. Sadly, Joe was battling cancer and had to cancel, so we did the gig for him with the New England Bluegrass Boys.

It was our farewell to Joe, who died that spring—one of the sweetest souls who ever lived. My mother had come to one of the concerts, and, in her usual fashion, seemed to know half the audience before it was over. She too became very ill not too long after, so I was spending time with her in Dedham when Nanci came up to Passim to launch her album for Rounder Records, which was another way the circle came 'round. My mother passed away in April, but she had lived long enough to know that I had found happiness following the path she had helped set me on back when she gave me Carl Sandburg's *American Songbag*.

In the summer of '85 Bill Keith, Mark O'Connor, and I did a tour of England and once again played at the Cambridge Folk Festival. Cambridge really lit a fire under us. Bill and Mark were feeding off of each other musically; I felt great vocally, and there was no stopping us when we went over to Dublin to play one night at Barry's Hotel. The place was packed, and the response was amazing—another "Mighty Night!" One good by-product of this visit was that I got to meet a songwriter named Mick Hanly. Mick had been encouraged to introduce himself to me by Phillip Donnelly and P.J. Curtis. A year or so earlier P.J. had come to Nashville to produce an album by a marvelous Irish singer, Maura O'Connell. Phillip had organized the sessions, so I played some rhythm guitar on it. Jerry Douglas and Bela Fleck were also there, and I could see the start of a bit of a romance between Maura and Bela. Thanks to Phillip Donnelly, this was the beginning of a lot of two-way traffic between Dublin and Nashville. Meeting Mick Hanly was another piece of the puzzle, and I encouraged him to feel free to send me songs, which eventually worked out well for both of us.

On our way home we played the Newport Folk Festival. After a fifteen-year hiatus, George Wein and the town had come to an accommodation. The new site was an old Civil War fort at the mouth of the harbor. There were two daytime concerts and attendance was limited to about eight thousand (with no wooden chairs!), so it was very different from the former setup, but it was good to be back and an honor to be playing on the inaugural concert. My buddy Robert L. Jones was in charge and all of George's team was still intact, including the dapper and irrepressible Charlie B.—Charlie Bourgeois—along with my old haberdasher from Harvard Square, Charlie Davidson. The Charlies were both impressed that bluegrassers could burn up Ellington's "Caravan." It was a good homecoming.

Once back in Nashville, I got together with Nanci, who, with a little encouragement from me, had decided to move into a small apartment in town. She had just returned from playing the Winnipeg Folk Festival and played me a song, "Love at the Five and Dime," that she had written as part of a songwriting workshop she had led there. I was knocked out, and it became the linchpin/clincher for another album. Pat Alger also had a new song he'd written with Fred Koller and Gene Levine called "Goin' Gone." Nanci and I both liked it and decided to add it to our list, along with Tom Russell's "St. Olav's Gate." When we got together in the fall to record, it was like a reunion. We all had the attitude of "Now we know what we're doing," and we were full of confidence as we started out in high spirits. Curt Allen was engineering this time. However, as can often happen when you're overconfident, we couldn't seem to get a groove going on the first song we tried, "Lookin' for the Time." We worked away for an hour and a half, but for some reason it wasn't jelling. Finally, I said, "Let's give this a rest and try something else," so we started in on "Goin' Gone," and then the power went out! All the lights—everything went out. (It turned out a car had hit a power pole down the street.) So there was nothing to do but go to lunch. We hadn't gotten a note on tape, but I did my best to stay calm. When we got back from lunch, the power was back on, and we picked up where we left off with "Goin' Gone." Half an hour later we had it. Boom—like that! Then we got into our rhythm and started sailing.

I had moved more solidly into my role as a producer. If I had an idea, I wasn't afraid to try it. On "Love at the Five and Dime" I went over to Lloyd Green and said, "Lloyd, this song is about a steel player who runs off with the bass player's wife, so you can play through the whole song." He laughed and was happy to run with it. On "Goin' Gone" I decided to get a fine autoharp player named Gove Scrivenor to come in and do a solo along with Mark O'Connor. Not too long after I'd left Bearsville, Randy Van Warmer had recorded his hit "Just When I Needed You Most," which featured John Sebastian on autoharp, and of course, John had used autoharp on the Lovin' Spoonful's "Do You Believe in Magic." I thought it would give a wonderful lift to our track, and I was right.

Once we got going, we rolled right along, recording eleven songs in three days and overdubbing for two days. Curt had been doing some engineering over at Jack's Tracks, so we went there to mix where there was a real echo chamber. As a result, Allen Reynolds heard this album quite a bit while we were mixing. He was working with Kathy Mattea, and both "Love at the Five and Dime" and "Goin' Gone" caught his ear. Allen asked Nanci if it would be alright with her if he played "Love at the Five and Dime" for Kathy. There was no conflict there. Nanci's record would be on Rounder, and there was no chance of her recording getting played on country radio. They weren't set up to promote a record like that. As a songwriter, Nanci realized that this was her opportunity for that to happen, so she said, "Yes." I don't know if any other producer in Nashville would have picked "Love at the Five and Dime" as a possible hit single. Allen heard it as a really good story song that would suit Kathy's honest voice. It was a top-10 single and opened the door for Kathy to make her third album.

As I listened to this album after we had finished, I became more and more convinced that it had moved Nanci up to a higher level. I thought it was more focused and had songs that could get out to a wider audience. After working at Jack's for a few years I was beginning to have more of an ear for a song that would have broad appeal. I definitely felt that about "Love at the Five and Dime" and "Goin' Gone." I also understood by this time that Nanci was very set on moving up, if she could, to a major label. I was aware that Tony Brown, who I had met when he was playing piano on the House of Cash demos that I engineered, and who had started working as a producer under Jimmy Bowen at MCA, felt that there might be an opening for an artist like Nanci on the radio. I also understood that MCA under Bowen was a closed shop. If she went there, I would no longer be able to continue as Nanci's producer.

As I was thinking about this, I ran into Jim Foglesong, who was head of A & R for Capitol Records, and asked him if he would listen to a new artist I was producing. He graciously gave me an appointment and I played him "Love at the Five and Dime" and "Goin' Gone." He was very complimentary and told me that he thought they were both good songs and were well produced, but that he didn't think they would be accepted by radio where artists like Lee Greenwood and Barbara Mandrell were having major success. I appreciated his honesty and thanked him for taking the time to listen. That was the only alternative I had, so ultimately Nanci did go to MCA, which was difficult for me. Totally understandable, but difficult. My work with Nanci had done what it was supposed to do—get her on a major label, which was where she wanted to be. I just couldn't go along. The lesson was that I wasn't producing for me, I was producing for the artist. The artist had to be free to do whatever they wanted. I couldn't disagree with that.

Meanwhile, Oh Boy! Records had been successfully launched, and John Prine already had enough new songs to make another album. This time we decided to go for a more acoustic sound, more on the bluegrass side of things, so I brought in Stuart Duncan on mandolin and fiddle and Alan O'Bryant on banjo and harmony vocals. Alan and Stuart were in the newly formed Nashville Bluegrass Band, which was fast becoming my favorite bluegrass group. In addition to John's songs, we did an old Carter Family favorite from our late-night picking sessions at John's house, "Lulu Walls" (that aggravating beauty) as well as Hank Williams's "They'll Never Take Her Love from Me," featuring the achingly beautiful steel playing of John's longtime friend Leo LeBlanc. John and Rachel were having a very up-and-down time of it, but the resulting songs might have been worth all the trouble. Perhaps the best song to come out of the turmoil generated by Rachel and John's relationship was the aptly titled "Speed of the Sound of Loneliness":

> You come home late
> You come home early
> You come home big
> When you're feelin' small
> You come home straight
> You come home curly
> Sometimes you don't come home at all.
> *Chorus:* What in the world's come over you
> What in heaven's name have you done
> You've broken the speed of the sound of loneliness
> You're out there runnin' just to be on the run.

Whatever that phrase "speed of the sound of loneliness" meant, you didn't have to be Dick Tracy to figure it out. It was funny, sad, and true all at once—a real John Prine song.

We also decided to recut John's best known song "Paradise" with this more acoustic sound. I assumed that everyone would be familiar with it, but after we ran it down once, Kenny Malone came up to John and asked, "Who's Mr. Peabody?" Kenny was a unique drummer in that he wouldn't play a song unless he understood the lyric. The feel had to relate to the meaning of the song. I loved him for that. So John told him the whole story about how his parents had come from this little village called Paradise in Muhlenberg County near Central City, Kentucky, and how the Peabody Coal Company had come in and bought everyone out and had strip-mined the land. "Okay," said Kenny. "Now I can play it."

We thought we were through, but John had one more song up his sleeve that he'd just written with Fred Koller—"Let's Talk Dirty in Hawaiian." As soon as John played it for me, we knew what we had to do. We played it for Jack Clement, who reached for his ukulele. We called up Lloyd Green and asked him to put on his Hawaiian shirt and bring over his steel guitar. If ever there was a sing-along song, this was it:

> Let's talk dirty in Hawaiian
> Whisper in my ear
> Kicka pooka moka wa wahini
> Are the words I long to hear
> Lay your coconuta on my tiki
> What the hecka mooka mooka dear
> Let's talk dirty in Hawaiian
> Say the words I long to hear

Naturally, as president of Oh Boy! Records, John made the executive decision to issue the song as a single—on green vinyl, with a gorgeous silhouette on the cover by our good friend Beth White of John sitting under a palm tree serenading a "wahini." To this day, collectors all over the world are fighting for copies.

Now that we were really finished, John asked the photographer, Jim McGuire, and me if we'd like to ride up with him to Central City and take some pictures he could use for the album. We rode up in John's 1949 red Ford coupe and got into the Rambling Rose Motel in Central City. After a couple of vodkas John said, "Okay, fellas, how would you like to take a ride to Paradise?" How could we refuse an invitation like that? We drove along a road in the dark, a chain-link fence on our left with some pine

FIGURE 19. John Prine "down by the Green River where Paradise lay."
Photograph: © McGuire.

trees planted inside it. John explained that the trees were there to hide the strip-mining. We were driving toward a big glow in the night sky. As we rounded a bend in the road, the source of the glow was revealed: a sign declared it to be THE PARADISE POWER PLANT—an enormous building with big smokestacks sending up clouds of steam, surrounded by huge mountains of coal. John drove right past the signs that read

NO ENTRY. AUTHORIZED PERSONNEL ONLY.

We bounced along on a frozen rutted road and came to a halt not far from "the Green River, where Paradise lay." We got out of the car. McGuire was taking pictures of John in the whole surreal scene. We could hear the whooping of alarm sirens in the distance, and soon we saw a big Suburban heading our way. We climbed back in the car and headed toward them. I could only wonder what they must be thinking as they saw this red '49 Ford coming up from the river. It was right out of *The Twilight Zone*. As we pulled up to them, John rolled down his window and simply said, "We just drove up from Nashville, and I was showing my friends where things used to be," and off we drove, leaving the guards to wonder if this had really happened or if they needed a vacation.

John had told me that he was going to call the album *German After-noons*. Sometimes I wouldn't really have a clue about what some of John's titles meant. When I asked him about *German Afternoons* he said that he had shown a list of possible titles to his mother and that she had liked that one. I couldn't argue with that. Maybe it had something to do with his time in the service over in Germany. Who knew? If John knew, he wasn't telling.

FORERUNNER

One evening at Cowboy's, Curt Allen and I were having a drink after our day's work. When he had a drink in him Curt could sometimes be a bit on the testy side. He looked at me and said, "Rooney! What are you gonna do?" I had no idea what he was talking about, so he said it again. "What are you gonna do?" Underneath the question, I suppose, was the unsaid, "You're getting old. Almost 50. You're 48 or whatever the hell you are, and you're still knocking around." There was certainly more than a hint of truth in that. I was skimming along, barely making a living. I was still a $12/hour engineer. I'd been doing albums for Jury Kruytiuk for $750. Nanci and John had paid me $1,500 for the first albums. I was going to get royalties sometime, but who knew how much? I'd be lucky to come back from a 4–6–week tour of Europe with $500 in my pocket. I didn't have a problem with this. I'd been brought up to do a day's work for a day's pay. When I was a kid this carpenter named Joe Dodge came to the house one day to do some work. I was a cute kid, so he gave me a 50¢ coin. I came in to my mother and said, "Look at this! Joe Dodge gave it to me!" She said, "Joe Dodge worked hard for that. Give it back to him." It was a lesson I never forgot. I try to be worth the money I'm paid. I don't like bullshit. I don't like inflated budgets. I want to pay everybody what they're supposed to get. I like to get paid too, but my basic thing is to help the artist get going. I was aware that there were people in Nashville who would take would-be artists from out of town and basically milk them. They'd pocket a few grand for themselves and move on. I didn't like that approach to things. I felt that if you did your work and did a good job, it would eventually pay off for you.

Realistically, however, I did realize that *I* could be asking Curt's question, "Rooney! What are you gonna do?" Then this little light went on in my head about publishing. Nanci Griffith and Lyle Lovett had both come through my hands. Lyle had slept on my couch. He had a fully finished eighteen-song tape. He'd written all the songs and produced them himself. Half of it was Texas-style stuff and half of it was sophisticated, slightly jazzy stuff. It was really good, but it was different. He would leave my apartment to meet with one publisher or another. The results weren't encouraging. One day he came back from a lunch meeting and showed me a napkin on which a fellow from a publishing company, after telling him his songs were too complicated, showed him the secret to hit songwriting success. On the napkin he had drawn a big V (for Verse) followed by 4 lines, then a lot of arrows pointed to a big C (for Chorus) also followed by 4 lines, and then back to another V! Lyle had to laugh. What else could he do? Eventually I introduced him to a good publisher, Bo Goldsen of Criterion Music, which led to a record deal with Curb, through Dick Whitehouse. I had had nothing to offer either Lyle or Nanci legitimately as a publisher, so I began to think about that.

As I thought more about publishing, the person who came to mind was, interestingly enough, Curt's wife, Terrell Tye. Terrell had come to work at Jack's as receptionist a little after the time I came into the picture. She was great-looking, had a lot of energy, and was a fun-loving girl. A lot of people might have been blinded by her looks and might not have given her credit for being smart, but they would have been wrong. Sometime in the year after Curt and Terrell married, Bob Webster got quite sick and was out of commission for a couple of months. During that time Terrell just kept looking after the books. When Webster finally came back to work he was impressed at how good a job she had done. One morning he looked up at her through his black-rimmed glasses and asked her, "Do you want to learn about this stuff?" She said, "Yeah, I think I'd like that." So Webster started teaching her about copyright administration, filling out the forms, how to check record label statements, how to do the writer's royalty statements, foreign sublicensing agreements and so on. She was learning from a master, but she was also bringing her own perspective to the material and started to learn how to organize it with computer programs.

I called Terrell up at home and said I'd like to talk to her about an idea I had, and we went to lunch. I said, "I'm thinking of starting a publishing company. You know all about administration. I seem to be working with a lot of songwriters. What would you think about that?" She said, "It's funny you should mention that, because Allen Reynolds has been talking to me about the work you've been doing with Nanci and John Prine." Allen had a small publishing catalogue, which Terrell had been doing the paperwork for, but he wasn't actively demoing and pitching songs. I was happy to hear that Allen was seeing a pattern in what I was doing and the kind of songs I was recording by Nanci and Pat Alger. Terrell suggested that we talk to Allen.

He was very receptive and said that he'd always wanted to have a real publishing company, but never had the time or inclination to do it himself. It made sense to him that we should join forces and that maybe a partnership would be the best way to go. He also said that he would want to bring in his engineer, Mark Miller, whose instincts about songs he had come to respect. Mark had succeeded Garth Fundis as Allen's engineer and had worked on Kathy Mattea's albums. I didn't really know him that well, but I totally trusted Allen's judgment, and if that's what he wanted, that's what we would do.

Allen then asked who I had in mind for writers. Right away I mentioned Pat Alger. Pat was making most of his money as a graphic designer, doing album covers for Rounder and exhibits for the Country Music Hall of Fame. He'd had the top-40 pop hit, "First Time Love," by Livingston Taylor, and Dolly Parton had also recorded "Once in a Very Blue Moon." A few songs he'd written with his friend Rick Beresford had been picked up by Rick's publisher, but no one had signed Pat as a writer. He had a son, Ryan, by now; his wife Chris was working; and he was beginning to wonder if he could afford to continue his songwriting habit. After our meeting with Allen I went to Pat and told him that we were thinking of starting a publishing company and asked him what it would take to keep him writing songs. He said that basically he needed enough to make his mortgage payments and a bit more. He also wanted to keep half of his publishing, since he had already created his own little company, Bait & Beer Music, and he knew how to fill out the copyright forms and how things worked. However, Pat realized that this was the opportunity he'd been waiting for. We came up with a figure of $1,000/month as an advance against future royalties, and he volunteered to include his share of "Goin' Gone," which Allen was about to record with

Kathy Mattea. I went back to Allen, Terrell, and Mark and told them what it would take to get Pat, and we all agreed.

I also suggested that we work with a singer-songwriter from Maine named David Mallett and a husband and wife team, Barry and Holly Tashian. Nanci had told me about Mallett, and we had just made an album together. He was good, and very much a State of Mainer—a bit abrupt when speaking but eloquent and somewhat elegiac in his songs. He was best known for "The Garden Song," familiarly known as "Inch by Inch," which had been recorded by everyone from John Denver to Kermit the Frog. Barry Tashian had been in the successful rock band from Boston, Barry & The Remains, back in the sixties, and more recently had been a member of Emmylou Harris's Hot Band, playing guitar and singing harmonies. When Emmylou decided to move to Nashville from California, Barry and Holly decided to make the move too. They had started working up old country and rockabilly songs to sing as a duo and were also starting to write songs in that style. The clarity and purity of their duets and the simplicity of their songs appealed to me as soon as I heard them.

Before he made a living as a songwriter, Allen had worked in a bank. He could add. He was a very straight, absolutely honest businessman. We formed a true partnership. As a result of his success as a songwriter and as producer of Don Williams and Crystal Gayle, Allen could have funded the whole thing himself, but we felt that it was important that we all share the financial burden. Each of us would put in $1,000/month, with Allen putting in $2,000. Allen also agreed to front us the office space for an agreed rent, which we wouldn't have to pay until we made some money. We came up with the name Forerunner Music (4 Runners!) and gave ourselves five years to see whether we could get something done. We all understood that it takes a long time, even if you have a hit or two, to get money coming the other way. Our annual operating budget would be $60,000. Terrell would get a salary as president and administrator of the company. We would also pay demo costs and advances out of the money. The rest of us would not be paid. We were starting out on a shoestring, so we'd do whatever had to be done ourselves. Mark and I were happy to do the demos. At one of our first meetings the subject of pitching songs came up. Allen immediately said, "Well, I wouldn't be doing that." Mark

FIGURE 20. The Forerunners (*l. to r.*: Jim Rooney, Terrell Tye, Allen Reynolds, Mark Miller).

said, "I wouldn't be good at that." I was looking at Terrell and Terrell was looking at me, so, by default, we were going to be our song pluggers.

In early 1987 we had a little show at the Bluebird Café to announce our arrival, and we went to work. Of course, at the beginning we didn't have that many songs to pitch. Mark and I did some demo sessions with Pat and Dave. Barry and Holly Tashian got a record deal at Northeastern Records in Boston, so I began working on an album with them as well, which also served to demo their songs. Every week we would get a tip sheet of who was recording. Terrell and I would go down the list trying to think of a song that might suit a particular artist. If we thought of something, we'd make up a cassette, copy a lyric sheet, and send them over to the producer or A & R person at the record label. Sometimes we would invite them over to listen in person. Of course, with only a few songs, we'd wind up pitching the same songs over and over! However, Allen had finished Kathy Mattea's next album and "Goin' Gone" was going to be the first single. Like good publishers, we decided to put some money toward hiring someone to promote the single to radio. We started checking the charts every week to see how it was doing, and it was doing well. Here we were, closing out our first year in business with a song climbing the charts! Curt's little kick in the ass had been just what I needed.

As exciting as this was and as busy as I was, my finances were still pretty sketchy. At times my $1,000/month contribution to the publishing company proved to be a challenge. The reliable old Valiant that I'd bought years before from James Talley was totaled one day by a kid running a red light. I was lucky I wasn't totaled too. I had bought another one, which had put an unexpected dent in my pocket book. One day I was talking to Pat Alger. His car had died, and he needed to get another one right away—and cheap. Without hesitating I said, "I'll sell you mine." That took care of that month's payment. A few months later we reversed roles, and I bought the car back from Pat to get him over his own cash shortage. We were sailing very close to the wind! However, the fact that we were financing our company this way and even sacrificing a bit made it all very real, because we really believed in what we were doing. Occasionally people would approach us from larger companies offering us deals of one sort or another, but we were pretty clear that we didn't want any outside partners trying to steer us in one direction or another. We trusted our musical instincts. We knew it would take time if we were to succeed at all, but we were committed and willing to be patient.

Some time before the release in September of 1987 of Kathy's album *Untasted Honey*, which included her first #1 hits, "Goin' Gone" and "Eighteen Wheels and a Dozen Roses," I remember Kathy's manager Bob Titley saying that if she could sell 250,000 albums that would be great. In fact, it turned out to be her first gold album, but that's the level of sales we were looking at that time. Unlike in earlier times when a songwriter was often the only writer and the publisher had 100 percent of the publishing, with Pat on "Goin' Gone" we had half of his publishing and he had two cowriters, so we were getting half of a third of the publisher's share, which was half of the total money generated by the song. In reality we were getting 1/12 of the total income. We weren't going to be getting rich quick that way, even with some hits.

Buoyed by our success with "Goin' Gone," we were trying to get songs recorded by other artists, but it wasn't easy, even when we felt it was a sure fire hit. Pretty early on Pat got together with Emmylou Harris's steel guitar player, Hank Devito, and wrote "Small Town Saturday Night":

There's an Elvis movie on the marquee sign
We've all seen at least three times
Everybody's broke, but Bobby's got a buck
Put a dollar's worth of gas in his pickup truck
Chorus: We're goin' ninety miles an hour down a dead end road
            What's the hurry, son, where're you gonna go
            We're gonna howl at the moon, shoot out the light
            It's a small town Saturday night
            It's a small town Saturday night.

Right away I thought it was a great lyric, and that we would have no trouble getting it recorded. When people heard it, they'd ask for a copy and show interest, but nothing happened. There was a group called Highway 101 who had a great singer named Paulette Carlson. Their guitar player, Jack Armstrong heard Pat play the song at a songwriter's night at the Bluebird Café. He liked it, so we brought him in to add his guitar to the demo, thinking that might improve our chances of getting it cut. Still, nothing happened. The song was going to have to wait to be discovered. This is where my experience at Jack's gave me some perspective, because I remembered all of those songs I had heard by Allen Reynolds, Bob Mc-Dill, and Dickie Lee that had never been recorded. I was beginning to get a taste of this myself. That's why they call it pitching. You're throwing the ball in there again and again and again and again. The hits are few and far between. It can be a very discouraging business if you take it personally. To add insult to injury, I would hear some of the songs that people did cut after rejecting our songs, and I'd say, "This is crap! There's no justice in this world!" Who ever said there was? That's the way it is, and you just have to keep plowing ahead.

THE TEXAS CONNECTION

Throughout this period, my work as an engineer and producer was what was keeping the bills paid and enabling me to keep my stake in Forerunner. I engineered and produced albums with Pat Alger's friend and songwriting collaborator, Rick Beresford; with David Grier, a brilliant young acoustic guitarist; and a singer/songwriter from Austin named Jane Gilman. I enjoyed helping writers and musicians give a shape and a sound to their work without having to spend a lot of money doing it. I was also starting to get some recognition for my efforts in the form of Grammy nominations for both *Last of the True Believers* and *German After-noons*. I decided to go out to Los Angeles for the awards show. By this time Judy and Johanna were living at Ocean Beach in San Diego, after spending four years near Judy's mother out in the Mojave Desert. Her plan to reconnect with her children hadn't worked out, and Judy was still having her ups and downs. I didn't want to miss the opportunity to have Johanna back in my life, so I decided to bring them both up to Los Angeles, and we had a big time with John and Nanci. Tracy Chapman won that year with her first album, which included the huge hit "Fast Car," but that didn't matter. It was my first encounter with that level of show business, and we made the most of it.

Nanci had celebrated the releases of her albums at her old stomping ground in Houston, Anderson Fair. Nanci, Lyle Lovett, Lucinda Williams, and lots of other artists had gotten their start there. I got a taste for the laid-back but very creative atmosphere of the place. Nanci also took me to the Kerrville Folk Festival down in the hill country between Austin and San Antonio. The whole focus of the festival was on singer/song-writers. The best thing about it was the late-night singing around the campfires. The songs seemed to rise right up with the smoke. At Kerrville I reconnected with Jerry Jeff Walker. He had started his own label, Tried & True Records, and had started recording a compilation of songs for a double album called *Gypsy Songman*. Jerry asked me if I could organize some sessions for him in Nashville. Stack had moved on and Curt was now producing Marty Stuart, so I started working with the engineer Rich Adler, who had done several albums with John Hartford and knew how to record acoustic music. Jerry Jeff was in fine form, his voice flexible and warm. In addition to some of his songs like "Railroad Lady," he did Paul Siebel's beautiful "Then Came the Children" and Michael Burton's classic "Night Rider's Lament." I had opened some shows for Jerry Jeff and the Lost Gonzo Band back when I was living in Massachusetts, and we were both pretty wild. Ten years later he was now married to a good strong Texas woman, Susan, and had two kids. He was still lots of fun, but marriage and fatherhood had probably saved his life. His music had a settled quality to it now, and it felt good to be working with him and to renew our friendship.

One day I came in to Cowboy's to see what was going on. I looked at the white blackboard studio schedule in the downstairs hallway and saw that Townes Van Zandt was going to be doing some recording. I went in to visit with Jack and asked him who was going to be engineering. He said, "What about you?" They were going to start the next day. I thought about it for about a minute and said, "I'm on." Nanci Griffith, Lyle Lovett, Richard Dobson, Rodney Crowell, Guy Clark—all the Houston songwriters—cited Townes as a major influence, and this was a good opportunity to really work with him. Jack and Townes had figured out what songs they were going to do and who would be playing. Townes had his old compadre Mickey White with him, playing acoustic rhythm and slide guitar, and Donny Silverman on sax. Jack added Kenny Malone, Roy Huskey, Charles Cochran, and Mark Howard on second acoustic guitar. I suggested Mark O'Connor for fiddle and mandolin. Although Jack was the producer, he seemed to be spending a lot of time downstairs "listening through the walls." There were decisions to be made, so I just started making them. On the morning of the third day I went in to Jack and asked, "Are we producing this album together?" Without missing a beat, he said, "Well, I suppose we are."

Even though we hadn't spent lots of time together lately, Townes and I had a very solid relationship. There were some people who almost worshipped him. A certain mystique had grown up around him, and whatever Townes did was beyond reproach or criticism. I watched him with some people, and he could be a bit mean sometimes. He'd play games with them and run them around a bit. It was almost a way to put them off. I think it made him uncomfortable to be the object of such adulation. I never had that kind of relationship with him. I think he knew instinctively that I wasn't a game player. I think he also felt that I understood where his music came from. He'd obviously soaked up the ballad tradition. He'd listened to bluesmen like Lightnin' Hopkins and Mance Lipscomb. I loved and respected that. I also knew that he could be as big an asshole as anyone else, but I wasn't interested in that, and there was never even a move in that direction. The result was that we had a great time making this record. Once again I brought in Rich Adler to help me mix it, to make it sound as good as we could. Jim McGuire took a couple of very straightforward photographs for the cover of the album, which was titled *At My Window*.

Together with the earlier albums that Townes did with Cowboy, I think this turned out to be one of his best, and it shows why all those other writers looked up to him. The songs came up through him from a deep source. He sang them to us in a voice as burnished and dark and light as the whiskey he loved. His was an old soul, telling and retelling the old stories that show us how to pass through this life and go on to the next. Townes closed the album with an exceptional song, "The Catfish Song," accompanied by Charles Cochran on organ:

Well, the angel of springtime
He rides down the southwind
The angel of summer he does just the same
The angel of autumn
She's blue and she's golden
And the angel of winter
Won't remember your name
Down at the bottom of that dirty ol' river
Down where the reeds and the catfish play
There lies a dream as soft as the water
There lies a bluebird that's flown away
There lies a bluebird
That's flown away.

That was Townes.

As a result of spending time with Townes, Jerry Jeff, Nanci, and Richard Dobson I found that I was being drawn more and more into the music of Texas. Nanci would regularly bring me up cases of Shiner Bock, which I dubbed "The Best Beer Brewed in America." Now, Texas came to me in the person of Robert Earl Keen Jr. Robert came from Bandera, Texas, "The Cowboy Capital of the World." He'd gone to Texas A&M where he had roomed with Lyle Lovett, which might have been his downfall, or vice versa. At any rate, Robert had come up to Nashville to try his luck, and we decided to work together. He'd done a studio album, *No Kinda Dancer*, back in Texas, but my instincts told me that it might be a good idea to do a live album with Robert to capture some of his humor, charm, and energy that came across when he performed. I asked Robert what his favorite place to play was and, without hesitation, he said, "The Sons of Hermann Hall in Dallas." The Sons of Hermann were an old fraternal order in Texas and thereabouts. There was a good-sized ballroom upstairs and a great old wood bar downstairs. My kind of place. Robert had been playing with Roy Huskey and a hot mandolin and fiddle player named Jon Yudkin, so we decided to bring them down to Dallas and record a couple of nights. The best laid plans can sometimes go astray. Roy missed his plane, so we had to do Friday without him. It gave me a chance to get used to the sound of the room and for Robert to get good and loose. Saturday night was a big night. Robert's audience was primed, and he was at his best. The atmosphere was perfect for Robert. I found out from someone at the bar that the place was indeed on Elm Street—the famous street in the song "Deep Elem Blues":

> When you go down to Deep Elem, keep your money in your pants
> 'Cause those women in Deep Elem they don't give a man a chance
> Oh, sweet mama, daddy's got them Deep Elem blues
> Oh, sweet mama, daddy's got them Deep Elem blues

I think Robert might have got some of those ghosts dancing that night, and we got it all on tape.

BRINGING IT ALL BACK HOME

Phillip Donnelly had moved back to Ireland and was helping to organize a couple of concerts for a television series called "The Session," bringing artists from Nashville and Austin together with Irish artists. I went over with Don Everly, John Prine, Jack Clement, Guy Clark, and Marty Stuart. We shared the stage with The Chieftains, Mary Black, and a great young band, Arcady, among others, and the mixture of American Roots music and Irish music showed how much we shared in common.

After the gig we went back to our headquarters at Bloom's Hotel and got the guitars out and started celebrating. During a break in the action, two friends I'd met before at Ballysadare—Donal Lunny and Phillip King—took me aside and told me about a project they were hatching about Irish music and its travels around the world; they were going to call it "Bringing It All Back Home." It was going to be a documentary series funded by the BBC and RTE, and they asked me if I would be willing to help put together some sessions to be shot in Nashville in a few months. I got in touch with Emmylou Harris, The Everly Brothers, Mark O'Connor and Ricky Skaggs, among others. In late April Phillip and Donal returned with a full BBC film crew headed up by director Peter Carr. We were going to be filming at Cowboy's. First up were the Everly Brothers. Don had been enthusiastic when I first mentioned the project in Dublin. He subsequently talked Phil into doing it. We were going to do "Down in the Willow Garden" with the piper Liam O'Flynn, Phillip Donnelly on acoustic guitar, and Roy Huskey on upright bass. They had originally recorded it on *Songs Our Daddy Taught Us*. A couple of weeks before the session I had talked to Don about what they were going to do, and he mentioned another song that they had sung back in high school but had never recorded called "Don't Let Our Sweet Love Die," an old York Brothers number. Don sang a bit of it for me, and I told him to work it up with Phil. They were going to be playing in Lake Tahoe just before coming back to Nashville, so I thought they'd have time to go over both songs. The first day of filming arrived. The crew took the morning to set up. Around noon Don and Phil showed up. We got them settled in with Phillip, Liam, and Roy, and Donal said he was ready for them to run down "Willow Garden." We were all in the control room looking at the speakers. At Jack's there was no control room window and no video monitor. The first thing we heard was Phil coughing and clearing his throat followed by, "What key do we do this in?" So much for running things over in Tahoe. We sat through a few faltering starts, more coughing and clearing of throats. I was beginning to wonder if this was going to be a bust. Here I had organized the whole week. We had this crew over from England and Ireland. I was getting nervous. Suddenly, out of the speakers came The Everly Brothers!

> Down in the willow garden
> Where me and my true love did meet
> It was there we went a courting
> My love fell off to sleep

Everyone in the room looked at everyone else. There they were. Such an unmistakably pure sound. Then came the sound of the pipes, beautifully played by Liam O'Flynn. It was the essence of the whole project,

"Bringing It All Back Home." The song had made its way over from Ireland to Kentucky where it was handed on by Ike Everly to his sons, who were now handing it on to us. When they finished, Donal said, "That's it!"

The rest of the week was smooth sailing. Emmylou Harris, Mary Black, and Dolores Keane did a stunning version of "Sonny's Dream," a song by Ron Hynes, who was from St. John's, Newfoundland. Ricky Skaggs and Mark O'Connor got together on some fiddle tunes with the Irish fiddler Paddy Glackin, backed up by Russ Barenberg on guitar and Donal Lunny on bouzouki. Mary Black and Richard Thompson did his classic "Dimming of the Day." We went up to Central City, Kentucky, to shoot some footage to go with John Prine's "Paradise." Everything came together beautifully.

Toward the end I asked Phillip King if he was going to be filming Peggi Jordan. I told him that it seemed to me that she was a pretty key figure in the folk revival in Dublin, having brought over Pete Seeger in 1963 and providing The Dubliners and others the space to get started with her late concerts at the Grafton Street Cinema. Phillip agreed, so I basically invited myself over to Dublin to join them when they interviewed Peggi. I hadn't laid eyes on her since 1964, but she was as energetic and classy as ever. Phillip had asked Barney McKenna and Sean Sheehan from The Dubliners to come along, and she immediately produced champagne to celebrate our reunion. In a way it was my own private version of "Bringing It All Back Home," as I sang her my own version of "One Morning in May." At the end she raised her glass to me and gave me a big hug. My homecoming to Ireland was complete.

Just after I returned from "The Session," the Irish connection continued in the person of Bono and Adam Clayton. The previous summer U-2 had asked Jack Clement to produce a session with them at the Sun Studios in Memphis. Jack had been breaking in a new young engineer named David Ferguson, so he took him along and threw him into the deep end of the pool like he had me. David did just fine. He was a born seat-of-the-pants engineer. The standout track from those sessions, complete with Wayne Jackson and the Memphis Horns, was "Angel of Harlem," Bono's tribute to Billie Holliday. The album, *Rattle and Hum*, was now finished and Bono and Adam were driving across the country on their own to soak up some of the atmosphere in Texas, Louisiana, and Tennessee. They decided to drop in on Jack and spend a few days in Nashville.

Johanna was now thirteen and had come to stay with me for a while. She and Judy weren't getting along. Judy's drinking was not good. In addition, Johanna had started going with a fellow ten years older than she was; he was supposedly tutoring her in math. I was afraid Judy would do something drastic, so I flew Johanna to Nashville. The year before, Jo and I had taken a trip together while Judy was in a rehab place. We drove from Nashville to Washington, D.C., where the Folklife Festival was happening on the Mall. We went to a Red Sox/Orioles game in Baltimore. We drove up to Atlantic City to see The Everly Brothers, with Nanci Griffith opening. Then we went into New York where I was going to be running a stage for Ethel Raim as part of the Statue Of Liberty Centennial Celebration.

That trip had solidified my relationship with Johanna. She was joy to be with—bright, positive, curious. I was becoming her real father, and I didn't want to lose her. I now hoped that some time and space between her and her mother and her boyfriend would help. She brought her schoolwork with her, which she would do every day over at Jack's Tracks while I was working in the studio. I knew that Jo was a huge U-2 fan. She'd turned me on to "Joshua Tree." When I found out that Bono and Adam were over at Jack's, I asked Jo if she'd like to come over to Cowboy's with me. Ever since she was a little girl, she'd loved that place, with its balconies and secret hiding places. When we got over to Jack's, his office door was closed, so I pushed Jo ahead of me and told her to walk right in and surprise Jack. Once in the door, her jaw dropped. She knew right away who she was looking at. Bono was terrific with her. Right away he noticed that she was wearing a Bob Marley T-shirt and started talking with her about him. When he found out her name was Johanna, he got a Sharpie and wrote on her T-shirt "Visions of Johanna," and he and Adam signed it. That shirt was never washed again.

After Jo got home Judy called me. She had heard that in Utah girls can get married at fourteen. I suggested that we call her boyfriend Ron's bluff and say that they could live together if they got married. Much to our surprise, he agreed, so Judy drove them up to Utah, and they got married. They're still married. I hadn't lost her.

FORERUNNER:
ONWARD AND UPWARD

At Forerunner we'd signed two more writers, a groove piano player named Pete Wasner and a lyricist named Charles John Quarto. Pete came to Nashville from Colorado and was playing with The Sweethearts of the Rodeo. Charles John had lived in various places, including California where he had worked with Graham Nash. Charles was a bit of a mystic and had another dimension to his writing. He fancied himself a poet, but I felt he was a better lyricist—not that I could have easily told you the difference. He'd written a fine song with Steve Gillette called "Grapes on the Vine," which had been recorded by Waylon Jennings. Charles and Pete had started writing together and had a song called "Mama Knows the Highway" that Allen really liked, so we decided to sign them up. "Goin' Gone" had gone all the way to #1, and Pat Alger had another song, "Like a Hurricane," on Kathy Mattea's *Untasted Honey* album and the title song of Nanci Griffith's first album with Tony Brown for MCA, "Lone Star State of Mind." In addition to Kathy, Allen was about to produce an album with one of the most popular singers in Ireland, Daniel O'Donnell, who had fallen in love with some of Barry and Holly Tashian's songs, which we had recorded for their first album. Our little company was starting to hum along.

That was our situation when Garth Brooks came in the door. Terrell and I didn't pay that much attention to him at the time. He was just an artist that Allen was talking to as a producer. They recorded a few songs, and Garth was eventually signed by Jim Foglesong to Capitol Records. They didn't record any of our songs for Garth's first album. Allen wasn't the kind of producer who would load a project up with songs he published. The songs had to work for the artist. We pitched him songs the same way we would pitch them to anyone, but we didn't connect. Hopefully, there would be a second album, and we'd have another shot.

During the year that Garth's first album was finding its way, Pat Alger and Garth had begun to collaborate. Two of the songs they wrote together, "The Thunder Rolls" and "Unanswered Prayers," not surprisingly, passed muster with Allen, and he added them to the list of songs they would record. When the second album came out, it went multiplatinum and set us as publishers on a new path. In addition to Kathy

Mattea's #1 parties (the most recent one for Pat Alger's "She Came from Fort Worth"), we started having some Garth Brooks #1 parties. We had demoed another of the songs that Garth and Pat had written, "Like We Never Had a Broken Heart," with a new singer, Trisha Yearwood. She, like Pat, was also from Lagrange, Georgia, and had been singing with him and his band The Algerians. We were all impressed with Trisha as a singer and encouraged Allen's former engineer, Garth Fundis to work with her as a producer, which, happily, he did. The following year Trisha had a big hit with "Like We Never Had a Broken Heart." Forerunner's circle of success was widening.

I was getting more and more of a feel for songs that would have melodic and lyric substance, as well as an appeal to a wide audience. One day Dave Mallett was running over some songs in the studio with the bass player Dave Pomeroy as they prepared for one of Dave's gigs at the Bluebird Café. I was in the control room sort of eavesdropping when I heard a song that I'd never heard before that knocked me out. It was called "The Summer of My Dreams" and was simply a gorgeous evocation of the ideal summer day in your life. Immediately I went in to Dave and asked him, "Did you write that last summer when you were back in Maine?" "Oh no," he said, "I've had that song a long time." "Then how come I have never heard it?" To which he replied, "That song's not for Nashville." I couldn't believe it. "Dave," I said, "you've got to go with your best stuff! Don't be trying to figure out what's 'for Nashville' and what's not. That song is head and shoulders above 'Sweet Tennessee' and some of these other songs you've been trying to write for what you think is the Nashville market. You've got to be yourself! Now would you please do it again so I could put it down on tape?"

> In the shade of this old tree in the summer of my dreams
> By the tall grass by the wild rose
> Where the tree stands and the wind blows
> As the days go oh so slowly, as the sun shines oh so holy
> On the good and gracious green in the summer of my dreams

This was David Mallett at his best. I immediately took the tape upstairs to Allen. The song came out on Kathy Mattea's next album, surrounded by a gorgeous string quartet accompaniment.

On the same album was another song I had heard the bluegrass singer

Laurie Lewis perform at the IBMA convention. Like David's, Laurie's song, "Love Chooses You," was a rich combination of a meaningful lyric and a beautiful melody. I asked her whether she had recorded it and whether she had a publisher. It was on her newest album, and she was publishing it herself. I asked her if we could have half the publishing if we succeeded in getting it recorded by a major artist. I told her that I had Kathy Mattea in mind, and she readily agreed. Once again, I went to Allen with it, and he agreed with me. We were completely trusting our instincts about what makes a good song and what kind of song would suit a particular artist. It was a hallmark of Allen's style as a producer that he wanted every song to have value on an album. Those songs gave the artist some depth and staying power. Those albums were the kind of albums that people kept and would come back to again and again. We weren't driven by the market, but, as it turned out, the market didn't seem to have a problem with our decisions.

My association with Allen was having an effect on me as a producer. I was more willing to be a bit more demanding of artists to make sure that their material was as good as it needed to be. Robert Earl Keen and I were in the process of gathering songs for a studio album. We both agreed that it wasn't a requirement that he write every song. He'd come up with a couple of songs that suited him: Blackie Farrell's "Sonora's Death Row" and a Shel Silverstein/Fred Koller collaboration "Jennifer Johnson and Me." I remembered a Bob McDill song, "Don't Turn Out the Light," one of those overlooked masterpieces in the Jack Music catalogue. Robert had some good songs of his own, including the amazing "The Five Pound Bass." However, when we got together right before we were scheduled to record, I had to tell Robert that I thought we were still lacking something and that it might be wise to cancel our sessions and wait until he had another great song. He looked at me and said, "I've got it! I'm still writing it, but it's there! Trust me. Don't cancel." That's all I needed to hear. I had challenged him, but he was solid in his conviction. He didn't disappoint me. The song was the career defining "The Road Goes On Forever."

I went back to Texas in the spring of '89 to record a live album with Jerry Jeff at Greune Hall, a quintessential Texas dance hall in Gruene, Texas, in the hill country about an hour from Austin—the best part of Texas as far as I was concerned. We had no problem having a good time while we were there and captured the essence of what had made Jerry Jeff a huge artist in Texas. In addition to being a master songwriter himself, Jerry knew a good songwriter when he heard one, and told me about a singer/songwriter named Hal Ketchum he had heard on KUT radio in Austin. I got a chance to hear him opening for Jerry at The Coach House in San Juan Capistrano when I was out visiting Judy and Johanna. He gave me a copy of an album he had recently done in Austin with Brian Wood called *Threadbare Alibis*. The songs on the album were well-written "story" songs. They weren't necessarily "hit" songs, but they were very good, and I could see what had gotten Jerry Jeff's attention. Eventually, Jerry Jeff and Hal came to Nashville to play at the Bluebird Café and I asked Allen, Terrell, and Mark to come down to listen to Hal. They were also impressed, and we invited him to come to Jack's Tracks the next day. We didn't try to sign him up or anything, but we told him that if he wanted to come up sometime to demo some songs, we'd be happy to help him, and he'd be more than welcome.

A month or two later, Hal called us up and asked if our offer to help him demo some songs still stood. I told him to come along and organized some players. This was my favorite thing to do in our publishing venture. Mark Miller and I had become a good team. He was fast, quiet, and had a good sense of humor and a good ear for where a song wanted to shine. We both enjoyed the process of taking a new song and coming up with a musical setting for it. We'd been turning the demos we had been doing with Pat Alger, Dave Mallett, and Barry and Holly Tashian into albums that were coming out on Sugar Hill, Rounder, and Flying Fish, which gave the songs another way to be heard. I now had a chance to really focus on Hal in the studio for the first time. As soon as I heard him on a good microphone in an environment I was familiar with, I turned to Mark and said, "Man! He's a great singer! What a voice!" His songs also seemed more focused and accessible than what I had heard previously, and we came out of that session thinking that Hal might have a real shot at a major record deal with radio potential. We also decided to offer him a writing deal, which he was happy to accept.

Hal started coming up from Texas on a regular basis and was writing with Pat Alger and Dave Mallett, as well as on his own, so we did some more demos and then organized a showcase for Hal at the Bluebird Café. A man named Walt Quinn heard him and stepped in as manager, and he eventually connected Hal to Dick Whitehouse, who signed him to Curb Records. Dick was a great A & R man. He'd signed the Judds, Hank Williams Jr., and Lyle Lovett to the label. He recognized original talent when he heard it and was very positive, very enthusiastic. Allen and I had agreed that if Hal got a deal, we would produce him together. Dick simply said to us, "All you guys need to do is to give me something I can go to radio with." He wasn't going to be looking over our shoulders. He trusted us to give him what he needed. Of course, Allen definitely knew what he was doing in this area. It was new territory for me, but I had been paying attention. When Allen recorded "Love at the Five and Dime" and "Goin' Gone" with Kathy, and I heard those records, in my heart of hearts I liked what I had done with Nanci better. However, I did understand what the difference was that had enabled Kathy's records to get played on radio. Her records had more of a bottom—a bigger bass, a bigger drum sound. I'd used an upright bass on Nanci's; Allen had used electric. Allen used Milton Sledge on drums for Kathy. Milton would have been a heavier drummer than Kenny Malone. I might have liked the acoustic subtlety of Nanci's record, but Kathy got played on the radio. I considered working with Allen on Hal to be a real privilege as well as an opportunity to learn and to be a full partner in producing at this level.

About the time we were starting to gather material for Hal, Mick Hanly showed up out of the blue from Ireland. Since meeting Mick at Barry's Hotel in '85, he had occasionally sent me songs. The songs he sent me were songs he thought would suit Nashville. A little like Dave Mallett, he was trying to figure out the market, and something about these songs just didn't ring true. I was happy and surprised to see him. Some person had convinced Mick that he knew everyone in Nashville and that he'd arrange for him to meet lots of people if he got himself there. So here he was. The only thing this fellow had set up was basically an open-mic six-thirty show at the Bluebird Café. Maura O'Connell and I and a handful of tourists were the only people who went. There were certainly no publishers or record people there. It was a waste of time, and Mick knew it. I was a little put out that he hadn't even called me in advance, but I told him not to worry and to drop by Jack's Tracks the next day. I introduced him to Allen, Terrell, and Mark. We listened to a couple of tracks from a new album he had with him, and I told Terrell to take it home and play it for Hal. (Against our better judgment Terrell and Hal had developed more than a professional relationship, but who were we to make judgments anyway?) Hal came in the next day raving about Mick's song, "Past the Point of Rescue." I told him to learn it, and we'd give it a try. As sometimes happens, Mick's trip didn't turn out the way he had planned. It was much better than he could have hoped.

I left it to Allen primarily to put together a band for Hal's sessions. Some I knew, some I didn't. We had Milton Sledge on drums and Bob Wray on electric bass, which insured a good solid bottom. Chris Leuzinger was the choice for electric guitar. Since our days in Cowboy's Ragtime Band, Chris and I had worked on lots of demos together. Allen was using him on Garth's records, and he was fast becoming one of the most sought-after guitarists in Nashville. When Chris played a track he already had in mind the parts he was going to add to it. He had lots of guitars and knew exactly which one to use and when to use it. I had learned to trust his instincts completely. Pete Wasner was on piano. Pete was not a flashy player, but he would give a track a beautiful swinging groove. On acoustic guitar we had Richard Bennett, who had moved to Nashville after working with Neil Diamond for many years. Richard had produced Steve Earl's breakthrough record "Guitar Town" and was going to be working with Allen on an upcoming Emmylou Harris record.

It didn't take long for Richard to make his presence felt. "Small Town Saturday Night" still hadn't been recorded by anyone and was first on our list. Hal had learned it from Pat's demo, which had sort of a Bo Diddley beat—boom ba boom boom. We had started running it down with that feel when Richard got up out of his chair, walked over to Hal with his guitar and said, "What about this?" and went voom, voom, voom, voom, voom, voom voom—straight 4's. In the control room I turned to Allen and Mark and said, "That's it! That's it!" We'd been trying to get that song recorded for nearly three years, and Richard had just unlocked it. It was so simple! That's the way it is sometimes with songs. You just keep fumbling along in the dark until you find the place where the song lives.

The sessions went really well. Hal seemed to always be in good voice, so we were able to cut his vocals live. He gave the musicians great performances, and they responded with great feeling tracks. We got a brilliant cut of "Past the Point of Rescue," as well as a strong new song of Hal's "I Know Where Love Lives." We also did a couple of Hal's songs that weren't destined to be hits, but which were an essential part of him. "I Miss My Mary" and "She Found the Place" were part of Hal's earlier work. We didn't want to abandon that side of him. By including them in the album Hal would come across as an artist who had some substance. One day Hal came in and told me that he'd been learning and singing "Five O'Clock World," which was the first song Allen had success with as a songwriter. It was a hit for a group called The Vogues, and it was Allen's ticket out of his day job. He was still working for the bank in Memphis when he wrote it, so he knew what he was writing about. The song has a kind of yodeling high part, which was what made it. Hal nailed it. Allen was surprised and pleased.

Once we had the album done, Dick Whitehouse heard it for the first time. He was just beaming, totally enthused. After nearly every cut he'd exclaim, "Hal! That's fantastic!" He needed no prompting. He and Curb's veteran record promoter Mike Borchetta settled on "Small Town Saturday Night" as the first single. Jim McGuire took the cover photos for the album. Hal had done a lot of carpentry work on McGuire's studio to make ends meet, and they had become good friends. Videos were just beginning to be used to promote records, and Hal asked McGuire to help him make one. McGuire asked Hal if he'd ever seen a movie called *Terror in Tiny Town*, a full-length black-and-white western with an entire cast of little people! It had all the stock western scenes—the barroom brawl, the stagecoach robbery and chase (on Shetland ponies), the diminutive Mae West–type heroine. McGuire's idea was to shoot Hal singing "Small Town Saturday Night" in black and white, walking in and out of *Terror in Tiny Town* as it was being projected onto a small screen. It was so simple and so effective. It got played all the time on the new CMT channel and is one of the few videos you can point to that definitely helped to sell a song. The other thing that helped to sell this song was the unflagging work of Mike Borchetta. It took sixteen weeks, and he had to beat out his own son Scott, who was promoting Reba McIntyre's current single, but Mike didn't let up until "Small Town Saturday Night" went to #1. Hal was on his way.

We followed "Small Town" with Hal's song, "I Know Where Love Lives," which went to #2, and then we came with "Past the Point of Rescue":

Last night I dreamed you were back again
Larger than life again, holding me tight again
Placing those same kisses on my brow

Sweeter than ever now, lord I remember how
Couldn't get enough of kissing, do you know how much
     you're missing
No you don't, but I do
The days like a slow train trickle by
And even the words I write refuse to fly
All I can hear is your song haunting me
Can't get the melody out of my head you see
Distractions I've been using, do you know how much you're losing
No you don't, but I do
Chorus: But I do, and I wonder if I'm past the point of rescue
        Is no word from you at all the best that you can do
        I never meant to push or shove you, do you know how
           much I love you
        No you don't, but I do

Not everyone would have heard that song as a potential single, but Allen and I had no reservations about it. Hal's voice embodied all of the passion and pain of the lyric. His performance was totally convincing. Chris Leuzinger came up with a great guitar riff, which immediately identified the song. As soon as the record started to get airplay we saw a huge jump in sales. People were genuinely moved by it and wanted to have it. By the end of that run Hal's album had gone gold! Of course, Allen had been there before, but this was all new to me. It was very rewarding to have worked with an artist from the ground up and to see all of the pieces fall into place.

All four of us felt that we were playing our parts and contributing to the growing success of Forerunner. In addition to releases by Hal, Kathy Mattea, and Garth Brooks, Trisha Yearwood was about to release "Like We Never Had a Broken Heart," and Vince Gill had recorded "Don't Let Our Love Start Slippin' Away," a song he had written with Pete Wasner, who was now playing in Vince's band. At the ASCAP awards in 1991, we went home with a pile of awards and in Billboard's year-end listing of Nashville publishers, we were in the top 10, right up there with Sony, BMG, Warner Brothers, and all the big boys. We'd been in business nearly five years, had financed everything out of our own pockets, and felt that we had achieved something—and that we'd done it with quality songs. These

FIGURE 21. #1 Party for *Small Town Saturday Night* (*l. to r.*: Jim Rooney, Pat Alger, Hal Ketchum, Mark Miller, Allen Reynolds, Terrell Tye, Hank DeVito).

FIGURE 22. #1 Party for *Unanswered Prayers* (*l. to r.*: Connie Bradley, Bob Doyle, Garth Brooks, Pat Alger, Allen Reynolds, Jim Rooney). Photograph © Alan L. Mayor.

songs were going to be around for a while and weren't just a bit of fluff. We were proud of what we were doing and the way we were doing it.

INFAMOUS ANGEL

I've had more than my share of lucky days: the day I met Bill Keith, the day I met Jack Clement, the day I met John Prine, the day I met Nanci Griffith, the day I met Pat Alger. I could go on and on. Among those days I would have to include the day I met Iris DeMent. It almost didn't happen. I didn't know Iris, but she called me up one day to invite me to come down to the Bluebird Café where she was going to be part of a showcase of songwriters from Kansas City who were now living in Nashville. The place was full, and I wound up standing around a corner near the bathrooms looking at the stage through a mirror, trying to hear what was going on. I heard a couple of people, but it wasn't capturing my attention, so I didn't stick around. A while later I was visiting Renée Bell, one of my favorite A & R people, who was working at MCA. Renée always knew what was going on and asked me if I had heard Iris De-Ment. I said, "I was supposed to, but I didn't." She said, "I can't believe you haven't heard her. Listen to this!" It was a board recording from that night at the Bluebird. I heard Iris sing "Our Town." Her voice went right to my heart. I shook my head. "What a fool! I guess I really missed that boat." A little while later Allen was working with Emmylou Harris on her *Cowgirl's Prayer* album and mentioned that he'd heard that Emmy's current steel player, Steve Fishell, was going to be producing Iris. My heart sank a little when I heard that. I finally got to meet Iris when she came over to sing some harmony on a song with Emmy. I introduced myself and wished her luck. That was that.

A month or two later I got a call from Ken Irwin at Rounder Records. They had signed Iris, and he asked me if I'd be interested in producing her album. It somehow hadn't worked out with Steve, so I jumped at the chance. When Iris called, I invited her over to my apartment. She was very quiet and shy. We sat down at my dining room table, and I asked her to sing me some songs. She had sort of a pained expression on her face and said, "Do I have to?" I said, "I don't know any other way to do this, do you?" So I sat there while Iris sang. The power of her voice up close was overwhelming. There was so much emotion in it. I was immediately taken back to the place where I first heard Hank Williams. The combination of simplicity, directness, and heartfelt emotion was what had started me on my musical journey nearly forty years earlier, and here it was again: this young woman sitting at my table singing her heart out. I gathered myself together as best I could, and we made a list of possible songs and started to work.

As I had at first with Nanci, I got Iris together with Mark Howard and Roy Huskey so that they would be in with her when it came time to record. Iris played guitar very simply, but it suited what she did. However, I also sensed that there was a piano somewhere in her background, so I asked Pete Wasner to play piano on the sessions. In addition, I got Stuart Duncan on mandolin and fiddle. For one session I had Jerry Douglas on dobro and for the rest Al Perkins, who had a beautiful, simple approach to his playing. I wanted to keep everything quite simple. All of these players knew how to stay out of somebody's way. That was the most important thing. Iris wasn't used to playing with other musicians, and I understood that she would be easily put off if somebody or something stood out. The day before we were to start, Iris and I got together to finalize what we were going to do. Looking at her list I noticed that her song "Let the Mystery Be" wasn't on it. When I asked her about it, she said she just didn't think it was as strong as some of the others. I said, "Iris! That's one of the reasons I'm working with you! I believe that life is a total mystery, and anyone who tells you they've got it all figured out is either a fool or a liar or a bit of both! Please do that song for me." So she did:

Everybody's wonderin' what and where they all came from
Everybody's worryin' 'bout where they're gonna go when the
    whole thing's done
But no one knows for certain and so it's all the same to me
I think I'll just let the mystery be
Some say once you're gone you're gone forever, and some say
    you're gonna come back.
Some say you rest in the arms of the Saviour if in sinful ways
    you lack.
Some say that they're comin' back in a garden, bunch of carrots
    and little sweet peas.
I think I'll just let the mystery be.

We recorded at Cowboy's where everyone could sit in a circle around Iris. Rich Adler was engineering. Recording Iris's voice was a challenge, but Rich did a great job of getting her on tape without overusing a limiter. She had a wide emotional range—from the wildness of "Hotter than Mojave in My Heart" to the sadness and resignation of "Our Town." There were times when I'd be holding my breath, hoping that nothing would break the spell as we neared the end of a song.

The source of all of this I soon discovered when I met Iris's mother, Flora Mae. It was part of Iris's plan to involve her mother in the recording. She had learned countless gospel songs from her, and there could be no doubt that this was the basis of her music. The family was originally from rural Arkansas but had moved to California when Iris was three. Out in California, the family maintained their lifestyle and went to church three or four times a week. The music in the home was all white gospel music. Hearing Iris and her mother sing "Higher Ground" was one of those times in a recording studio when you are capturing something very real and emotionally true:

> Lord lift me up and let me stand
> By faith in heaven's tableland
> A higher plane than I have found
> Lord plant my feet on higher ground

When Rich and I were mixing the album, I was struck by the simplicity and clarity of the playing. Although Iris's music reminded me of the music of people like Hank Williams, Lefty Frizzell, and Wilma Lee Cooper, I was never inclined to try to copy those records and go for a retro sound. I wanted to record music in a way that feels normal to me now with players who play musically and are not just playing licks borrowed from other players in other times. The emotions and underpinnings don't change. The retro approach would have put Iris's music in a box it didn't need to be in. It's music. The players I chose were responding to her songs musically. Her voice and her songs were the most important thing. Once people heard this stunning album, *Infamous Angel*, they never forgot it. I certainly never did.

FIGURE 23. Big hug with Iris DeMent at Jack's Tracks, 1991.

OLD FRIENDS

When I was first in Nashville in 1974, David Olney—along with Townes Van Zandt, Richard Dobson, and the crew that hung out at Bishop's—was obviously a kindred spirit. David was originally from the Northeast—Rhode Island—and I suppose we shared some of that somewhat harsher, slightly cynical outlook on life that set us apart from most southerners. David liked his music raw. He reminded me a lot of Eric Von Schmidt that way. When he had his rock-and-roll band The X-Rays, it was an all-out, no-holds-barred affair. Over the years, Olney, along with Pat McLaughlin, Sam Bush, and others had been part of The Nashville Jug Band, fronted by an absolutely manic, fabulous character named Ed Dye. One of my crowning moments as a recording engineer had come when I recorded the Jug Band's album for Rounder. If there ever was one, this was a "live" recording, with people all over the studio singing and playing as if they were on fire. In charge of this menagerie was a lovely, quiet, soft-spoken journalist/guitar player named Tommy Goldsmith. I guess I had gained Tommy's confidence as a result of that experience, because he called me up one day and asked if I'd be interested in working with him as a coproducer on an album with Dave. Without being aware of it, this was something I had hoped would happen for a long time.

Our approach on this album was sort of a combination of jug band music and country blues. The players included Stephanie Davis, who played the unlikely combination of fiddle and trumpet; the ever funky Mike Henderson on National steel body guitar and mandolin; Pat McLaughlin, also very funky, on his own style of jug band mandolin; Tommy Goldsmith and Dave on acoustic guitars; and the rock solid combination of Roy Huskey and Kenny Malone on upright bass and drums. Right from the start, David took no prisoners with a southern epic combining General Robert E. Lee and a bad, bad girl named Bama Lou. Maybe southern rock was what they were all fighting for. There were ample helpings of Dave's sarcastic wit in songs like "Luckiest Man" ("Your life stinks, but my life's just like a dream"), "Love's Been Linked to the Blues" ("In case you haven't heard, I'll give you the bad news / Love's been linked to the blues"). As I had learned years earlier with Chance Browne, a steady stream of sarcasm, no matter how witty, can pale after a while, but underneath that hard shell of David's is an insistence on the truth and endurance of love as expressed in the lyrics of the title song "Roses":

> The old oak tree began to shudder
> But he held his ground like some old soldier
> His ancient pride was burnt and shaken
> But something deep inside did waken
> He raised his limbs just like Moses
> And blossomed roses
> He blossomed roses

That image still stays with me.

As with David Olney, Pat McLaughlin was someone I never tired of going to see "live." After hearing him play one weekend, David Ferguson and I decided that it was time to talk to Pat about making another album like the one I had done ten years earlier with Curt Allen—"live" in the studio. Since recording U-2 at Sun, Ferg had become Cowboy's main engineer and, like me, loved to capture music on the fly before it had a chance to get stale or studied. Pat had done a couple of albums for Capitol, but they didn't have the same feel that he had when I heard him in a club. I guess we caught him at the right moment, because we were over at Cowboy's before Pat could think about it too much. From the first count-off Pat got into a deep groove on "Down to Memphis." His cutting electric rhythm, Dwight Scott's B-3 organ, and Jay Patten's sax wove in and out of each other in a beautiful dance. We were blessed on this album to have two of the most soulful singers in Nashville singing harmony—Pebble Daniels and Claude Hill. When they let loose on the Norman Whitfield classic "I Wish It Would Rain" you really did wish it would rain all day and all night. Every song had its own special feel, always set up by Pat's guitar, giving Pat's quirky lyrics a space to be:

> Who went and broke your heart
> Don't tell me, baby
> That was my favorite spot
> Don't tell me, baby
> In the time it takes for you to think it over
> I'll be closer than the seatbelt on your shoulder
> Whyn't you come on over, baby
> I'm the Repo Man, it's sad but I'll have to do
> It's the same old plan, but your name's been engraved in blue

Pat has that special knack for making soul music sound slightly country and country music sound soulful. "Burning Memories" took me right back to Joe Tex's Nashville recordings of songs like "The Love You Save Might Be Your Own":

> Burnin' memories just to feel the flame
> Of a love gone cold, no one to blame
> Wishful thinkin' things were still the same
> I'm burnin' memories just to feel the flame

At some point in the proceedings we came up with a title for the album, *Party at Pat's*, and what better closer than the rockin' party song cryptically titled "Hymn #122"?

> She looks like a number to me
> I've got a feeling really strong
> I want a table for three
> She's brought her girl friend along

FIGURE 24. "Lonesome" Pat McLaughlin.
Photograph: © Catherine J. Flanagan.

FIGURE 25. Townes Van Zandt and David Olney.
Photograph: © Catherine J. Flanagan.

Could be something. Could be nothing. You never know when you party at Pat's. Just to calm things down at the end, Pat did one of his dad's favorite songs, "Blue Room." A lot of Pat's heart and soul came from his dad—right out of that rich, black Iowa soil. One of the great things about Nashville was that people came there from all over, bringing a piece of their geography with them. When I first showed up and started hanging out with Pat, David, and Townes, I loved how different we all were and how much we could learn from each other. The music we would create individually and together would make friendships which were lasting and true.

CAROL AGAIN

I had become involved in the development of the Folk Alliance as a member of the board of directors in 1989. Although some people compared trying to organize a bunch of folkies to trying to herd a bunch of cats, I felt that it would be helpful to those trying to make a living playing folk music to approach it in a more organized fashion. The executive director was Phyllis Barney, one of those people who knows how to bring people together to work for a common cause. She insisted that we create a solid structure that would be inclusive of all the various people working in the field—from amateurs who loved to play and listen to folk music to professionals like full-time artists, managers, promoters, those running record labels, and record producers. I had certainly benefited from the efforts of so many others and now it was time for me to put some time and effort into helping the folk music world continue to expand its influence and its audience. One of my efforts, which bore fruit and of which I am proud, was the creation of a Lifetime Achievement Award to honor those people on whose shoulders we were standing. With woodblock artist Paul Ritscher, I came up with the image of a full-grown tree in a circular frame, symbolizing a lifetime of growth and productivity with no end. The first two recipients were, appropriately enough, Pete Seeger and Alan Lomax.

One benefit of becoming involved in the Folk Alliance was that it lifted my head above the Nashville world in which I was becoming increasingly immersed. Each year our annual conference was in a different city in the United States or Canada, and it was a great way to connect with music happening in different regions. At our meeting one year in Toronto I struck up an acquaintance with a real live wire with copper-colored hair named Rosalie Goldstein. Rosalie ran the Winnepeg Folk Festival, and she invited me to come up that summer as her guest. Whenever I played, Canadian musicians would come up to me and start talking to me about the old Blue Velvet Band record. It had evidently made quite an impression in Canada. You would have thought it had just come out. When Rosalie asked me to come back, I told her that playing solo really wasn't my thing, but that it might be an idea to reconstitute the Blue Velvet Band since so many people seemed to remember it. So the New Blue Velvet Band came into being, with Kenny Kosek replacing Richard Greene.

We played at several of the major Canadian and European folk festivals, and in the summer of '91 were booked to play a Bluegrass festival in the town of Athy, Co. Kildare, Ireland. When a gig in London fell through, I decided to come to Dublin a day early to hang out and called Phillip King to get me a hotel. While he had me on the phone he mentioned that he'd run into Carol Langstaff the night before at a wake for her mother, Diane Hamilton, who had just died. Phillip picked me up at the Dublin airport. Bloom's was full, so we went to The Gresham, an upmarket business-man's hotel on O'Connell Street, not a place I'd ordinarily be staying. As I was checking in at the desk, a phone rang and the woman behind the desk said, "It's for you." Who could possibly know I was here at The Gresham, of all places? It was Carol! I told her that I was sorry to hear about her mother. She thanked me and said, "Can I be blunt? I'd like to come in to see you this afternoon, but I'd have no way to get back to my mother's out in the country. Would it be alright if I spent the night?" I didn't have to think twice. "Of course. Come ahead."

Later that afternoon there was a knock on my door. There she was! Just as always, her face beaming, her eyes laughing. We had a big hug and stood back, taking each other in. The last time had been at a big party after Tom Rush's Christmas shows at Symphony Hall back in 1984. Carol had just shown up, and we had a couple of dances. I never forgot the feel of my hand on the small of her back as we whirled around the floor that night. Now, years later, here we were in Dublin. I was a mess. The airlines had lost my bag; I was unshaven and had been up for two days, but she didn't seem to mind and looked at me with the greatest expression of joy on her face. However, we were not alone. Carol had brought along her brother Colm and her sister Catroina. I had no idea what they were thinking, but they seemed to be happy to go along with whatever was happening. It was a fine summer day, so I suggested that we get out of the hotel and start walking around Dublin.

Since my time at Peggi Jordan's, Dublin always had a pull on me. I loved walking along the Liffey, up Grafton Street, through Stephen's Green, by O'Donoghue's, back through Trinity, to Temple Bar. Now, walking along with Carol holding my arm, it all seemed fresh again. We wound up at Claddagh Records, browsing through the stacks of Irish and World Folk Records. Occasionally Carol would pull out an album her mother had been involved with. I had never met her, although I had bought many albums on Tradition Records that she had recorded, such as *Instrumental Music of the Southern Appalachians*, *Lark in the Morning*, and *So Early in the Morning*. Carol told me that when her mother realized she was dying she decided to have a party and had invited many friends, including Carol's mentor, Jean Ritchie, and the actress/folksinger Robin Roberts. Sadly, or perhaps not so sadly, she died just as everyone was arriving for the party, so it had turned into a musical wake.

Phillip King had arranged that we should meet up with Jean Ritchie, her husband George Pickow, and Robin Roberts at the Olympia Theater for a concert that night by Mary Black. The day just kept unfolding before me. I couldn't have planned it. Having already gotten to hear Mary at The Session and then at the filming of "Bringing It All Back Home," I was looking forward to the concert, but having Carol beside me seemed to heighten the experience. It was extraordinary. Mary did a version of "The Dimming of the Day," which she had sung with Richard Thompson in Nashville as well as Mick Hanly's "Past the Point of Rescue," which she had recorded before Hal Ketchum on her *No Frontiers* album. By the end of the concert Carol and I were beaming. After we said our goodnights to Jean, George, and Robin, we walked arm in arm up Dame Street, past Trinity, across the bridge, up O'Connell Street to The Gresham. The doorman took a look at my unshaven face, jeans, and sneakers, but I produced my room key and he let me in, possibly wondering if standards everywhere were going to hell.

Like lots of Irish hotels at that time a double room came with two single beds. Carol and I were happy, each in our little bed, talking through the night, sometimes reaching across to each other. It felt right. We had a lot of catching up to do. She was still in the same house in Vermont and now had three kids, but was divorced from her husband Peter. She and her dad, John Langstaff, had created shows celebrating the Solstice, which they called "Revels" and which they had been putting on in Cambridge for the past fifteen years. They had branched out to other cities around the country, and she had started one up in Hanover, New Hampshire, near where she lived. I told her something of my life since I'd settled in Nashville, engineering, producing, publishing, and still—she was happy to hear—singing and playing. So we talked and thought back to the old days in Cambridge at the Club 47, the Sweezy's house, the snowball fights, the walks on the beach at Green Harbor. It was all good. We lulled each other to sleep with these happy memories. All too soon, it was time to get up and get moving. Carol was going to take a train and rejoin her family and friends. They would be scattering her mother's ashes on a favorite hillside up in County Louth. Her mother had spent much of her life bringing people together. It seemed right somehow that her final act of dying had brought Carol and me back together. It was a gift we were ready to accept.

When I got back to Nashville, I said to myself, "Jim, pay attention. Don't let this chance go by." I wrote Carol to tell her how happy I had been to connect with her again and said that I hoped we would stay in touch. I was pleasantly surprised when she wrote back and said that it had somehow seemed more than mere chance that we had come together in Dublin, and that she looked forward to continuing our conversation. It took me a little while, but I had an idea. Earlier that summer I had reconnected with my old friend Dewey Balfa, who now played with his daughter Christine in a group called, appropriately enough, Balfa Toujours. He was down in the dumps because he had been diagnosed with cancer, and the prognosis wasn't good. Before I left I told Dewey that I was going to come down to Louisiana and visit him in the fall. It was something I'd been meaning to do for years, but I meant what I said. I would take that trip. As it happened, Carol was working on starting a Revels in Houston and was going to be there in late October. I called her up and asked her if she'd ever been to Louisiana. She hadn't, so I told her about the trip I was planning and said, "If you're interested in dance, music and ritual, in Louisiana it happens every day of the week. How would you like to come with me and see for yourself?" To my great delight, she took me up on my offer. We were going to have an adventure.

I flew to Houston, rented a car, and we set out for New Orleans. On the way over we'd stop for some gumbo, oysters, and crab claws, wasting no time getting into the local cuisine. We were listening to a road tape I'd made with music by Lefty Frizzell, Flaco Jimenez, Doctor John, the Dirty Dozen Brass Band, Clifton Chenier, and the Balfa Brothers, and the miles flew by. In New Orleans we checked in to the Richelieu Motel in the French Quarter, where I'd stayed with John Prine. It had just the right atmosphere—a courtyard café, deep crimson wallpaper, French doors in the room opening onto a small balcony overlooking The Quarter. We spent the next two days exploring, visiting my friend Richard Allen, dropping in to Preservation Hall, and dancing the night away at Tipitina's to the loose, wild, chaotic sound of the Rebirth Jazz Band.

Our final day in New Orleans was Halloween. It's sort of like Mardi Gras without all the tourists. Everyone dresses up. Carol got into it. She made up her eyes, wore glow-in-the-dark earrings, and a beautiful black lace dress, which had belonged to her grandmother. She topped herself off with a black velvet hat. She looked beautiful. I, on the other hand, had only a trick arrow through the head that I'd bought that afternoon for a dollar at a flea market. Nobody ever said a word about Carol's outfit. They were too busy saying, "Get a load of Custer!" "Need some Tylenol?" I got my money's worth out of that arrow. Early in the evening we went to see a pretty bizarre Sam Shepherd play at a little theater, which, for some reason or other, gave us a fit of the giggles. I think we were getting slightly hysterical in the unreal atmosphere of New Orleans on Halloween. That atmosphere became totally magnified when we went into the Municipal Auditorium just before midnight. What a scene it was! The stage was dressed to look like a swamp, with moss and vines over everything. The Neville Brothers were just getting started. Aaron Neville sat on a huge throne center stage holding a staff. The Master of the Revels. Massive. Everyone in the audience was in full costume. The music immediately swept us away, and we joined everyone else moving, swaying, dancing. Toward the end they were joined by Dr. John, looking totally centered, singing "Right Place, Wrong Time." The finale was an incredible medley of "Amazing Grace," "By the Rivers of Babylon," and Bob Marley's "One Heart." It was healing music, healthful music. Carol and I had touched a piece of the soul of New Orleans. Music, dance, and ritual had come together for us on that night—All Hallow's Eve.

The next morning we headed out of New Orleans listening to Dr. John and the Dirty Dozen Jazz Band. As we passed through Lafayette, we switched to the Balfa Brothers, leaving the refineries and oil-rig yards behind, and suddenly were in the midst of rice fields or "prairies" as they are called locally. Before long we were in Eunice, pulling up in front of Dewey's house. He came out to greet us, and right away we were hugging and weeping, weeping and hugging. I had come as I said I would, and it obviously meant the world to him. We were welcomed into his home. He told us that it was ours for as long as we wanted, and he meant it. The smell of food cooking enveloped us. Dewey and his lady friend Pat had been at it all afternoon. We settled down for a drink. Lots of memories washed over Dewey and me from our days together at Newport and the Smithsonian Festival, but always touched with sadness because of the loss of Dewey's brothers Will and Rodney in a car crash twelve years earlier. It had broken Dewey's heart. I had wanted to record "Only the Best" with them, but we didn't get to it in time.

We forgot our sadness at the table. A chuck roast laced with garlic and jalapeño peppers was as good as it gets, served along with some Cajun corn and cabbage, and washed down with a few glasses of wine. Soon it was time for a little music. Dewey's face was wreathed in smiles. Melodies just floated from his fingers as he let himself go deep into the music. Pat and Carol were dancing in the kitchen. After a while, Pat lay down in her big lounger chair. Carol went off to bed, leaving Dewey and me to play down until we were through. Carol and I weren't through, though. We still had the giggles and seemed to be exploding with energy. We were so happy to be together in that bed. Late into the night we discovered that we seemed to be forging a relationship deeper than either of us had had in years. We felt safe and blessed in Dewey's house.

After a hearty breakfast the next morning, we followed Dewey at a pretty good clip over to Marc Savoy's music store, where they have a Cajun jam session every Saturday morning. Marc builds accordions and his wife, Ann, has written a definitive book called *Cajun Music: A Reflection of a People*. At Marc's place, things were in full swing. Dewey and I joined in, while Carol tried out a few steps with a great old guy—his hat at just the right jaunty angle—and a damned good dancer.

That evening Dewey got dressed up in a jacket and tie to go play on the *Rendez-Vous des Cajuns* radio show at the Liberty Theater in Eunice.

FIGURE 26. Playing some tunes with Dewey Balfa.

We dressed up too. Carol put on a long dancy dress and put some honey-suckle in her hair. We were ready for a big Cajun Saturday night. The stage backdrop, once again, was a bayou swamp scene. There were people in the audience from all over, including some French Canadians, but the bulk of the audience were just folks from the area looking for some fun on a Saturday night. They were ready to go when Dewey and his group started to play. Immediately, the area in front of the stage filled with dancers. Carol and I got in there with them. We went through waltzes and polkas and two-steps. Every so often Dewey would just let it go, and Carol would go with him. She was in heaven.

The honeysuckle was still working. When we danced close together I'd get a whiff, and I'd be filled with its sweetness. "Sweet" was a word I found myself using a lot on this trip. Dewey was a sweet man. There was a certain sweetness in the air in New Orleans. People were sweet to each other. Pat called Dewey "Daddy" in a sweet way. Aaron Neville's voice was so sweet—like trickling honey. The centuries of hardship had not hardened these people's hearts. Music, food, dancing, loving, and laughing won out over the sorrow and pain in their lives. Carol and I felt blessed to be among such sweet people. We finally danced the last dance to the sound of Dewey's fiddle, had a final gumbo and a drink with him in a joint across the street, hugged and cried one more time, and pulled out into the night to go to the airport in New Orleans.

What a week it had been! We both felt very nourished by each other and by the culture we had chosen to explore together. There was a fundamental reality which we both felt in our renewed relationship. Carol's mother, Diane Hamilton, had brought us together by her death. Dewey Balfa, too, would be gone six months later, but he had blessed us with his music, his honesty, and his generosity, and had sent us on our life's journey together. We knew it would not be easy. Carol had three teenage children. I had no idea how we would work things out, but I was ready to try.

OTHER VOICES

Going into 1992 Forerunner was flying. We were also gaining a reputation as a "writer's house." Some publishing companies would have quotas for their writers. If you wrote with another writer that only counted as half a song toward your quota. If you were supposed to write twenty-five songs a year and you cowrote all the time, it would mean that you'd have to write fifty songs. We felt that was a foolish approach. We assumed that writers wanted to write. The fact that they wrote fifty songs or ten songs was meaningless if the songs weren't any good. That whole mentality seemed stupid and counterproductive to us.

As a result, writers started coming to us. Tony Arata was one. We had long admired Tony as a writer and as a person. His song, "The Dance," had set Garth Brooks on another level as an artist. Matt Lindsey, who had worked with Tony as a song plugger at another company, had come to work for us, and when Tony's other publishing deal had come to an end, Matt was very key in Tony's decision to come with us. His new home seemed to agree with him. Patty Loveless would have great success with several of Tony's songs, including "Everybody's Equal in the Eyes of Love," "Nothing but Love," and "Long Stretch of Lonesome." Garth Brooks put everything he had into "The Change," written with Wayne Tester:

One hand reaches out and pulls a lost soul from harm
While a thousand more go unspoken for

And they say to you what good have you done by just this one
It's like whispering a prayer in the fury of a storm
And I hear them saying you'll never change things
And no matter what you do it's still the same thing
But it's not the world I am changing
I'll do this so this world will know that it will not change me.

That lyric was one example of why we were so proud to count Tony as a member of the Forerunner family and why Tony was recently inducted into the Nashville Songwriters Hall of Fame.

Another writer to join our fold was Tim O'Brien. Allen had recorded his songs "Walk the Way the Wind Blows" and "Untold Stories," which had been hits for Kathy Mattea. I had known Tim as a member of the Bluegrass band Hot Rize for a long time. It didn't take much encouragement on my part to convince him that Forerunner would be a good place for him to hang his hat and develop as a writer. Some of Tim's songs written while he was with us became my favorites as well as a lot of other people's. Garth Brooks recorded "When There's No One Around," written with Darrell Scott. I would record it with Sean Keane. I would also record "Like I Used to Do," written with Pat Alger, with both Sean Keane and Charley Landsborough. Charley also recorded "Time to Learn," a beautiful gem by Tim and Pat that quietly touched your heart:

It takes time to learn when someone's gone for good
They're not coming back like you wish they would
In the empty hours when you miss them so
It's time to learn to let them go.

Tim could brighten up our day any time he was around with his wit and air of good cheer, but it was his heart which really informed every song he wrote.

Steve Gillette was another writer who was intrigued by what we were doing at Forerunner. I had become friendly with Steve and his wife Cindy Mangsen at the Kerrville Folk Festival. Like many others I had thought that "Darcy Farrow" was an old folk song until I discovered that Steve had written it with Tom Campbell. With Charles John Quarto, Steve had written "Grapes on the Vine," with its unforgettable first verse:

There are songs that birds don't sing to people
Secrets that keep right through to the end
There are heroes that hide until forever
And I'm singin' this song for one of them

I invited him to come by whenever he was in Nashville. He took me up on that offer, and before we knew it we had decided to do an album together. We recorded "Grapes on the Vine," plus two more gems written by Steve and Charles John Quarto, "The Old Trail," and "Always a Train in My Dreams." Eventually Steve's connection with us led to Don Williams recording "The Old Trail" and Garth Brooks recording "Unto Us This Night" on his *Beyond the Season* Christmas album. It was another case of a writer finding his own way to us at Forerunner and the songs finding their home.

One of the highlights of my Fourth Annual 50th Birthday Party in January that year was when Nanci Griffith and Emmylou Harris sang a Kate Wolf song, "Across the Great Divide." Something about it just grabbed me and held me. It might have had something to do with the beginning of my new journey with Carol:

I've been walkin' in my sleep
Countin' troubles 'stead of countin' sheep
Where the years went I can't say
I just turned around and they've gone away.
I've been siftin' through the layers
Of dusty books and faded papers
They tell a story I used to know
And it was one that happened so long ago
Chorus: It's gone away in yesterday
         Now I find myself on the mountainside
         Where the rivers change direction
         Across the Great Divide

Something special about that performance had struck Nanci as well, and she asked me if I'd be willing to go into the studio with her and her band and record that song and two or three others as demos for a new album project. It had been six years since Nanci and I had worked together, and

I had some misgivings about being able to surpass that work, which I felt was some of the best work either of us had done, but Nanci told me that she thought that I had always understood her as an artist and that she felt it was the right time for us to come back together.

We decided to record with Mark Miller at Jack's Tracks. From the very beginning everything felt right. Nanci had been working with her Blue Moon Orchestra for a while, and had settled into a very good groove with them. The band consisted of James Hooker, keyboards; Pete Kennedy, guitars; Peter Gorisch, bass; Fran Breen and Pat McInerney on drums and percussion; and Lee Satterfield, harmony vocals. For this session we also had Stuart Duncan on fiddle and mandolin. Two gems came out of the session, "Woman of the Phoenix" by Texas songwriter Vince Bell and "Across the Great Divide," the song that would launch us into this project with full hearts. That was in March. We didn't record again until July, but Nanci and I got together from time to time to listen to songs and build a list. Fairly soon, Nanci settled on the idea that there were so many songs by writers she admired like Kate or Vince or by writers who had influenced her in some way like Tom Paxton or Pete Seeger, there would be more than enough material for an album.

When we recorded again in July, we added Frank Christian to the band. His excellent fingerpicking guitar style gave us another distinctive voice in the tracks. When I first started working with Nanci she would drive from Austin to New York by herself to play in a coffeehouse. She had connected with several writers in the New York folk scene, Frank fore-most among them—the quintessential Greenwich Villager. Nanci had chosen to record one of his songs, "Three Flights Up," which painted the real picture of Village life:

> In the winter, a-chatterin' cold
> While the building shook like ragweed in the wind
> Stories from the heat pipes
> We were told
> But now they only leave me
> With a half-enchanted grin
> It was always three flights up
> Cathedral bells kept time.

Nanci chose to do a song from another denizen of the Village, Bob Dylan's "Boots of Spanish Leather." We did this simply with guitars, bass, and percussion. When Nanci sent a copy to Jeff Rosen, Bob's manager, she got word back that Bob liked it and would be happy to add his harmonica to it if we sent the track to him in Los Angeles. It was good to reconnect with Bob, even from afar. We finished this batch of sessions with two more songs, the first a song of Jerry Jeff Walker's that Jerry later told me he had nearly forgotten, "Morning Song for Sally." It was absolutely beautiful—about as far from Gonzo as you could get. The second song was one of Townes Van Zandt's best ballads, "Tecumseh Valley." I had long loved the song after hearing both Townes and Bobby Bare do it, but Nanci's performance was riveting. She put everything she had into it and was close to tears at the end:

> They found her down beneath the stairs
> That led to Gypsy Sally's
> In her hand when she died
> Was a note that cried
> Fare thee well . . . Tecumseh Valley
> The name she gave was Caroline
> Daughter of a miner
> And her ways were free
> It seemed to me
> The sunshine walked beside her

All I could do when it was over was go into the studio and put my arms around Nanci. We would later get Arlo Guthrie to come and sing harmony with her, which gave the story even more strength. By the time we finished these sessions, Nanci had come up with a perfect title for the project: *Other Voices, Other Rooms*, taken from the title of Truman Capote's first novel.

The next sessions were in Dublin at the end of July, after Nanci, John Prine, and I, with The New Blue Velvet Band, played the Cambridge Folk Festival. Carol came over, and we were delighted to return to the place where we had reconnected only a year earlier. Phillip Donnelly was going to be joining Nanci's band for these sessions at the Windmill Lane Studios. The studio we were in was huge and it took Brian Masterson, the top engineer in Ireland for this kind of music, a while to figure out a setup so we could get Nanci's vocals live. We finally got started with Tom Paxton's classic "Can't Help but Wonder Where I'm Bound." Phillip immediately made his presence felt with a ringing acoustic guitar solo. We then carried on with a new song by Janis Ian and Kathy Mattea's husband Jon Vezner, "This Old Town." Just the two songs we did that day illustrated perfectly Nanci's idea that folk music was continually growing and evolving from one generation to another.

The next day Brian was ready to go. He'd gotten the picture that both Nanci and I liked to work fast. The first song we did was a clear favorite of mine, John Prine's "Speed of the Sound of Loneliness." Phillip had played the song so many times with John that he got us into just the right groove. I missed having him in Nashville. We'd done so much work together, and his guitar had played such an important part in the records Nanci and I had done that it felt like we'd picked up where we'd left off. Nanci gave the song a heartfelt performance. She had made it her own. Close on the heels of that, we did another song I had played with Phillip many times, Ralph McTell's poignant song of emigration "From Clare to Here." As a result of the success in Ireland of her recording of Julie Gold's "From a Distance," Nanci had come to consider Ireland a second home, and the emotion she put into the lyric of the song was real. After Phillip added his keening electric guitar and the great Dublin singer Pete Cummins had sung a harmony part, we knew we'd done something special.

We didn't get back in the studio in Nashville until the fall. Nanci and I were still listening to lots of songs and our list seemed to be getting longer. There were going to be many we would not do for one reason or another, but it was a total immersion in the wide and deep pool of "folk" music. When we gathered again at Jack's Tracks, we had settled on three songs to do with the band. The first was Gordon Lightfoot's funny/sad song about a road-worn picker, "Ten Degrees and Getting Colder," something many of us could relate to. Next we did Michael Burton's classic cowboy song "Night Rider's Lament," with its catalogue of wrangler wonders that the city folk know nothing about:

They've never seen the northern lights
Never seen the hawk on the wing

Never seen the spring hit the Great Divide
Oh they never heard old Camp Cookie sing

"Camp Cookie" in this case was the incomparable cowboy singer and
yodeler, Don Edwards. Some might find it strange that Nanci would fly
someone all the way from Texas to yodel for one minute at the end of a
song. That's the way she was. She wanted the best, so she got the best.
That little bit of yodeling turned out to be the opening Don and I needed
to strike up what was to become a lifelong friendship.

Finally, we did a song by a young songwriter named Buddy Mondlock,
"Comin' Down in the Rain." Guy Clark had been the first one to turn me
on to Buddy. He was soft-spoken and gentle, but with an underlying
intensity to his lyrics. As soon as she heard the song, Nanci knew it was
a story she could tell:

Strung out and hung out to dry
Laughin' under the line
It's not such a dignified place
But he really don't mind
He says with his feet on the ground
He'd have nothin' to gain
Claims he likes it up there
And he'll only come down in the rain.
Chorus: Comin' down in the rain
            Washin' out of the sky
            Loaded down with the pain
            There just ain't no way to fly
            You can read him as clear
            As the wall where he once wrote his name
            It was right next to hers
            But it'll only come down in the rain

We were definitely close to having our project surrounded. Everything
we had recorded so far held up. What were we missing? We were talking
about this one morning at the studio. One hole became obvious. How
could a collection of songs like this be complete without a Woody Guthrie
song? Nanci thought of "Do Re Mi" and thought she remembered Guy

Clark singing it one time. We called Guy up on the spot. He knew the song, and said he could come over, so I then called Roy Huskey and got him to come as well. McInerney was already there doing some percussion overdubs and Pat Flynn, the brilliant flat picker with the Newgrass Revival, was coming in to play on the Lightfoot song, so we had it figured out in about fifteen minutes. If we'd planned it for months, it couldn't have come out better. The two Texans gave the lyric every bit of humor and bite that was in it, and Pat Flynn's guitar sparkled throughout. It was over in a few minutes. Guy listened back and said "All that practice sure paid off!" and out the door he strode.

Almost since we began, Nanci had wanted to involve Chet Atkins. We had finally settled on two songs for him to play on, "Are You Tired of Me Darling," an old Carter Family song, and the Malvina Reynolds song, "Turn Around," which Harry Belafonte first made popular. Naturally, I was looking forward to meeting and working with Chet, but I was a little bit nervous too. Who was I, next to him? The doorbell rang, and there he was, Chet Atkins, with a guitar case in each hand, alone, no entourage, just himself. He came in, introduced himself, unpacked, told a couple of quiet jokes and asked Nanci what she'd like to start with. She suggested the Carter Family song. Of course, Chet knew it. He'd started working in Knoxville with Maybelle Carter and her daughters before they all came to Nashville to be on the Opry. He asked Nanci to run it down for him. She fingerpicked it on the guitar when she played it. Chet said, "That's fine. You do that. I'll just back you up." When Nanci started to say something, he said, "I like what you're doing. Let me just back you up." There was no "I'm Chet Atkins and you're not." If playing backup was what was needed, that's what he'd do. I was impressed. For "Turn Around" he had brought a custom-made Del Vecchio resonator guitar with a stereo pickup. It had a very distinctive sound. Before we started, he went over to Pete and said that he'd be playing certain chord inversions, so Pete might want to play the bass notes to go with them. His part was very simple, very beautiful, and suited the song perfectly. When he listened back he quietly told Mark how he liked to place the stereo pickups in the mix. Mark did what he said and asked him how it sounded. Chet just said, "That's fine." He then turned to Nanci and said, "Is that okay? Are you happy?" Needless to say, she was. I was. We all were. While he was packing up I started talking to him about his payment. He said, "All my union checks go to the W. O. Smith Community Music School," and that was that. He picked up his cases and went out the door. He was a total professional in the highest sense of the word. It was one of the great privileges of my life to work even that little bit with him.

After we had Nanci's original "folk hero" Carolyn Hester come in and join Nanci on "Can't Help but Wonder Where I'm Bound," Emmylou Harris joined Nanci and Lee Satterfield on "Across the Great Divide" and then sang a gorgeous, heartbreaking trio with Iris DeMent and Nanci on "Are You Tired of Me Darling." Finally, Bela Fleck added a totally unique banjo part to "This Old Town." We were getting down to our last song and it was a big one—"Wimoweh." One of the first records Nanci listened to at home with her parents as a young girl was "The Weavers Live at Carnegie Hall." Another big record in her life was Odetta's first album. Just as she had been so encouraging to Bill Keith and me when we did our first gig at the Ballad Room, Odetta had encouraged Nanci ever since she first drove from Texas to Greenwich Village to try her luck. There was no doubt in Nanci's mind that Odetta would be the one to lead us in "Wimoweh" to cap off this wonderful collection of songs. While she was at it, Nanci wanted a full house of singers to give it everything they had, so we wound up with a packed studio, all under the direction of Marlin Griffith, Nanci's dad, who was a champion barbershop quartet singer and had given Nanci her schooling in harmony singing. We had The Indigo Girls, Pam Rose and Mary Ann Kennedy, John Prine, Barry and Holly Tashian, John Gorka, and Dave Mallett; James Hooker and I sang bass. The music was provided by the great Leo Kottke on 12-string guitar, John Hartford on banjo and tap dancing, Roy Huskey on upright bass, and Pat McInerney on percussion. Once we got our parts sorted out and Odetta set the tempo, there was no stopping us. Nanci sang high shouts next to Odetta, whose surging voice was carrying over all of us. The journey we had started nearly a year earlier with "Across the Great Divide" was complete. We were finished.

While we were mixing the album, we got a chance to relive the whole recording experience of the past year. Going into the project I had no idea how much it would come to mean to me. I tried to express my feelings in the liner notes:

Nanci conquered my fears with her clear vision. She had in mind to bring together in an album many of the voices, words, and melodies which had entered her soul starting as a young girl growing up in Texas and continuing to this day. My own soul made a similar musical journey starting in Boston and Cambridge in the '50's and '60's up until the present. This album is full of the musical voices of friends old and new. It is a true collection of the "folk" spirit, which speaks to us constantly in a voice that is personal and compelling. It has been my pleasure to share in the fulfillment of Nanci's vision and my pleasure to listen to all of the voices gathered here together.

Nanci reinforced the connection to the continuing folk tradition by inviting David Gahr to provide photographs of many of the writers, as well as to take photographs of Nanci and me. I had known Dave since my days at Newport. There is no doubt in my mind that the most beautiful and telling photographs in *Baby, Let Me Follow You Down* were his. The joy he captured in his cover photograph of Nanci holding her copy of *Other Voices, Other Rooms* needed no words of explanation.

I felt the effects of this album for a long time. Nanci brought many of the artists and writers who had been a part of the project to the Paramount Theater in Austin for a celebratory concert, which was also being filmed for television. Among those gathered was Tom Paxton. Tom and I had known each other since the sixties. After hearing the results of Nanci's album and spending time together backstage at the Paramount, Tom asked me if I'd be interested in helping him make an album. Naturally, I was more than delighted, and so we set out on a journey of our own, which has resulted in four albums to date, two of which were nominated for Grammys. Every time we have recorded I've been moved by the quality of Tom's songs and his singing. His lyrics range from being topical like the silly and humorous "Short Shelf Life Songs" or the heartbreakingly real, "On the Road from Srebrenica" to the timeless "Spin and Turn." When Tom and Iris DeMent sang his song "Along the Verdigris," it sounded as if their voices had come right up from that river deep in America's heartland. Just as Nanci had envisioned, through Tom I was being led ever further into the roots and branches of folk music. There was no better guide.

FIGURE 27. Celebrating with Nanci Griffith
after completing *Other Voices, Other Rooms*.
Photograph © Estate of David Gahr.

After the Paramount concert was over many of us gathered in the bar
of the Driskil Hotel. James Hooker sat down at the piano and before long
Odetta, Paxton, Nanci, Carolyn Hester, Iris, Emmylou, and Jerry Jeff were
singing all the songs we've known forever. Eventually, there was a lull
in the action, and without saying a word Iris sat down at the piano and
started to sing:

My life, it don't count for nothing
When I look at this world, I feel so small
My life, it's only a season
A passing September that no one will recall
But I gave joy to my mother
I made my lover smile
And I can give comfort to my friends when they're hurting
I can make it seem better for a while

Everything in the room stopped. There were tears in my eyes, and I wasn't the only one. What more could we say? What could we add to that? The song said what was in all of us in one way or another. The collective experience and wisdom in that room acknowledged that a new voice was among us. A new branch was growing on the old tree. It was an enormous boost to Iris's confidence that Nanci included her in *Other Voices*. It was yet another way that Nanci's vision was helping to move many of us further down our path. The final confirmation for Nanci came when the album was nominated for and won a Grammy. The Grammy wasn't only for her, it was for all of the writers, singers, musicians, and engineers gathered together by Nanci to join her on this journey. We were all encouraged by it to carry on the tradition.

GROWING PAINS

The response to Iris DeMent's *Infamous Angel* was greater than I dared to hope for. For a record on a small independent label, it started to sell pretty well. Rounder eventually released the album in England, where my old friend Andrew Wickham heard it. I hadn't heard anything about Andy really since the Blue Velvet Band days when he introduced me to Joe Smith. Miraculously, Andy was still with the company, working for Warner Brothers in London. Iris's music was just what Andy thought country music should be. He loved it and wasted no time in calling Lenny Waronker, now head of A & R at Warner Brothers in Los Angeles and urged him to sign Iris. As it happened, she was booked to play at the Ash Grove in Santa Monica, so Lenny made a point to go hear her. When he got there, he was surprised to find Peter Asher, manager of Linda Ronstadt and James Taylor, there as well. The word about Iris was definitely spreading. The upshot of it all was that Lenny made a successful offer to Rounder to buy out Iris's contract for *Infamous Angel* and signed her to Warner Brothers, and Peter Asher became her manager. Iris was now going to be able to reach a much wider audience with her music.

That is one of the points of the exercise—to get your music out to lots of people, and people were definitely responding. More than one person told me that they had first heard Iris while driving in their car and had to pull over because they were so moved. Carol and I went to see her do a solo, sold-out concert at Sanders Theater at Harvard. At the end the audience was on their feet. Andy Wickham had come over from London. It was a triumph. However, all of this success was not without its down side. Iris had never felt totally comfortable performing. She had also recently married a retired captain in the Kansas City Fire Department, Elmer McCall. Show business was not a life he had envisioned for himself. Suddenly they both had to deal with all of the demands of a successful performing career—press and radio interviews, sound checks, hotels, airports, lots of travel. And then you had to go out on a stage by yourself and perform. The response of the people would always make it worthwhile in the end, but there was no denying the pressure that went with success.

I'd say that both of us were feeling some of that pressure when we went to record Iris's second album. Working for Warner Brothers was not like working for Rounder. There were contracts and budgets to be worked out. We had more money to spend, but that could be a mixed blessing if you were worried about trying to please other people. Despite having gotten so busy, Iris had a good bunch of new songs. She wrote me a detailed letter going over what she thought we should do with each one. Some were similar to the ones on *Infamous Angel* but others she called "Departure" songs, which she wanted done in a different way. Reading the letter, I got the feeling that Iris might be trying too hard to prescribe in advance what would happen with each song. That went against my inclination to let the musicians participate in finding out where a song lived. We had basically recorded *Infamous Angel* in three days. It was over almost before Iris got a chance to think about it. I think that was still my mindset when we started the second one. The first day went smoothly enough. I had the old crew back together, and we recorded an old Carter Family song, "Troublesome Waters," Lefty Frizzell's "Mom and Dad's Waltz," and a new "traditional" song of Iris's, "The Shores of Jordan." When we started in on the second day, Iris came back to me in the control room. She was upset. We were doing one of the "Departure" songs with the same players, but it wasn't working for her. I suggested that we take a walk and talk about it. I told the guys to take a break, and we went outside. What was wrong was that I really hadn't paid close enough attention to what she was saying in her letter. I needed to listen to Iris and not get in a big hurry (as Jack Clement would say). We decided to send everyone home that day and make some plans.

I had had it in mind that Richard Bennett's guitar style might be suited to some of the "Departure" songs, so he and Roy Huskey came over to rehearse with Iris. We wound up recording three songs, "You've Done Nothing Wrong," "Easy's Gettin' Harder," and "No Time to Cry" with just the two of them, adding keyboard or accordion later. I then put together a larger group, including Jack Clement on acoustic rhythm guitar, Charles Cochran on piano, and Kenny Malone on percussion, along with Stuart and Roy. This group had a slightly beefier, more rhythmic approach, which worked with "Sweet Is the Melody," "Calling for You," and "Childhood Memories." Finally, for "My Life" it had to be Iris playing piano herself with a beautiful cello accompaniment played by John Catchings. Once I started to listen and we really worked together, we got to that place Iris had imagined.

Second albums are always a test, because usually an artist has songs stored up for the first one and can sometimes have a hard time coming up with songs that are as strong for the second. Not so in Iris's case. If anything, she was digging deeper into the mystery of her music this time. She sang about it in "Sweet Is the Melody":

> Sweet is the melody, so hard to come by
> It's hard to make every note bend just right
> You lay down the hours and leave not one trace
> But a tune for the dancing is there in its place

She also sang about the difficulties of her new life as a working performer:

> My father died a year ago today
> The rooster started crowin' when they carried Dad away

There beside my mother, in the living room I stood
With my brothers and my sisters knowin' Dad was gone for good
Well, I stayed at home just long enough to lay him in the ground
And then I caught a plane to do a show up north in Detroit town
Because I'm older now and I've got no time to cry.

With "My Life" Iris grew into herself. If, even as she said, "easy's gettin' harder every day," she was determined as ever in her faith:

I'm gonna let my feet go dancin' to my very favorite songs
'Cause I know my time for leaving is bound to come before too long
And there ain't no way of knowin' how tomorrow's gonna be
So I'll just dance the shores of Jordan till the angels carry me.

All of Iris's hard work and determination was rewarded when *My Life* received a Grammy nomination.

Like Iris, Hal Ketchum faced the challenge of making his second album. Encouraged by the success of *Past the Point of Rescue*, we set our minds on finding just the right mix of songs. Hal was in a good place. He and Terrell were married and had bought a little fishing cabin out of town near the Caney Fork River. One day he came in and played us a new song, "Sure Love," which he had written with Gary Burr:

I would chase old ghosts and watch them scatter
Drop old dreams and watch them shatter
Lose myself and all I own
To find sure love

We were on our way. Hal also came in with a great radio rocker that he'd written with Ronny Scaife, "Hearts Are Gonna Roll." Like the first album, this one was a collaborative effort involving the Forerunner family. Pete Wasner and Charles John Quarto contributed "Mama Knows the Highway," an amazing "road" song about a female trucker (Large Marge?) and the atmospheric "Ghost Town." "Softer than a Whisper" was a lovely, soft ballad by Pat Alger and Austin Cunningham. Dave Mallett and Hal wrote the poignant "Daddy's Oldsmobile" about a child's view of a family living in their car. "Trail of Tears" was an older song by a new Foreunner writer, Randy Handley, about one of the saddest stories in America's history. It seemed appropriate to follow that with one of Hal's earlier songs,

"Someplace Far Away," about a man following the dream of the wagon trains traveling west:

> And the dream that makes a sparrow fly can make an eagle fall
> One that makes a rich man money, it ain't no dream at all
> It's a cryin' shame to wake up just to find it's all been broke in two
> Careful what you're dreamin' cause it someday may come true.

When we were through we were confident that we had songs for radio and songs that revealed Hal as an artist and a first-class writer.

The success of "Past the Point of Rescue" and "Sure Love" was rewarded in early 1994 when Hal was inducted into the Grand Ole Opry. It was a big moment for all of us. I never imagined in my wildest dreams that I would have a part to play in someone making it to the Opry. It was a big moment for Hal as well. He had started out in the small town of Greenwich (not to be confused with Greenwich Village!) in rural upstate New York. He had as "country" an upbringing as anyone: hunting, trapping, fishing, and making a living as a carpenter. He started playing in a little rock-and-roll trio in high school and would feel most comfortable with that configuration his whole performing career. Life was not easy, and Hal didn't take life easy. His mother was ill for many years with multiple sclerosis, eventually dying from it, and Hal and his dad didn't always see eye to eye. He eventually made his way to Texas to follow his musical star, which led him to Jerry Jeff and ultimately to me. Now, here we all were, our Forerunner family, and, best of all, Hal's dad, sharing this moment with him, as he went out on that Opry stage and sang "The Wings of a Dove" with the great Ferlin Huskey.

OUT WEST

Pat Alger had gotten to know Ian Tyson and went out to his ranch in Alberta to write with him. He had left the music scene for a while after he and Sylvia broke up and had become involved in raising cutting horses at a championship level. When he came back to music, it was through his life as a cowboy. The first album he came out with in this new incarnation was the brilliant *Cowboyography*. When Pat was out visiting Ian he mentioned that he was involved with me as a publisher and producer and suggested that Ian get in touch with me if he ever wanted to record in Nashville.

When we started working together, I was impressed by Ian's focus and commitment. Here he was thirty-five years into it, in wonderful voice, still writing songs of the highest quality. He was a man who did not believe in taking shortcuts. He took pride in his work and approached it as would a fine craftsman. Taken all together, the songs told the story of the cowboy life in all its glory, in all its heartbreak, in all its tough determination and pride. When we were through, Ian invited me to the annual Cowboy Poetry Gathering held each year in Elko, Nevada. Don Edwards would be there, as well as a poet named Paul Zarzyski, whose poem had been the basis of "Rodeo Road," one of the songs we had recorded about a rodeo cowboy at the end of his road.

Carol had actually been to the very first Cowboy Poetry Gathering back in the mideighties when she was researching material for a "Cowboy Revels," so she needed no persuasion to join me. Her son Matthew was about seventeen and had been writing poetry, so we decided to take him with us as well. During the daytime, Carol took a Native American cooking workshop, and Matthew signed up to take a poetry workshop with Paul Zarzyski. I decided to take a "gambling workshop" and went up to the casino at the Red Lion Inn, got a $10 roll of quarters and sat down in front of a machine. I was about $8 in when a big pile of coins tumbled out—about $250 worth! After I spent my next $10, I decided that that was all the luck I was going to have that day and left. The motel bill was paid. I was a pretty lucky cowboy.

Matthew had really enjoyed his workshop with Paul Zarzyski, so we went to a reading Paul was doing that afternoon. Paul was from the Iron Range country in Wisconsin, a volatile mix of Polish and Italian, a bronc rider on the rodeo circuit for fifteen years. I came away from this session feeling like I had just witnessed someone special. His energy was undeniable. Later in the weekend Don Edwards gave a concert. I had only heard him yodel when he came to do the Camp Cookie part on "Night Rider's Lament." Now I heard his voice, an absolutely beautiful warm baritone, reminiscent at times of Elton Britt, at times of Marty Robbins. After his concert, Don asked me if I'd be interested in working with him on an album. Having been drawn into this world by Ian, I felt myself wanting to get further in. It was a new reality for me to explore, where music, words, and dance were an integral part of the fabric of life, just as they were in Appalachia and Louisiana.

Don lost no time in following up and wrote me a detailed letter about his vision for the album. I suggested that if he felt more at home recording in Texas that would be fine with me. I also said I'd leave it up to him to pick the musicians. He knew just the guys, starting with Rich O'Brien, an excellent western style guitar player who I had heard and met at Elko. I visited Don on his small ranch out in Weathersfield, west of Fort Worth. The house was full of all sorts of western musical memorabilia, and it was clear that he was a thorough scholar of the music. He wanted his album to be a true reflection of its depth and breadth, ranging from old poems set to music like "The Habit" or "Bad Half Hour /Annie Laurie"; to well-known cowboy songs he'd arranged like "Gypsy Davey" or "Run Along, Little Dogies"; to country and swing songs by Fred Rose, Cindy Walker, Marty Robbins, and Stuart Hamblen; to the contemporary "Freedom Song" by Andy Wilkinson. Don was proud of this music and gave it the respect, care, and love it deserved.

Before we started recording, Don took me into Fort Worth to visit his old stomping grounds around the old stockyards and especially the White Elephant Saloon. While we were talking about our musical wanderings over a beer, we couldn't believe how close we had come to running into each other back in Boston in the fifties. For a time Don's dad was working in the area. They lived in Milton, just a few miles from Dedham. Like me, Don was dreaming of another life. I wanted to be Hank Williams; he wanted to be Tom Mix, Roy Rogers, Gene Autry—or all three! He had actually worked with Elton Britt and with Herb Hooven, who had played on "Livin' on the Mountain." Ultimately, Don got himself to Fort Worth, soaking up the music while he worked driving trucks for the oil riggers. Now here we both were, brought together as a result of Nanci getting him to come sing on the "Night Rider's Lament." It was meant to be.

Don and I were together in our thinking about what we wanted to do, but, with the exception of Rich, I hadn't met any of the musicians, so I was a bit nervous. Don very graciously made a point of introducing me, telling them about my work with Nanci, and making it clear that I was his choice to run things. Bob Boatright and Snuffy Elmore had both played fiddle with the Texas Playboys. Mark Abbott was a heavy equipment operator who was as solid as his bass fiddle. The one fellow who really caught my eye was the steel player, Tom Morrell. He played a steel guitar (what they used to call "the old ironing board"), not a pedal steel. The instrument had lots of battle scars and a built-in ashtray. Nobody had to tell me that this was an old-fashioned, no-nonsense guy. If I couldn't cut it with him, I was going to have a hard time. Once we started to work, it became clear that I wasn't the type of producer to tell everyone what to play and that I was happy to let them get to a place with a song where Don could really sing it and relax. In a very short time, we established a good working rhythm and came out of the day with five songs under our belt. It was a scorcher outside, easily over 100 degrees, so a frosty, cold beer seemed like a good idea. Tom Morrell beat me to the punch and bought me the first one. It was the start of a good friendship with the man they liked to call "Wolf."

At the end of our three days, we had 12 tracks and twelve fantastic live vocals by Don. We got Peter Rowan and Tim and Mollie O'Brien to sing some harmonies, as did Stephanie Davis and the western harmony experts in Nashville, Dennis Wilson and Curtis Young. Waddie Mitchell did an emotional recitation on Cindy Walker's classic "Jim, I Wore a Tie." Joey "The Cowpolka King" Miskulin played on that and on Don's own tribute to Tom Mix, *West of Yesterday*. Mark Miller mixed the album, taking full advantage of the echo chamber at Jack's Tracks. Don's voice was as rich and supple as well-worn leather. Many months later I got a call from Don. He was excited. "We've won The Wrangler Award!" I said, "That's great! What's the Wrangler Award?" There was a bit of a pause, as Don came to terms with my ignorance. The Wrangler Award, as it turned out, was the highest award given out each year by the Cowboy Hall of Fame in Oklahoma City for achievement in western arts and culture. I was now being led by Don still further into the world of the West.

CHANGING TIMES

Led by the phenomenal success of Garth Brooks, all album sales were well above what they had been just a few years earlier when we had started. In addition to Matt Lindsey, we added another, equally enthusiastic and committed song plugger to our ranks, Leslie Barr. There was more than enough work for two people to keep up with all of the songs in our growing catalogue. However, it seemed that the pitching process itself was getting harder. More and more there were a lot of middlemen coming into the process. Some producers hired assistants to listen to songs. Then there might be the assistant to the A & R person, before you got to the A & R person. Sometimes we'd connect directly with an artist or producer and they would actually record the song. Then some marketing person would jump in and say, "No! No! No! That's not the kind of song we can sell," and that would be that. It was a far cry from the days of Chet Atkins, Jack Clement, or Owen Bradley when it was a fairly straight shot from the writer and publisher to the producer and the artist. They'd either say, "No," or they'd cut it and put it out. If people bought it, fine; if they didn't, they'd try something else. Now, we often felt like songs were being sent off to limbo. It could be frustrating, but we had to believe that quality would have to be our hallmark, and we'd stick to our guns.

Two more writers joined us at this time, Herb McCullough and Shawn Camp. Herb had been a friend of mine since I first came to Nashville. We met at the Kountry Korner at the time when Judy was living in the basement. He was as quiet and soft-spoken as some of the other denizens of the place were blustery and loud. We called him "Herbal." Over the years we would run into each other. He'd had some writing deals and had cuts by artists like John Anderson, Mark Chestnut, and Diamond Rio. He'd been keeping his eye on us and the way we were operating and came to me and said he wanted to write with us just because he liked us. He wouldn't take an advance; he'd just take his chances.

Herb had befriended a very talented young country artist and writer named Shawn Camp. Shawn was from Arkansas. He could play fiddle, mandolin, and guitar, as well as sing. He was also a fine writer. Shawn had had a record deal with Sony and had some luck with a song called "Fallin' Never Felt So Good," but marketing people at the label started wanting Shawn to work more on his image than his music. It all went down the drain when the label decided not to release his second album, and Shawn understandably got very frustrated and discouraged. Herb had been trying to help him and started bringing him over to Jack's Tracks to write with him. We all liked Shawn and were happy to see him whenever he came around. Eventually Allen and I sat down with him and formally invited him to join Forerunner. He was so gun-shy at this point; he didn't trust anybody. I could see it in his eyes, but our offer stood, and eventually he came with us. He had found a home.

About the same time that Herb and Shawn were coming, Pat Alger and I started working on an album. Our good friend Renée Bell was now at Liberty Records and had conceived of a songwriter series. Pat was first on her list. We had done two albums previously for Sugar Hill Records. Like them, this album demonstrated Pat's skills not only as a writer, but also as a singer and guitarist. We cut some of Pat's better known songs like "That Summer" (Garth Brooks), "Like We Never Had a Broken Heart" (Trisha Yearwood), "Somebody's Love" (Hal Ketchum), and "I'm Taking My Time" (Brenda Lee). We also cut other songs, just as good, that we wanted to bring into the light of day. Songwriting was much more to Pat than just writing "hits." He wanted to reach people's hearts. He had the ability to craft words and music which expressed the full range of our emotions. He could call up every mother's worry:

Fifteen going on twenty
I knew all there was to know
I could start a Ford without the keys
I loved to wind 'em up and watch 'em go

He could laugh about the mistakes in love that we make over and over:

You'd get down on your knees
And you would beg me please
And I would take you back just like that
And I would leave the door open wide
Once again for you
It was an open invitation to the blues

He could take us outside ourselves to look at the bigger picture:

And you can read it in the news
On any city street
People go to sleep each night
With not enough to eat
And if we took a little less
And gave a little more
Someday we might forget

Chorus: We've heard it all before
We've heard it all before
Like the beating of a drum
If we open up the door
Someday peace will come
We must find a way
To make a flower from a sword
Then we'll never have to say
We've heard it all before

This is what made me proud to be a publisher and a producer. I was in a position to help bring this quality of art into people's lives. Working with Pat gave me the certainty that this was work worth doing.

However, like many great artists, Pat was never totally satisfied. There was no doubt in his mind about the success of our partnership or the depth of our friendship. He just had the notion that there might be more to achieve elsewhere. He had become very involved in the Nashville Songwriter's Association, in NARAS, and in the Country Music Association. In the process he had a better understanding of the truly global nature of the music business. We were a small independent company almost entirely focused on Nashville. Pat had been talking to David Conrad at Almo/Irving, which also had offices in Los Angeles, New York, and London. It looked like a step up to Pat, and he decided to take it. We had just finished mixing the album when he told me. Naturally, I was not thrilled to hear the news, but if that's what he thought was best for him and what he wanted to do, what point was there in me arguing with him? He'd played a major role in our success, and we had no complaints. As it turned out, his years at Forerunner were his most successful years—bigger wasn't necessarily better—and his work with us eventually led him to be inducted into the Nashville Songwriters Hall of Fame.

Since I'd been making my life up now for about thirty years, you'd think I'd be used to change, but it could still get you in the gut, as it had with Pat. I was about to get another blow—this time from Iris. Sometime in 1994 Tom Russell and Dave Alvin came up with the idea of an alternative singer/songwriter tribute to Merle Haggard to be called *Tulare Dust* and asked Iris if she'd do a song for it. She asked me what I thought, and I was all for it. She settled on "Big City." I had Merle's album, but I purposely

FIGURE 28. Pat Alger and Jim Rooney enjoying a brew.

didn't listen to it, because I didn't want to get intimidated by it. We didn't have a big budget—only $500—so Barry Tashian, Roy Huskey, Iris, and I sat in a circle at Jack's Tracks and recorded it in about fifteen minutes.

A few months later the album came out. Iris was home in Kansas City one night when the phone rang. She answered it and the voice at the other end said, "Iris?" She answered, "Yes." "Do you know who this is?" "No." "This is Merle Haggard," and Merle then told her how hearing her sing "Big City" had restored his faith in country music. He went on in that vein for about half an hour! The upshot of it all was that he had invited her to sit in with him when they came to Kansas City and they became friends. Later in May a concert was set at the Fillmore West in San Francisco to celebrate *Tulare Dust*. They invited Haggard, and he asked if Iris was going to be there. They assured him that she would, so he agreed to come and to bring his band The Strangers as well. I had to go to this. On the night, Iris got up and sang with Haggard and The Strangers backing her. She sang "Big City" and the Jimmie Rodgers song "Hobo Bill's Last Ride." She was so relaxed up there. She looked like she'd been singing with the band for years. And this was someone who could only play by herself when we first met!

Afterward, I had an idea. Iris had seemed so comfortable with his band that I wondered if it might be something for her to record with them. She thought about it and asked Merle. He said that she'd be welcome to come up to his place near Redding any time. I was delighted. I asked Bobby Wood, who had played piano some with Haggard (as well as Garth Brooks, Elvis, and everyone in between) if he'd go out there with me. I thought it might be a good idea to have someone I knew in the band.

Haggard had a compound up near Lake Shasta. He had his house there as well as a studio with living quarters for The Strangers. The band was on call, ready to go any time Merle was—24 hours a day. Lou Bradley, who had worked at Columbia in Nashville, was the resident engineer. I figured we'd try three or four songs, starting with "Hobo Bill's Last Ride," since they'd already played it together. It was a special treat to listen to Norman Hamlet on dobro and steel. He'd played on every Merle Haggard record I had. Iris sang a Haggard song I didn't know, "Here in Frisco." We then tried a couple of her new ones, "This Kind of Happy" and "Walking Home," which I especially liked, although it was late in the day and I wasn't sure we had totally figured it out. However, I was happy. I had looked on this as sort of a test drilling to see how it would go. I knew we had a great cut of "Hobo Bill's Last Ride" and good solid cuts on two of the other three. It had been a good day. About two weeks later I was up in Vermont helping Carol get ready for a Connecticut Riverfest that she was putting on. The phone rang. It was Iris. "Jim? This is Iris. Jim, I don't think we should continue working together." The wind went out of me. She'd called as I was literally walking out the door. What could I say? I said, "Iris, if that's what you want, it's alright with me. It's up to you." Carol asked me who had called. I said, "Iris. She fired me." Carol started to say something, but I headed her off. "She's the artist. It's up to her. She'll figure it out. Let's go."

PART IV
THE LONG
RUN

A NEW LIFE

Since our amazing trip to Louisiana, Carol and I had been doing our best to weave our lives together. When I came into the picture Sarah was nineteen, living in Boston, and getting ready to go to Indiana University to study recorder and early music. Matthew was fifteen and Sonya was thirteen. They were in the local schools and lived part of the time at Carol's and part of the time at their dad's. Carol and her former husband Peter had been divorced for about five years and she had had two or three relationships during that time, so it was no surprise that my arrival was not greeted with any great enthusiasm by the kids. As I have often said about the time Sonya first laid eyes on me, "If looks could kill, I'd be dead." I had my work cut out for me. If I couldn't gain the acceptance of these three people, Carol and I would have to respect that. All I could do would be to get to know them, help them if I could, and have them accept me for who I was. It would have to come naturally over time.

This was a big change for me. I'd been getting used to the idea that I might be a bachelor like Uncle Jim or Bob Webster. I'd given up chasing the girls (pretty much). Instead, there were annual trips to Spring training in Florida with Webster, Pat Alger, and whoever else showed up; trips to Keeneland, Churchill Downs, and Ellis Park to watch the horses run; baseball junkets to Chicago, St. Louis, Cincinnati, Milwaukee (for Nolan Ryan's 300th win), the Baseball Hall of Fame in Cooperstown (the year Johnny Bench, Carl Yastrzemski, and Harry Caray were inducted). I could do as I pleased. Come and go when I wanted. So why would I want to change all this and complicate my life at this late date? Because I knew instinctively, down deep inside, that it would be worth it. It would require me to think about people other than myself. It would stretch me. It would challenge me. It would make me grow.

Going with Carol meant quite a change in lifestyle. I'd been an apartment dweller for fifteen years. Carol lived in a 200-year-old farmhouse with woodstoves for cooking and heating. The wood had to be stacked and split. She had a big vegetable garden, which had to be dug, weeded, and watered. In the summer she lived in a tepee out by her pond. It was all very picturesque, but it was a lot of change to deal with. As time went by, though, we began to work things out between us. There was another me still alive under the "bachelor" me. There was the kid who helped his dad saw down big trees with a two-man crosscut saw and then bucksawed the branches into firewood. There was the kid who'd worked on the farm picking berries in the summer. There was the kid who oiled the porch and painted all the trim on the house in Green Harbor. There was the young man who bought the *Whole Earth Catalogue* when he moved to Woodstock, and, with his wife Sheila, planted a vegetable garden and transformed their cottage in the three years they lived in it. Gradually, this other "Jim" began to surface. He didn't like to exercise, but he liked to work. He liked the Zen of digging the garden row by row or stacking wood piece by piece. Carol made some adjustments too. When I explained that I was too tall to hunker down and sit cross-legged all the time and that the smoke and mosquitoes and dampness in the tepee were too much for me, we settled on an L. L. Bean tent with air mattresses. We built an outdoor pantry and stone circle campfire with a round iron grill on it. I could get up in the morning, start a fire, cook breakfast and later on take a swim in the pond. I was living a new life.

One way I had to connect with Sonya and Matthew was through the music I was bringing into their lives. Right away, Sonya loved Iris DeMent. I had brought up a cassette of *Infamous Angel* before it came out, and

Sonya and Carol nearly wore it out playing it in the car every time they went to town. Matthew loved Robert Earl Keen's *West Textures* album. He had a beat-up old pickup truck and was just breaking into the Strafford Volunteer Fire Department, and Robert Earl's music spoke to him. They already knew about Nanci. Carol had heard "Once in a Very Blue Moon" and "Goin' Gone" on a local folk radio show long before she knew I had anything to do with them. Eventually, Carol brought the kids to Nashville and they got to meet Iris, Nanci, John Prine, Pat Alger, and Hal Ketchum. At one of my many "50th" birthday parties, Sonya and Matthew showed off their swing dancing skills, Matthew recited a poem, Sarah played a recorder/gamba piece with her friend Tim Merton, and Carol sang one of Jean Ritchie's songs. I felt that they were happy to come into my world. My friends were also happy to see the new me—the family man.

It wasn't all roses. Once or twice I bumped heads with Matthew when I'd get between him and Carol. I lost it with Sonya and one of her friends one day when they were acting up and I told them to "shut the fuck up." I had to apologize, which I did right away, but I heard about it from Sarah, who was going to protect her little sister. Carol would call me out when I dominated the conversation too much or would get pissed off and "bully" her. I was used to having my own way and to running things the way I wanted to run them. If I wanted this to work, I'd have to learn to listen more and to communicate better. I hadn't been ready to do that with Sheila. I was ready now.

I wanted this new life. I wanted Carol and me to become true partners. I wanted it so much that I jumped the gun. Carol and I were visiting my sister Eileen in Cincinnati and were in a place up on the Ohio River. I was feeling romantic and got a couple of roses for Carol and me. We dropped them into the river and as we watched them float down together I asked Carol to marry me. Naturally, she was surprised, but she was romantic too, and I think she was happy that I felt that way. Not content to let matters take their course, I wrote the kids and asked what they thought about this idea of mine. The silence was deafening. I knew without asking that we had a lot further to go before that happened.

A couple of years later around Labor Day Carol asked me to take a walk with her to a special place she wanted to show me. We walked up the road past her neighbors and up into the woods on a long out-of-use road. Eventually we came up on a large fenced off area that enclosed a commercial deer ranch. Carol asked me how I felt about climbing over the fence. It was about eight feet high, but it looked climbable, so I said, "Sure." I managed to make it, and we continued on.

We came to a knoll with a beautiful view of the surrounding hills, but the most arresting feature of the place was a large, white, rounded quartz rock jutting out of the ground like a giant egg. This is what Carol brought me to see. I exclaimed about its size and whiteness, and she took my hand and asked if I would join her in some "hocus pocus." I said that I would. We knelt on either side of this rock—a rock formed millions of years ago in unbelievable heat and pressure, subsequently emerging from the earth in this particular place, containing within it all of that vast and ancient energy. Carol extended her arms with one palm up, one palm down. I reached across the rock and joined my palms with hers, one up, one down. We stayed like that for some moments, our eyes closed, absorbing the energy of that place. We then opened our eyes, and she said to me,

"I feel worthy of our relationship.
I feel a deep commitment to us.
I am ready."

Then I said it too, and that was it. We embraced and kissed, and I said to Carol, "I think we just married ourselves!" And, indeed, we had. We were laughing and crying as we went back down. I might have flown over the fence. I have no memory of it. All I know is that I was filled with a joy the likes of which I had never experienced before. One reason for that was that I was sure that this time Sarah, Matthew, and Sonya would be happy that we had made this commitment to each other, because it meant that my commitment to them was permanent. We had come to the point where we truly loved one another.

We barely had time to let this all sink in, because I was supposed to go to Ireland in three weeks to record some songs with Nanci Griffith for an *Other Voices, Too* album we had started work on. I decided that this would be a perfect opportunity for us to take a honeymoon. Carol was in a bit of a happy daze and instantly agreed, so over we went. After a night in Dublin, where it had all started five years earlier, we headed off to Cork, at the suggestion of Phillip King, a true Cork man. There we met up with Mick Daly and The Lee Valley String Band; I'd heard them on the "Bringing It All Back Home" CD. Mick invited me to sit in with them at their weekly session in the Corner House. They played a mixture of old-timey, bluegrass, and country songs and reminded me in some ways of the Charles River Valley Boys. The session was well lubricated with endless pints of Murphy's stout. I'd only been in Cork a few hours, and I already liked it. After a day spent walking around the city, we headed down to Baltimore in West Cork. We were off on our own, having a private time together, walking on the isolated beaches of Sherkin Island, still taking in the meaning of our "married" state.

Back in Dublin, we met up with Nanci, Phillip Donnelly's new wife Jessica, Pat McInerney, and James Hooker. Nanci immediately ordered champagne, so that was the first of several celebrations of our wedding. After we got back from Dublin my sister Eileen, my sister Kathleen and her partner Doug, my brother John and his wife Ulli, and cousin Bill Driscoll and his wife Kathy all joined us to offer their support and congratulations. John gave us a wonderful drawing of us "climbing the fence" to commemorate our achievement. Just before Christmas we had a big party at the house for all of Carol's family, friends, and neighbors. What especially pleased me was the way Sarah, Matthew, and Sonya joined in helping to make it their party. They all pitched in to make the house look beautiful and to make sure there was lots of great food. Sarah played her recorder. Carol's dad, Jack Langstaff, led us all in singing. Then at some point Carol and I said, "We're all going outside!" and we grabbed hands and led everyone out to the side yard where we formed a big circle. Carol and I stepped to the center of the circle. We stretched out our arms and laid our palms on each other's and repeated what we had said over the big quartz egg back in September. Sonya then handed us wedding rings we'd had made in Ireland and we placed them on each other's finger. Everyone cheered. We'd done it in public this time, with them as witnesses, giving us all their love and support. We could feel it flowing into us. After the New Year we went to Nashville and did it one last time for all of the friends I had made there in the course of the past twenty years. We were now well and truly married for all the world to see. Our new life together had begun.

BLUEGRASS AND
FOLK VOICES

On September 9, 1996, just after I had returned to Nashville from our "wedding at the rock," Bill Monroe left this world. He had been incapacitated by a stroke a few months earlier and had been living in a nursing home in Springfield, Tennessee. Two or three weeks before he died, I went out to pay him a visit. Over the course of the past few years Bill had had a series of health problems. I had seen him when he looked weak and barely able to get to the stage, but once on stage, he would come to life and be dancing at the end of his set to "Uncle Pen" and do endless encores to "Swing Low, Sweet Chariot." Now, however, he was in a wheelchair and unable to speak. Still, his eyes had the same intensity as he took my hand in his. There was no point in trying to make small talk, so I took out my guitar and sang him some songs I knew he would like—Bill Monroe songs. Two or three of the nurses and a couple of other patients came around. Bill was smiling and moving his hand in time to the music. That time never left him. When I saw him next he was lying in state at the Ryman Auditorium as thousands passed by to pay him their last respects. When we sang "Swing Low" that day we knew he was where he wanted to be.

Back in 1985 I had worked with Peter Rowan on an album of all Bill Monroe songs called *First Whippoorwill*. It was what I like to call a "hardcore Bluegrass" album, featuring former Bluegrass Boys Bill Keith, Buddy Spicher, and Richard Greene. Earlier this spring I had worked with Peter on another hard-core album, which he called *Bluegrass Boy*. Although the songs were all new and written by Peter, he was definitely channeling Bill Monroe's style and energy in his writing, singing, and playing.

He covered the whole range of Monroe songs starting out with a good up-tempo number called "Nighttime," followed by the lonesome-sounding "Wild Geese Fly Again." "A Jealous Heart and a Worried Mind" could have come out of the Monroe/Jimmy Martin period, while the racy "Stable Boy Blues" was out of the early Bluegrass period with Clyde Moody. There can be no doubt that Bill drew great strength from working the land. He had talked to Peter about the concept of letting the harvest go to seed to provide sustenance through the winter for the birds and "little critters." Peter asked Del McCoury, one of the greatest singers to ever work with Monroe, to join him in singing "Let the Harvest Go to Seed":

Oh I feel like that old mountain
Standing lonesome in the sky
Where the cries of the wolf
Hungry wind's mournful sigh
High above our little cabin
Lay my bones there to rest
Where the wild birds and critters
Still make their little nest
You have been my true companion
Since the day our love was young
Darling, stand beside me
And watch the setting sun
If I die before you do
One request I ask you please
Pray Jesus take my soul
Let the harvest go to seed

Peter chose to close the album with the title song, a lullaby, "Bluegrass Boy." When we started making this album, Bill hadn't had his stroke, but his health was failing and the chances of his making a comeback were slim—although, tough as he was, none of us would have been totally surprised if he had. *Bluegrass Boy* was a chance for us to quietly and gently let Bill go. The sound of Richard's droning fiddle and Peter's sweet, trilling mandolin created a hypnotic setting for the lyrics:

Hushabye my bluegrass boy
Put away your little toys
All the stars in the heavens we will count them
Hush the fiddle, hush the bow
Mandolin, guitar, banjo
All is sleepy from the schoolhouse to the mountain
Hushabye now don't you cry
While I sing this lullaby
All is peaceful now where darkness spreads her mantle

Stars are blinking one by one
Now your busy day is done
Close your eyes in the light of this candle
Soon the night will pass away
And the dawning of the day
Will awaken you with joy my bluegrass boy
And the birdies on the wing
Melodies upon the wind
Will be songs for you to sing, my bluegrass boy
Hushabye . . . Hushabye . . . my bluegrass boy

With that, the band came in playing the melody as a beautiful, fading bluegrass waltz, the kind Bill Monroe loved best.

Since I had first seen Bill in person at Watermelon Park in 1960 and met him at "The Bluegrass Home" in Nashville in 1963, he had played an important part in shaping my approach to music and to living. Music for

FIGURE 29. Bill Monroe cradling his mandolin.
Photograph: © McGuire.

Bill was an essential part of life and enabled him to deal with whatever it might bring him. Peter Rowan's genius lies in his ability to absorb different kinds of music and make them his own, but I believe the music that affected him most deeply was the music of Bill Monroe. In the making of this album Peter and I were able to acknowledge Bill's tremendous influence on us and to let him know that we would be following his wish to "let the harvest go to seed" in order to create new music and new songs from the old traditions.

Bill and Bonnie Hearne are prime examples of artists who are continually reinterpreting and refreshing the song tradition. In the late sixties and early seventies Bill and Bonnie were an important part of the developing folk scene in Austin. In those years they were very supportive and helpful to younger performers like Nanci, Lyle Lovett, and Tish Hinojosa. Nanci had introduced me to Bill and Bonnie in the fall of '95 when they played at the Bluebird Café, and several months later they asked me to help them make an album. When I listened to the records and tapes that Bill and Bonnie had been doing on a shoestring over the years, I was continually struck by the quality of the songs they chose to sing. What their recordings lacked in polish or technical finesse, they more than made up for in content and emotional truth. In April, I finally got to visit Bill and Bonnie where they now lived in Santa Fe. At their gig at the La Fonda Hotel, people were on their feet dancing from the first note to the last. Their music obviously moved these people, and the songs had entered their lives.

After listening and talking for three days we came up with a long list of songs to consider and started to reach out to their many friends in the musical community to help make this project a celebration of their twenty-five years of making music together. We decided to start out back in Austin, where it all began, and there was no problem getting people to join us. The generosity and kindness Bill and Bonnie had extended to so many was not forgotten. Jerry Jeff joined us, as did Christine Albert and Tish Hinojosa. The solid pedal steel guitar player Lloyd Maines headed up the band, which included Paul Pearcy on drums, Spencer Starnes on bass, and Bill and Bonnie's good friend, songwriter John Egenes on mandolin. I loved the feel we got on the tracks we recorded there at Cedar Creek Recording. Bill and Jerry Jeff's singing on "Muley Brown," John Egenes's song about an old bronc rider, perfectly captured the Austin sound, which Jerry Jeff had helped to put on the musical map. Bonnie's own "Bluebonnet Girl" combined a polka with a beautiful evocation of the Texas hill country. Bill and Bonnie joined their harmonies with Lloyd's singing steel on Ian Tyson's little known but beautiful "Wild Geese."

In Nashville Nanci herself joined Bonnie on "Georgetown," a song by Gerry Spehar that she used to sing when she lived back in Austin. Then Bill and Nanci did her song "Going Back to Georgia." Bill's vocal is totally believable as he sings:

> I been blinded by the sun, washed in the rain
> Scattered in America, I'm scatterin' again
> But if you're goin' south darlin
> I guess I'm travellin' with you

That was their gift. Bill and Bonnie could make you believe that they lived every song that they sang. When Bonnie sang the chorus of Eliza Gilkyson's "Rose of Sharon," you knew that she was that woman who was in total rapture:

> Rise up, my love, and come away
> The rain is over and gone
> Your love is the fruit of my darkest day
> And I am your rose of Sharon

Bill could stand next to Lyle Lovett and split the vocal on Lyle's "Walk through the Bottomland" without giving up any of his own personality. He'd half talk it, half sing it; he'd make it real:

> She never married and she never would
> (you know) all of the people they'd say
> (aw) the New Jersey lady she just ain't no good
> To follow a cowboy that way.

Then Bonnie would join Bill on the chorus with total conviction:

> Sing me a melody, sing me a blues
> Walk through the bottomland without no shoes
> The Brazos she's runnin' scared
> She heard the news
> Walk through the bottomland without no shoes

The joy in Lyle's face as he sang with Bill and Bonnie told the whole story. Bill and Bonnie got many of their songs out of albums. They were careful listeners, and knew what songs spoke to them. Such a song was "Every Drop of Water" by Allen Shamblin and Steve Seskin. When Bill and Bonnie heard it on a Ricky Skaggs album, it jumped out at them:

> Life is kind of like a roller coaster
> Up and down, over and over again
> The way I figure it, it's all grist for the mill
> There's a lesson to learn with every hard spill that we take
> There are no mistakes
> *Chorus:* We're all diamonds in the rough
> But we'll shine soon enough
> It's the struggles in life that make us strong
> It weighs the good times and the bad
> Keep in mind when you're sad
> Those tears of joy and sorrow lead you home
> Every drop of water shapes the stone.

This was their story and they made it their song so much that we called the album *Diamonds in the Rough*." In their singing and playing Bill and Bonnie brought to all of these songs an innate strength, optimism, and determination, which was their gift to all who listened to them, who danced to them. It was their gift to me.

Since the time we recorded *Other Voices, Other Rooms* it seemed that Nanci and I had never stopped exploring the world of folk music, which was such a big influence on both of us. Working with Nanci had directly led me to working with Tom Paxton, Don Edwards, and Bill and Bonnie. There seemed to be no end to it as we plunged into making *Other Voices, Too (a Trip Back to Bountiful)*. We started with a group some people might not have thought of when they thought of "folk music," but Buddy Holly's original band, the Crickets—Sonny Curtis, J. I. Allison and Joe B. Mauldin—who came right out of the West Texas country around Lubbock, are as down to earth and "folky" as they come. Their music went right into Nanci's bloodstream as a young girl, and she wanted them with her as we began our new adventure. They all came over to Jack's Tracks on our first day, and we recorded Sonny's classic hit for The Everlys, "Walk Right Back," and then did Johnny Cash's "I Still Miss Someone" with an

East Texas boy and one-time Cash son-in-law, Rodney Crowell. We closed the day out with a "newer folk," Pat McLaughlin, doing "Try the Love," a song we'd recorded on his first album. It was a circular waltz, which somehow seemed to spring from the same well the Crickets and Johnny Cash were drinking from.

A month or so later we gathered with the Crickets again to record Harlan Howard's "The Streets of Baltimore," with Harlan himself doing the narration. He'd worked in the factories up in Michigan and out in California and knew what he was talking about:

> I got myself a factory job
> I ran an old machine
> We bought a little cottage
> In a neighborhood serene
> But every night when I came home
> With every muscle sore
> She would drag me through the streets of Baltimore

Back when Nanci and I were working together in the mideighties I would hear her talking about Harlan. He had befriended her, and she had become one of his "pals." I was jealous. I wanted to be his pal too. After all, I'd been in love with his songs ever since I bought *Buck Owens Sings Harlan Howard* back in 1961! I just needed to be patient, and eventually I got to sit with Harlan, Nanci, and Harlan's pals during happy hour over at Maude's Courtyard. Once I got in the door, we hit it off. He liked people who had their own voice.

One day he called and asked, "Hey, pal, want to go to a hockey game?" Of course I did. Coming from Michigan, Harlan loved his hockey. His favorite man on the ice was the "enforcer," the man who kept the other team honest, who wouldn't tolerate any bullshit. Under his cheerful, joking exterior, there was a bit of the enforcer in Harlan. He'd come up the hard way, and he was a competitor. He wanted those songs of his to get cut. He wanted hits. He believed in himself and worked hard to get where he had got and was still very much in the game, still wanting more. He had what all great competitors have—desire. Desire to be the best. I would soon find out about that first-hand.

After the game, Harlan invited me back to his house for a drink. "Do you like to play Scrabble, pal?" Sure. Why not? I used to play some with my dad. We both liked words, so this seemed like a great chance to play with a real wordsmith. The game was fun. We were both enjoying ourselves. Showing off a bit. Competing a bit. Getting down to the last letters I pulled a couple of good ones, and things were looking up for me. Then Harlan gave me a great look. "Hate to do this to you, pal." He cleaned his slate with a triple score involving a couple of Qs, Xs, Zs, and who knows what else. He beat me. With a flourish. "Great game, pal. Let's do it again sometime. You almost had me." I walked home that night, laughing all the way. If anyone had told me in 1965 that someday I'd be playing Scrabble with Harlan Howard!!! And almost beat him!!! ALMOST. That old enforcer couldn't allow *that*. Even if I was his "pal."

In September Nanci and I headed back to Dublin to cast our nets into the waters around Ireland and the British Isles. Nanci gathered quite a crew, including Iain Matthews, an early member of Fairport Convention; Brian Willoughby from The Strawbs; and Clive Gregson, for many years with the Richard Thompson Band. Appropriately enough the first song we launched into was Richard Thompson's "Wall of Death":

> You're going nowhere when you ride on the carousel
> And maybe you're strong
> But what's the good of ringing a bell
> The switchback will make you crazy
> Beware of the bearded lady
> Oh let me take my chances on the wall of death

This is the song Nanci chose to lead off the album. I guess it summed up our feelings about taking our chances and taking no prisoners while we were at it. It definitely got us going.

Certainly one of the most moving songs to come out of the entire English folk revival scene was Sandy Denny's "Who Knows Where the Time Goes." Just as "Wall of Death" sings of the necessity of living life to the fullest, this song sings of the inevitability of leaving as part of living. In addition to Iain, Brian, and Clive, Nanci invited Sharon Shannon on button accordion and Nollaig Casey and Mary Custy on fiddles to create a beautiful, floating sonic bed for the song. She was joined in harmony by Dolores Keane. When we listened to the playback, there was not a sound in the control room. We had no doubt that the spirit of Sandy Denny was very much alive:

249

So come the storms of winter
And then the birds in spring again
I have no fear of time
For who knows how my love grows
And who knows where the time goes.

We closed out the Dublin sessions with Stephen Foster's "Hard Times," one of the most popular songs in Ireland because of their memories of their own "hard times" after the Famine of 1847. Phillip Donnelly joined Dolores, Sharon, Nollaig, and Mary for this one. There was no shortage of soul in the room.

From Dublin we flew to New York for a real hootenanny. We chose "He Was a Friend of Mine," which had been popularized by both Dave Van Ronk and Eric Von Schmidt, and Pete Seeger's "If I Had a Hammer." We could have been in Newport in 1963. On "He Was a Friend of Mine," in addition to Dave and Eric, we had Odetta, Jean Ritchie, Rosalie Sorrels, Nina Gerber, Lucy Kaplansky, Julie Gold, Caitlin Von Schmidt, Eric Taylor, Frank Christian, and Tom Russell. For "If I Had a Hammer" we had Odetta, Jean Ritchie, Rosalie Sorrels, Lucy Kaplansky, Nina Gerber, Gillian Welch, Eric Weissberg, Frank Christian, Matthew Ryan, Ted Jones, Jay Joyce, Richard Thompson, Glen Phillips, Eric Taylor, and even me. Pete Seeger had helped most of us get started and kept most of us going. He kept us focused on making life better for everyone. We wanted to sing this for him.

Back in Nashville Nanci's traveling hootenanny continued on without any letup. Tom Rush started us off with "Wasn't That a Mighty Storm." Eric Von Schmidt had passed this song on to Tom when they were both playing at the Club, and Tom had made it a keystone of his performances ever since. Lucinda Williams and Nanci sang Woody Guthrie's "Deportee (Plane Wreck at Los Gatos)" along with Steve Earle, John Stewart, Odetta, and Tish Hinojosa. Guy Clark came in to sing "Desperadoes Waiting for a Train" with Nanci, Jerry Jeff Walker, Steve Earle, Jimmy Dale Gilmore, and Eric Taylor—a Texas hootenanny of its own. Ian Tyson and Tom Russell traded off singing each other's songs with Nanci—Tom sang "Summer Wages" and Ian sang "Canadian Whiskey." Completing the Canadian "hat trick" Nanci, Tom Russell, Susan Cowsill, and Maura Kennedy sang Sylvia Fricker's "You Were on My Mind," one of Ian & Sylvia's classic songs. Not every song had a cast of thousands. Lucinda Williams and Nanci did a beautifully simple version of "Wings of a Dove." Nanci, Lyle Lovett, and Eric Taylor sang a haunting new song by John Grimaudo and Saylor White, "Dress of Laces." Emmylou Harris, Carolyn Hester, and their daughters joined Nanci on Texas songwriter Mickie Merkens's "old-sounding" "Yarrington Town." Both generations blended together in the never-ending continuum of folk music. Finally, though, we came back to Nanci, the solo folk singer, as she was when I first met her, driving her car from Austin to New York to play a coffeehouse. She chose to sing "Darcy Farrow," by Steve Gillette and Tom Campbell—another new "folk song," which captures the tradition of balladry:

> They sing of Darcy Farrow where the Truckee runs through
> They sing of her beauty in Virginia City too
> At dusty sundown to her name they drink a round
> And to young Vandy whose love was true.
> Where the Walker runs down into the Carson Valley plain
> There lived a young maiden Darcy Farrow was her name
> The daughter of old Dundee and a fair one was she
> The sweetest flower that bloomed o'er the range

We were done!

PRINE COUNTRY TIME I

John Prine was a happy man. He had a new woman in his life. Fiona Whelan was working at Windmill Lane Studios in Dublin when John happened by one day. He caught her eye, and when she heard that there was a good chance that he'd be at Bloom's Hotel after The Session show, she made it a point to be there. Her strategy worked. Here it was, several years later, and they were getting married in Nashville. Everything was working for John. Oh Boy! Records was doing great. We had done three albums together, two of which, *German Afternoons* and *John Prine Live*, had been nominated for Grammys. Since then John had won a Grammy for *The Missing Years*, produced by Howie Epstein. All of the albums were selling well and John was selling out all of his shows. A large Irish contingent came over, and the wedding went on for days. Maura O'Connell, Roger Cook, Sandy Mason, and I sang "Only Love" in the church. There wasn't a dry eye in the house.

The wedding was a good chance for Iris and me to get together. I hadn't seen her since we had parted ways, although she had called me once or twice to ask my advice about other producers! Carol and I were happy to see Iris and Elmer again at such a happy occasion. Our love for each other hadn't gone away. John had been having Iris open a lot of his shows. They would usually sing a song or two together, and he came back from one of those tours all excited: "I've got to record some duets with Iris! It's so good when we sing together, I can't stand it!" That was the seed of the album that became *In Spite of Ourselves*. As he thought about it, John decided to do more than just duets with Iris. He made a list of some of his favorite female singers and showed it to me. I added a few of my own. We then started thinking of all our favorite country duet songs and were starting to get excited. However, when we talked to John's manager, Al Bunetta, about it, he wasn't so sure. "John Prine's fans want to hear him sing John Prine songs." John gave Al a look and simply said, "John Prine hasn't got any John Prine songs." So that settled that. John rented an apartment at the Spence Manor across from BMI on Music Row. Every afternoon we'd hole up listening to Porter and Dolly, George and Tammy, George and Melba, Ernest and Loretta, Conway and Loretta, Don and Phil. If this was work, we were loving it. In the meantime, John sent a letter to about a dozen or so of the women on his list, inviting them to join him. Everyone came back and said, "Yes."

Naturally, we decided to start with Iris and scheduled a time for her to come to Jack's Tracks to record with John and his band. The day before, I got a call first thing in the morning. It was Iris. She didn't sound too happy. She had spent the day before trying to record a song for "The Horse Whisperer" movie soundtrack and it evidently hadn't gone well. I asked her what the song was. It was "Whispering Pines," an old Johnny Horton song. She wanted to know if I could help her. I told her to come over. It was barely 9:30 in the morning, but she showed up a few minutes later. I told her to sit down and sing me the song, which she did. "What's the problem?" I asked. "It sounds fine to me." She said, "It does?" I assured her it was just fine.

FIGURE 30. Iris and John on the road with Jason Wilbur (*l.*) and Dave Jacques (*r.*). Photograph by Mitchell Drosin.

Garth Brooks was in the studio and someone was over at Cowboy's, so I called Mark Howard and asked him what was going on at his place. It was tied up until the evening. So I booked it for 7 o'clock—Mark to play guitar and mandolin, Mike Bub to play bass (Roy Huskey had recently passed away from cancer—a very sad day in my life), and Ferg to engineer. The man from the movie company came by around 7:45 and asked, "How's it going?" I said, "It's done. Do you want to hear it?" He couldn't believe it. He'd spent the day before watching a studio full of musicians spinning their wheels—and spending a lot of money while they were at it. He listened. It was beautiful, just Iris singing a simple song with a voice full of simple emotion and truth. I was so happy to have her back in my life again.

The next day, we started on John's project. The first song we did was George Jones and Tammy Wynette's classic "(We're Not) the Jet Set." When we listened to the original, we were amazed to find out that it was less than two minutes long! As a matter of fact, lots of those great hits from that era were less than three minutes long. They said what they had to say and got out. It was definitely before Jerry Jeff, John Hartford, and Kris Kristofferson changed the songwriting rules. Hearing John and Iris together just made me smile. This was the country music I loved. Phil Parlapiano's Italian mandolin and accordian set the song up so beautifully as they sang about their love blossoming in Rome, Athens, and Paris—Rome, Georgia; Athens, Texas; and Paris, Tennessee. Then we were off:

> We're not the jet set
> We're the old Chevro-let set

Iris and John followed that up with Felice Bryant's "We Could," as simple as a country song can get:

> If anyone could find the joy
> That true love brings a girl and boy
> We could
> We could you and I
> If anyone could ever say
> That their true love was here to stay
> We could
> We could you and I

One of my all-time favorite country duet albums was by George Jones and Melba Montgomery. Onie Wheeler's "Let's Invite Them Over" jumped out at me the first time I heard it. When country folks moved to the suburbs, there were lots of new things to deal with:

> I know why you're lonely
> And I know why you're blue
> You're lonesome to see him
> And you long to see her too
> We're not in love with each other
> We're in love with our best friends
> So let's invite them over again.

This was pretty steamy stuff. It was evidently pretty true stuff too, because lots of people loved this song. John and Iris weren't born yesterday, and they made the song real. We had achieved liftoff.

We didn't miss a beat. The next day Melba Montgomery herself came in. As a singer and a writer she had been in the top rank of female country artists. We were absolutely thrilled when she agreed to join John in singing her classic "We Must Have Been out of Our Minds," which had also been on that album she did with George Jones. Soulful writing and soulful singing was at the heart of country music, and Melba Montgomery had it all. John asked her to kick up her heels and let it all hang out on "Milwaukee Here I Come." She had a ball with it:

> We were watching T.V.
> Ernest Tubb was singing loud
> I said that's the man for me
> I love him, there's no doubt
> I'm leaving you and going now
> To find out where he's at
> If I can't get him I'll settle for
> That bluegrass Lester Flatt

Backing Melba on these tracks was the great pedal steel guitar man, Buddy Emmons, who I now knew because he was in the Everly Brothers band. Buddy had played on the original recordings, but he didn't act as if he'd already done this. His playing was fresh and full of energy. He had a smile on his face the whole time as he kept his focus on Melba and John.

Another one of the greatest female country singers, Connie Smith, had also replied to John's letter. She came over to Cowboy's and right off the bat blew me away as she sang Don Everly's "So Sad (to Watch Good Love Go Bad)." Her voice was so rich, so full, so true. I had heard Don sing it many times, but Connie's version with John gave me something I hadn't heard before. Back in Cambridge, the first time I heard Buck Owens, he was singing a duet with Rose Maddox on Freddie Hart's "Loose Talk." Betsy Siggins and I used to sing it at the Club, and I had mentioned it to John to put on our list. He asked Connie if she knew it, and she didn't hesitate. It was already in her:

> When I go out walkin'
> There's lots of loose talkin'
> They say we're unhappy and we'll break apart
> But darlin' it's not true
> Because I still love you
> And I do with all of my heart.

Chorus: We may have to leave here
            To find peace of mind dear
            Some place where we can live a life of our own
            For I know you love me
            And happy we could be
            If some folks would leave us alone

With Iris, Melba, and Connie under our belts we took a break for Christmas. We were elated with the results. This was turning into something really special. John had one more tour to do before the holidays. When he got back he noticed a little sore had developed at the base of his neck where his guitar strap went over his shoulder. After the New Year he got the word back that it was cancerous. He had been thrown a big curve ball. Then began the process of trying to figure out what the best course of action was. It was frustrating. A surgeon would recommend surgery; a radiation man, radiation; a chemo man, chemo. At one point I suggested that if he went to a car mechanic, he'd have him up on the lift! It was no joke, and finally John opted to go to the M. D. Anderson Center in Houston where he underwent surgery and some radiation. The prognosis was good, but we didn't know if we'd ever finish this album which had started out so well and meant so much to both of us. We were in for a big lesson in patience.

IRELAND CALLS

Carol's oldest daughter, Sarah, had been studying recorder in The Hague in Holland, and Carol and I went over for a visit in December of '96. As long as we were that close, I insisted that we spend a couple of days in Amsterdam. Among other things, the Michelin Guide recommended three "coffeehouses." We picked one and found it. It was a nice little place with lots of potted plants and lovely music playing. You went to a high counter to order your coffee, tea, or pastry. Behind the bar was a big chalkboard menu listing all of the various kinds of hashish on offer. It seemed to be pretty much the same idea as a wine bar, so I just ordered the cheapest—the "house hash." They fixed us up with a water pipe and gave us a sizable chunk of hash. We got some tea and a pastry and sat down to have our tea and puff away.

We started to have what Carol likes to call "big ideas." I looked at her and asked, "What would you think about living in Ireland half the year?" By this time Sonya was a senior in high school and would be graduating. Matthew was in college in Maine. Sarah was getting along with her musical career. We were looking forward to being a bit free, so I guess that's what was in the back of my mind when I came up with this "big idea." The more we thought about it, the better we liked it. Carol had been going to Ireland since she was eleven, starting when her mother was over with the Clancy family in Carrick-on-Suir in the late fifties. Eventually her mother had married an Irish man named Bill Meek and had a family in Ireland. So over the years Carol had been back and forth to Ireland a good bit. We both felt that it was her mother who brought us together in Dublin through her death.

Of course, I had loved coming to Ireland ever since my total immersion experience with Peggi Jordan back in 1964. Since coming over to Ballysadare with Don Everly and Phillip Donnelly in 1980, I'd been a pretty frequent visitor and had struck up good friendships with quite a number of people. The previous summer Carol's sister Sorcha Meek had gotten married, and we went over for the wedding. Afterward we took a little ramble and wound up in Galway during the Arts Festival. We got into a little B&B in town and saw four plays in two days and just loved the place. The center of town had retained a lot of its medieval character and the streets were swarming with lots of university students. A few years earlier I had come over in the winter with John Prine and his new love Fiona Whelan. I had been told where my grandfather Patrick Flaherty's house was on the Barna pier just outside of Galway City, so we visited that and my great-grandfather's grave. This was my home place. Sitting in the coffee shop in Amsterdam, all of these memories came in on me, so there was fertile soil for my "big idea" to take root and grow.

When I returned to Nashville, I began to think of another reason to shake things up a bit. I was definitely beginning to feel burnt out by the song business. The early years of building our company had been very exciting and rewarding. As a result of our success, we had grown. We now had eight or ten writers. They were all writing songs and, naturally, they all wanted you to listen to them, to demo them, to pitch them. Even though Matt Lindsey and Leslie Barr had taken up a lot of the load and almost all of the pitching, I felt an obligation to listen to everything and, with Mark, to be involved in demoing. In addition, one of my basic functions producing Hal was to listen to all of the songs that would be submitted for him to record. I would wind up with grocery bags full of cassettes to listen to. One of my listening places was my car. Sometimes I would drive up to Lake Malone in Kentucky and listen to these songs as I drove. I'd throw the rejects over my shoulder into the back seat. I'd get worn down after a while and say, "That's not too bad," and keep one in the front seat. Often, when I got back and listened to the keepers again, I'd say to myself, "What was I thinking?" You wanted so much to hear a great song or even a good song. In Nashville it was also part of your daily life to listen to writers or artists who are your friends or friends of friends. You don't want to close the door on people. I remembered what it meant to me when I first came to Nashville and Jack Clement opened his door to me. You live in hope. You're always thinking, "There might be that special song here." The world is full of stories about people who didn't listen, who didn't pay attention, and missed the boat. However, even with the success and the quality of the songs of our own Forerunner writers, I had come to the place where I needed to freshen up. I looked forward to going to a place where I would be open to something new. I needed to grow again.

We were taking a blind chance, really, but we finally decided that we'd try it for six months and see what happened. Naturally, I talked it over with my partners. Our accountant Kent Harrell gave me a bit of perspective. He said, "You're one of the owners of the company. If you want to go off for a while, you can." I'd never thought of it that way, but it helped. Once we'd made up our minds, I set to work to see about how to find us a place to live. We'd decided on the Galway area, and I got a brochure of furnished houses for rent. I circled about half a dozen places around Galway City. I also figured that John Prine's friends Richard and Bridie Hackett, who had Hogan's Pub in Galway, might be some help.

Sarah was going to be doing her master's recital in May. Neither her father Frank Cantor nor Carol was able to go, so I got a ticket on Delta from Atlanta to Amsterdam and came back through Shannon for no extra charge. That gave me a couple of days to check out houses around Galway. On my way from Shannon to Galway I saw a sign to a place called "Moran's on the Weir," a famous oyster pub I had once visited with John Prine and our friend Pat Kelly. It was a lovely afternoon in May, so I said to myself, "I think I'll go in there and have some oysters and a pint." I was sitting outside watching the swans go by, enjoying my pint and the delicious native oysters. I thought, "This is very nice right here." I went inside and asked the barman if he knew of any houses to rent in the area. He gave me a phone number for a woman named Kathrein Curtin. I gave her a call when I got into Galway and set up a time the next morning to look at the house. Her husband Barney met me out on the main road in Ballinderreen and drove me in. The road was enclosed in hedges and wound around, eventually coming to a T-junction with a beautiful little bay on the left where a fellow was just coming up with what looked like a bucket of mussels. Things were looking up. The house itself was just up the road. It was beautiful, fairly new, faced with stone, with a big skylight over the entrance hall that let in a lot of light. It dawned on me that it was one of the houses I had circled in the brochure—quite a coincidence!

After I looked it over, Barney took me down to meet Kathrein, who actually did the business. She was from Germany originally and was very organized. She explained the terms very clearly. I said that I'd talk to my wife after I got back to the States and would call them in a week or so. The night before I left I went for a couple of pints with Richard Hackett at Hogan's. He said there would be a session later on and that he'd arranged for a guitar for me. Eventually two women came in with instruments and sat down near the end of the bar. I overheard them talking and one of them mentioned that she'd brought her guitar in for a "Yank," who was coming in to play. I went over and introduced myself as "The Yank." They were Mary Staunton, a box player, and Ailish O'Connor, a fiddler. The session got under way. They were both excellent players, and Mary also had a lovely voice. I sang a few songs. Gradually, the session built up a head of steam as more people joined in. Richard kept the pints flowing. There was a giant of a man named Brendan Begley, who was a wild box player from Kerry who also had the sweetest singing voice. Eventually, another fellow with a rubber face did a hilarious recitation. He turned out to be Mick Lally, one of Galway's and Ireland's greatest actors. I was lucky to get out of there with my life about four in the morning. I could see that living in Ireland might prove to be a challenge. When I got home, I showed Carol a picture of the house. Her face fell, and I knew exactly what she was thinking. I said, "Carol, they don't rent hovels in Ireland anymore." I knew she wanted an old thatched cottage with chickens running in and out the door, but she went along with me. I called Kathrein up and booked it from late September to early April. We took the blind plunge.

My partners seemed to be okay with me not being around so much. I was already going up and down to Vermont, and I'd always gone off here and there to play, so it wasn't a total shock. After she graduated from high school, Sonya was drifting a bit, not sure what she wanted to do. I suggested that she could go to Nashville, live in my apartment, and get work in a restaurant. She knew the Prines and Pat Alger and some of my friends, and I knew they'd look after her. Matthew and Sarah were set, so we were free to go. We arrived in Ireland the last week of September and got into the house. Immediately Carol responded to how much light came into the house and how close we were to the water. We woke up the first morning and were greeted by a beautiful full rainbow, which ended in the water out back. We took it as a good omen. We bought a couple of bicycles right away, threw them into the back of a station wagon John Prine had lent to us and started exploring the area, discovering old forts, holy wells, ancient ruined churches, hidden places.

Before I left Nashville, a friend of mine from the old days in Cambridge, Billy Burke, called. Sadly, he had cancer and was dying, but he wanted to tell me that he'd been to the area in Ireland where we were going and had met the singer Sean Tyrell and thought I'd like him. Interestingly enough, I had just been listening to an excellent album by Sean, *Cry of a Dreamer*, produced by my friend P.J. Curtis and given to me by Joe Boyd. Joe had also been part of our Cambridge crowd and had long been involved with Fairport Convention, Richard Thompson, and the McGarrigle Sisters; he also had his own label, Hannibal Records. Here was Billy in his dying days asking me to look up Sean and to send along his best wishes, so I felt that I owed it to him to get in touch with Sean.

He lived not too far away in a place called Bell Harbour, in the middle of this beautiful limestone landscape in County Clare called The Burren. Sean and his wife Connie were very welcoming and took us to a great music session that night. Before we left he told me that he was going to go up to a place called Letterfrack in Connemara the following weekend for a gathering with music sessions and talks called "Sea Week" hosted by the local schoolmaster, Leo Hallissey. Sean thought we'd enjoy it, so we decided to go. The ride took us through the heart of the "Twelve Bens," the marble and quartzite pointed mountains of Connemara. It was breathtaking to watch the mountains appear and disappear as sunlight and showers alternated, punctuated by rainbows of all states of completion. Finally, as we drove on a winding road out to the end of the Renvyle Peninsula by the sea, white with foam, a final rainbow plunged into the heaving water, the colors absolutely fluorescent. This was a magic landscape. The B&B, run by Virginia and Maurice Davin and their family, was next to a ruined tower house once inhabited by one of my forbears, Roderick O'Flaherty. This was my home country, wild and stunningly beautiful.

That weekend was a great gathering of musicians, poets, marine biologists, explorers—all sorts. We didn't know a soul except for Sean Tyrell and P.J. Curtis, but it didn't matter. There was a session in a pub on Friday night where we met the organizer Leo Hallissey, a soft-spoken man who welcomed us warmly. On Saturday morning sixty or so people gathered in a small classroom where Leo led the day's series of talks. To begin with, he doused the lights, and we sat in total darkness listening to a flute play an old Irish air. One by one, Leo lit some candles, bathing the room in a lovely warm light. A poet named Moya Cannon then read a couple of poems, followed by two or three tunes on fiddle and flute. Then Leo introduced the first speaker. There were talks about whales, the local history, exploring expeditions, ecology. You name it. Then we all went for a walk along the coast listening to people talk about the seaweed, the rocks, the history—often with Leo turning to one person or another for a "blast of a song" or a "blast of a poem"—oblivious to the wind or the odd shower. That night we all had a delicious meal at the local hostel followed by a concert in the living room by Sean Tyrell, Mary Staunton—I remembered her from my wild night at Hogan's—and more poems by Moya Cannon. Afterward we introduced ourselves to Moya, and she invited us to come along that week to the launch of a new collection of her poems at Kenny's booksellers in Galway. We took her up on that and after her reading she took us to a postlaunch session with none other than Sharon Shannon! Thank God for Billy Burke! His call led us to this wonderful gathering, which over the years has generated deep and lasting friendships with a wide variety of interesting and talented people. We hadn't been in the country a month, and it seemed as if we were being led in some mysterious way.

Barney Curtin had told me that there was a music session the first Friday of the month at O'Connor's in Ballinderreen, so on the first Friday in

November I headed down, bringing my guitar along just in case. The pub was packed, but I was welcomed into the session. My entry was eased by the presence of another American, Sue Fahy, who played fiddle. She was from Michigan and had worked for The Mandolin Brothers there. She knew of Bill Keith and me, so that helped. She was married to Mike Fahy, a flute player. There was another fiddler, Rena Small; a harmonica player, Paul Moran; Brendan O'Loinsigh (Lynch), who played banjo; and a fine box player named Mary Francis Dervan. Of course, I didn't know any of the tunes they were playing, except for a few like "Mrs. McCloud's Reel," which had traveled over to America, but I've always loved fiddle tunes and have a pretty good ear, so I just strummed away. Toward the end they asked me to sing a song. For some reason I picked "Blue Ridge Mountain Blues." Sue knew it, and by the end they had all joined in. This was to become my new musical home in Ireland.

As Christmas approached, Sue mentioned that on the day after Christmas, St. Stephen's Day, the group from O'Connor's would go out and do "the wren." Carol knew all about this ancient tradition of mummers going from house to house, dancing, singing, playing tunes and enjoying some hospitality, and collecting some money. They asked if we wanted to join them, and we said that we'd love to. As it turned out that was what really cemented us into the village. Carol made us some masks and we met the others at O'Connors for a hot whiskey before we set out. Everyone was all dressed up in great costumes and spirits were high. We probably went around to twenty or thirty houses in the course of the afternoon and night. We'd come up to the door playing "Jingle Bells," burst into the kitchen, immediately do a small set dance, and then Sue or I would sing a song, Paul would do the "broom dance," and we'd play a waltz and get people in the house dancing. It was especially wonderful to visit some of the older people in the village. Their kitchens were still homely and simple. Everyone offered us hot whiskey or tea, cakes and sandwiches. Then we'd be on to the next. By ten or eleven, we were back at the pub for a session until one in the morning. By doing that, the place opened up to us. From then on, people in the village knew who we were. They appreciated the fact that we were there in the winter and that we wanted to be part of the reality of their life as opposed to just being tourists—rich "Yanks" coming over to show off.

FIGURE 31. Ballinderreen mummers getting ready to make the rounds
(*front, kneeling*: Breandan O'Loinsigh; *first row l. to r.*: Sue Fahy,
Mary Francis Dervan, Paul Moran, Catherine Linnane;
second row l. to r.: Miles O'Kane, Rena Small, Mike Fahy,
Carol; *back, standing*: Jim Rooney).
Photograph courtesy of Breandan O'Loinsigh.

There's no doubt that we were enjoying ourselves in our new environment, but both Carol and I like to be working. I remember looking at her one day after we'd been there a couple of months and saying, "Do you think we'll always just be tourists here?" As if in answer to my question, a few days later the phone rang. It was Sean Keane, Dolores's brother, who had been in Arcady at The Session. He said, "Welcome to Ireland!" He had heard that I was in the area from a recording engineer in Galway named Pat Neary; I had looked up Pat in case I ever wanted to do some recording. Without too much small talk, Sean asked me if I'd be interested in working with him on an album. My first question was, "What about

Arty McGlynn?" Arty had produced *Turn a Phrase*, an album of Sean's we had bought after first hearing it playing at McCarthy's pub in Baltimore on our "honeymoon." Sean assured me that Arty was busy producing an album with Liam O'Flynn, so that wasn't a problem. I asked Sean where he lived, and he said, "About two miles away." Everything about our Irish experience was so serendipitous. Sean came right over, and we sat in the kitchen. When I asked him if he had any songs in mind to record, the very first song he showed me was "Like I Used to Do," by Pat Alger and Tim O'Brien. I looked at Sean and said, "I publish that song!" He had no idea. He'd heard it on an album of Tim's. The next song he played was "Killin' the Blues." I said, "I was in The Woodstock Mountains Revue with Roly Salley, and we used to play that song every show we did. Where did you hear it?" He'd heard it on a Chris Smither album. I told Sean that Chris was another old friend of mine. He also wanted to do Bob Dylan's "Lay Down Your Weary Tune," the only Dylan song I ever sang back in the sixties. Right off the bat it seemed that Sean and I were on the same wavelength. An idea popped into my head, and I asked him, "Have you ever heard a song called 'I'm No Stranger to the Rain'"? He hadn't. "It was a good hit in the states for a singer named Keith Whitley," I told him. "My friend Sonny Curtis wrote it. I think it might suit you." I called Sonny up on the spot. It was morning in Nashville, and he answered his phone. I explained that I was in Ireland with this singer Sean Keane and asked him to send me a copy of the song. Like the good professional songwriter that he was, Sonny sent it over right away. Sean loved it. We recorded it, and it turned out to be a hit for Sean.

After talking to Sean, I called Arty just to be sure that he wasn't available to produce Sean's album. He assured me that he was busy with Liam, but that he'd be happy to play the sessions if the timing was right. That was great news. At this time, Arty was one of the top acoustic guitarists playing Irish traditional music. However, he had also spent eighteen years on the road with some of Ireland's top showbands playing electric guitar and pedal steel and seven years with Van Morrison. Through Arty I connected with some of the best studio musicians in Ireland—James Blennerhassett on upright bass, Rod McVey on keyboards, and Tommy Hayes on percussion. I wouldn't have known who these people were. Unlike Nashville, they were scattered all over the country, so you really had to know who they were and where to find them. Arty knew. In addition, we used his wife Nollaig Casey on fiddle, Johnny Og Connolly on accordian, Tommy Keane on pipes, and Sean's brother Matt and sister Dolores on harmonies. Hearing Sean sing surrounded by his family and friends made me realize how much of a traditional singer he was. His singing style had deep roots in Galway, but it wasn't a thing of the past. It was ongoing, and Sean could lead you into whatever musical world he chose to explore, be it Bob Dylan or an ancient lament. All of a sudden, after being in Ireland for three months I was working, doing something I really liked to do. But it was in a fresh setting, with different instruments and a different sound.

Before I went back to Nashville, I went down to Cork for a couple of weekends to work with Mick Daly on an album with the Lee Valley String Band to celebrate the thirtieth anniversary of the session first started in 1968. DanDan Fitzgerald was the engineer; he had done sound for Bill Keith, Mark O'Connor and me when we played at Barry's Hotel in Dublin back in '85. He had a studio set up in his house in a recently built housing estate on the outskirts of Cork. It was the only place with the shades drawn down. I don't know what the neighbors thought was going on in there, but it was all very innocent. We set up the boys in the kitchen, which suited the music, and DanDan and I set up shop in the living room. Each person in the group was a real character. Each voice was totally identifiable: Chris Twomey had an ethereal, weathered high tenor; Mick Daly a lovely smooth baritone; Mick Murphy, a butcher by trade, a hearty, rough and ready, almost vaudevillian style; Brendan Butler a clear high tenor; Mick "Tana" O'Brien a jug band, bluesy voice; Pete Brennan a perfect harmony tenor. The material ranged from Charlie Poole and the Carter Family through Bill Monroe and Flatt & Scruggs all the way up to Tim O'Brien and The Amazing Rhythm Aces. It made for a great show, which is how I approached mixing and sequencing the album with Mick and DanDan. The album had all of the energy, simplicity, and emotion that brought me to this music in the first place. I now had two albums under my belt, so it looked like I didn't have to worry about being only a tourist in Ireland any more.

FIGURE 32. With Sean Keane at the Ballinderreen Community Center.
Photograph: © Ik Mellick.

FIGURE 33. The Lee Valley String Band recording session at
DanDan Fitzgerald's, Cork (*front, kneeling*: Kevin Gill and DanDan Fitzgerald;
front sitting: Mick Murphy, Mick "Tana" O'Brien; *back, standing*: Chris Twomey,
Jim Rooney, Mick Daly, Pete Brennan, Brendan Butler, Hal O'Neil).
Photograph: © Marcus Connaughton.

BACK TO BUSINESS

After being away for a while, I got a bit more perspective on things in Nashville. I was already aware of the difficulties presented to us by the infiltration of the recording process by middle management types and marketing people. However, I wasn't really aware of our own situation until one day at one of our periodic meetings when our accountant Kent Harrell opened up by saying, "You guys lost about $200,000 last year." This was news to all of us. Terrell was on a salary because she was running the company, but Allen, Mark, and I were not dependent on the company to make our living. Once in a while we had declared a dividend after a particularly good year, but Allen made his living as a songwriter and producer, Mark as engineer and studio manager, and me by producing and playing. So this news came as a bit of a shock. It brought it home to us how quickly the worm could turn. It had been more than a year since we'd had a single in the charts. At the same time we had developed a very healthy overhead. When we started we had no song pluggers and were paying minimal advances to Pat Alger and Dave Mallett. By now advances to writers had climbed to significant numbers. We had three full-time employees and one part-time, health insurance, rent, the works. It occurred to me that it could all go away as fast as it came.

Later that spring something else started me thinking. Carol had retired from doing Revels and had started a "Connecticut Riverfest." There was a group of us helping Carol organize things. At the beginning of every meeting someone would start off by reading a poem or piece of writing about a river to focus our minds. One day someone read a piece out of Mark Twain's *Life on the Mississippi* describing the river at dawn. It was a gorgeous piece of writing, and I decided to get the book out of the library and read it. The first part described how Twain had grown up in Hannibal, Missouri, wanting to become a river pilot and how he achieved that (like my friend John Hartford). The second part is an account of how he returned to the river a quarter of a century later when he was a celebrity writer. He brought a group of people to St. Louis to accompany him on a trip down the Mississippi to Hannibal. Where the river had been literally covered in steamboats when he left, there were now only three in sight! They'd been put out of business by the railroads.

Having grown up and lived in New England as I did, where towns were full of empty mill buildings from the textile business that went away, you'd think I would have had some awareness of how dramatically things can change, how something that seems so solid and lasting can vanish from sight, but it was this piece of writing by Mark Twain that put the idea in my head that technological changes can pull the rug out from under you in a hurry. It was beginning to dawn on me that the digital revolution was a *real* revolution—probably the first such thing in my lifetime. My parents had gone through all kinds of things—the motorcar, electric light, the telephone, movies, radio, television, recordings. In my lifetime all the new things were variations and improvements on existing inventions. In the recording business we went from 78s to 45s to 33s to cassettes to CDs, but they were all basically something that was sold to people physically. Artists, producers, writers, and publishers were all living on royalties generated by those sales. I was now beginning to understand that this digital thing was affecting everything. It was showing up in the way we recorded. At Jack's Tracks we were all wedded to the analog recording process. We were still using two-inch tape and loved the quality of the sound reproduction. However, lots of people were starting to move into the digital realm because it was cheaper. If the sound wasn't quite as good, who would notice? I was already running into this in Galway where I was forced into using the A-Dat recording format. In Nashville, people were changing to ProTools with hard drives. It was happening all around me. The days of editing tape with razor blades were over. It was now "cut and paste." I had also noticed the beginnings of downloading happening, especially with college kids who were being provided with high-speed internet access for free by their schools. Now they could download songs right onto their computers by "sharing" files rather than the old-fashioned way of paying for a CD. Somebody called "The Napster" was considered a major threat to the recording industry. The response of the multinational companies dominating the business was to sue the customers and threaten them with dire consequences if they persisted in their "sharing." This approach seemed futile to me. The genie was out of the bottle and no number of lawyers could put it back in.

The more I thought about all of these things, the more it became clear to me that it was quite possible for our company to go from a position of being worth something to being something we couldn't sell. Personally I couldn't let that happen. I didn't have the resources to wait this one out and hope for things to improve at some point. I was too old. If I'd been younger, I would have had to figure out this brave new world, but I couldn't honestly look our writers in the eye and tell them not to worry, that we'd figure it all out, no problem. It was a sobering time—time to make a move. I came in to one of our meetings and told my partners that I was thinking of ending my participation in the company. We had a structure for this eventuality that had been in place since we started. After explaining my reasons, I invited them to think about our situation and come back to me with their thoughts. The next day Allen came to me. Of all of us he had the most business sense; he was very thoughtful and observant as well. He said, "Pal, I think you're right." He'd put a pencil to paper the night before and thought about it and had come to the same conclusion as I had.

One of Jack Clement's little sayings is, "If you're not having fun, you're not doing your job right." The fun had gone out of it for us. As publishers we felt that our writers were wonderful, but we couldn't seem to get anywhere with their material in the environment that had developed in Nashville. Even with all of Garth's success, we knew that it wouldn't last forever and quite probably would never be repeated. The new regime at Curb had not been good for Hal. Dick Whitehouse had retired and his replacement didn't share his enthusiasm for Hal, who was having difficulties too. Things were not going well for Hal and Terrell. We had come to a parting of the ways with Dave Mallett. Although we had gotten him good recordings of his songs on good selling albums by Kathy Mattea, Hal, and Emmylou Harris, he seemed to feel that we hadn't done enough to get him a single. Allen and I had a heart to heart with Dave, but, since he wasn't happy with us, we let him know that we wouldn't renew his contract at the end of the year. It wasn't easy. He had three kids and a good wife. I believed in him as a writer, but it was time for a change.

We had got lucky with a song by Shawn Camp, Sandy Mason, and Benita Hill called "Two Pina Coladas." When I first heard it I said, "Didn't Jimmy Buffett already do this?" I just thought it was nothing. Garth Brooks thought it was something. He recorded it. It was a #1 record, and it saved our ass. That kind of summed up our position. If we'd had a lot of songs like that maybe we'd have been in better shape, but I just couldn't see it. I had to follow my instincts. When Allen agreed with me, it became much easier to make a move. Terrell was sentimentally inclined to keep the company going. We all were. It was our baby. But I just couldn't let the only equity that I had built up after more than thirty years of working in the music business evaporate.

ALL THIS WAY FOR
THE SHORT RIDE

A year or so earlier Carol and I had gone out to the Cowboy Hall of Fame in Oklahoma City to collect the Wrangler Award for Don Edward's *West of Yesterday* album. The actual award was a bronze statuette of a wrangler on a horse. If you didn't show up in person, they wouldn't send it to you, so we definitely had to go. As it turned out, the whole thing was a pretty big deal. They had a reception for the honorees and guests at the Hall of Fame and Museum. The Museum alone was worth the trip. It had a stunning collection of western art, including many works by Frederick Remington, Charles Russell, and Harold Von Schmidt, Eric's father. In the crowd were some favorite cowboy movie actors like Richard Farnsworth, Wilfred Brimley, and the host for the awards show, Tommy Lee Jones. It was a real honor to stand up on stage with Don. Two dreamers were seeing their dreams come true. The winner that year for poetry was Paul Zarzyski's collection "All This Way for the Short Ride." When Paul got up wearing his black hat and trademark hand-painted tie and recited the title poem, he brought the house down. I turned to Carol and said, "I've got to do something with him." Afterward we were exchanging congratulations with Paul and his partner Liz Dear when Don came up and asked if we'd all like to go out to dinner with him and his wife Cathy and Tommy Lee Jones. A long white limo pulled up to the entrance and we all piled in. Tommy Lee had a friend with him named Cliff. Cliff evidently had a ranch next to Tommy Lee's in west Texas and was what Cowboy might have referred to as Tommy Lee's "comical sidekick." (Every cowboy movie star had his Gabby Hayes or Festus.) Cliff wasn't that comical, but he helped us in and out of the limo and smoothed the way. Carol wound up sitting next to Cliff. Conversation was going on smoothly around the table when suddenly Cliff said in a loud voice, "I don't ask you how much money you have in the bank!" Conversation stopped in time for us to hear Carol say that she had once had a cow in Vermont and was just interested in how many cows Cliff had. Big mistake. Never ask a cowboy how many head he has. It's not done. Gradually, conversation resumed and somehow or other Tommy Lee mentioned that he loved the music of the Carter Family and had once been lucky enough to see Maybelle Carter in person. I asked him where that was. He had heard her at the Club 47. I said, "I was running that club at the time. I guess that's was when you were going to HARVARD!" I wanted to make sure Cliff heard that his pal had been to that effete eastern school.

The next morning Carol and I had breakfast with Paul and Liz. We shared a big laugh over the goings-on at the previous night's dinner. Finally, I took the plunge and told Paul that I was going to have to do something with him, and he told me that he'd be up for it. One of the ways I get myself to do things is to say that I'm going to do something out loud to other people. Then I have to do it. So now I had to do it. Ever since the days of the beat poets reading poems while a sax wailed or congas throbbed, people have tried combining music with poetry. The other extreme would have been Rod McEuen with lush strings in the background. I hadn't found that much of it worked for me, so I was going to have to figure this out. I also had a feeling that I would have a tough time finding a label to pay for such a venture, so I decided to pay for it and put it out myself. For the first time in my life I seemed to be making some money, so what better way to spend it than on a great artist like Paul?

Over the course of the next few months I read Paul's poems and had him send me cassettes of him reading them. Gradually, things began to sort themselves out for me. There were some of the more western "cowboy" ones that seemed suited for the same guys who had played with Don Edwards. Some of Paul's other poems had a bit of a rock-and-roll attitude to them. One day I was over at Georgetown Masters, where I had been mastering most of my albums with Denny Purcell, who was a big fan of my work. He introduced me to the great Duane Eddy and was talking me up to him. Duane was very soft-spoken and opened up a bit when I told him of my past involvement with Don Everly. He gave me his card and said that if I ever needed him to do anything to give him a call. That had been months earlier, but as I listened to Paul recite a couple of his poems, "Monte Carlo Express," and "The Bucking Horse Moon," I thought they might be something for Duane, so I called him up and asked if he'd listen and tell me if he'd be willing to try putting some of his guitar with them. When Duane called me back and said that he loved the poems and would do it, I was thrilled. Things were falling into place. I had ideas for John Hartford, Pat Alger, and a few more pickers. Paul knew of a flamenco guitarist in Santa Fe. We were ready to go.

My thought was that Paul would recite the poem and then we would decide whether they'd play before, during or after the recitation, but that it would all be done "live." For me, the secret to recording Paul was to capture the energy he put into performing each poem. His fifteen years of getting up on broncs, waiting for the chute to open, gave him an edge. Each poem was going to be an exciting ride, and I wanted the musicians to be in it with him. My instincts were right. I listened as each musician responded to him and came up with his own ideas. Duane Eddy duplicated the twists and turns of Paul's cowboy driving on "Monte Carlo Express"; John Hartford matched Paul's tongue-twisting list of favorite pies in "The Heavyweight Champion Pie-Eatin' Cowboy of the West" with his own hail of banjo notes; Mark Abbott played a simple bass coda to follow "All This Way for the Short Ride"; Tommy Morrel introduced "Montana Second Hand" with the refrain of Hank Williams's "I'm So Lonesome I Could Cry" on the solo steel guitar; Sam Levine provided the sad wail of the clarinet as prelude to "Shoes" and Bill Miller the equally sorrowful answer on the Native American flute at the conclusion; Rich O'Brien answered Paul's tribute to him, "And All the World Would Call Me *Rich*," with his own heartfelt instrumental tribute, "Prayer for Buck Ramsey"; Bob Boatright came up with a beautiful rendition of "Darlin' Nellie Gray" as a fitting farewell for Paul's rodeo compadre, "Staircase"; the guys collectively came up with the "Flintstone's Theme" in response to "Benny Reynolds's Bareback Riggin'"; Mike Henderson's electric slide guitar *became* Stub, "The Whale in My Wallet." I loved it all. The musicians loved it. Paul loved it. We had figured it all out together, and it was live as it could be. It was the one and only Paul Zarzyski (rhymes with "bar whiskey"). We titled the album *Words Growing Wild*, after a poem Paul wrote about his earliest memories of the music of words, which described his father's fishing flies and the flowers his mother loved:

> I still go home to relearn my first love for words
> echoing through those woods: *I caught one!*

Dad! I caught one! Dad! Dad!
skipping like thin flat stones down the crick-
and him galloping through popples, splitshot ticking,
to find me leaping for a fingerling, my first
brookie twirling from a willow like a jewel.

I felt the same way. Paul's poetry, with all of this music surrounding it, was twirling, glittering like a jewel.

HERBAL AND ME

Back in January of '98, I'd come over from Ireland on a visit. One morning Herb McCullough told me that he'd made a New Year's resolution to write a song with everyone in the building—"and that includes *you!*" Right away I started backing up and making excuses. I hadn't written anything in ages. I was going right back to Ireland and wouldn't be back in the States until April. But Herb wouldn't let go, so finally we got out our calendars and picked a date. As it turned out, I was going to be mixing Sean Keane's album on the day Herb and I had agreed. He accused me of "blowing it off," but there was a tornado brewing and I really needed to get cracking in case the power went off, so we said we'd do it the next week, and I promptly put it out of my mind. Next week rolled around. On the appointed morning I was down in my office. Once again Herb showed up. I tried the lame excuse that I'd forgotten to bring in my guitar, but he was having none of it. "I brought two." The jig was up. I said, "Okay. Let's see what we can do."

We had a small room downstairs for writers to use. Hal Ketchum had painted a scene of an endless highway on one wall so you could forget you were in the cellar and gaze off into the distance as you tried to come up with something. Herb and I settled in. I wasn't lying to Herb when I said that I hadn't written anything in ages. Listening to songs day and night for years wasn't conducive to writing more songs. I'm sure Herb understood all this, and he got us started by just talking like the two good old friends that we were. He started asking me about Ireland and, like many Americans, was curious about the violence in Northern Ireland. I had only been to Belfast once, so I was no expert, but I started talking about how all of these situations, like our own racial problem, were basically the same. If you asked people what they wanted out of life—Catholics or Protestants, blacks or whites, Serbs or Croatians—they would always say the same thing. They wanted to make a living; they wanted to provide for their families; they wanted their kids to grow up safe, get a good education, and have a better life. It was all the same basic stuff. The problem came when people, often encouraged by politicians, either could not or would not put themselves in someone else's shoes and try to see life from their point of view. That last phrase rang some sort of a bell. I started to strum my guitar. An hour or so later we had a song, "Point of View":

> If I were you and you were me
> Do you think we could agree
> To get along
> Could we get along
> Would left be right and right be wrong
> Could we sing a simple song
> In harmony
> Sweet harmony
> *Chorus:* We're all trying to make a living
> Trying to find a way to be true
> It wouldn't be so tough if we were willing
> To open up and change our point of view
> Just open up and change our point of view
> If your future's in the past
> There's no need for you to ask
> Which road you're on
> Or where you're going
> Is that the best that you can do
> When your child looks up at you
> With hopeful eyes
> Such hopeful eyes
> *Chorus:*

We went to lunch and came back. We played it again. It was still there. We made a little cassette to take with us. I said to Herb, "That was good. I enjoyed that. Thanks for dragging me in there." He pounced. "Does that mean you'll do it again?" He had me.

After putting him off once or twice, I finally got back in the little room with Herb. We had it in our heads that maybe we should write some kind of positive love song. We both felt lucky to have good women in our lives, but after an hour or so of trying to be positive, we kept coming back to that time when we met at the Kountry Korner and were living the honky-tonk life. I said, without thinking, "Well, you know, Herb, when you're living on the devil's level, you're living on the devil's time." Only a tone-deaf fool would have let that line get away. It was a gift. We both jumped on it:

If misery loves company, you'll never be alone
He's always out there callin' you, you'll never stay at home
You think you're pretty lucky, you're trying to play it smart
You never see the sunshine 'cause you're too busy stabbin'
    in the dark
Chorus: When you're livin' on the devil's level
       You're livin' on the devil's time
       When you're livin' on the devil's level
       He's gonna make you walk that line
Some day you'll meet an angel
She'll teach you how to fly
You'll walk out on that party
Never even say goodbye
Chorus:

I had always liked the simplicity of J. J. Cale's music, and this song seemed to call for something similar, so I just basically stayed on one chord all the way. It doesn't get much simpler than that. We were batting a thousand, so I beat Herb to the punch and said, "Do you want to do it again? Or should we quit while we're ahead?" "Let's go for it," he smiled. "We're on a roll."

The third time we actually did get that positive love song we had been searching for when the devil distracted us. Herb and Joanne loved the Southwest and rural Florida where he came from. Carol had definitely gotten me back in touch with life in the natural world where you could smell and touch and feel. Carol's favorite dance was the waltz, and I naturally started strumming in 3/4 time:

A light in the night lights up the dark
Inside my little room
It might be the stars, it might be the moon
Hello, baby, it's you
A whisper of wind kisses my skin
A fragrance of flowers in bloom
Cedar and sage sweep me away
Hello, baby, it's you

In hockey, it's called "the hat trick." We'd scored three in a row. I think Harlan Howard would have approved. I eventually recorded all three songs and Sean Keane had a single of "Point of View," which got a very favorable response in Ireland just as the peace process was finally taking hold. If it hadn't been for Herb's perseverance it wouldn't have happened. He was a true friend, and he knew that I needed this. I needed to get away from the business and back to the music.

PRINE COUNTRY TIME II

John Prine's recovery from his surgery and radiation was slow but steady. They'd taken a pretty good chunk out of his neck behind his jawbone. The radiation had fried his saliva glands, so he needed to drink water all the time. His voice was pretty much a whisper, but John was determined and optimistic. He had lots of reasons to come back, none more important than his two young sons, Jack and Tommy, "Irish Twins," born eleven months apart. John treasured his new life as a husband and a father. That was all the motivation he needed.

In July of '98 I went over to Ireland to help Sean Keane launch *No Stranger*. John and Fiona and the family were renting a house for the summer in Salt Hill in Galway. Fiona was up in Donegal for a few days visiting her family and John was on his own. Richard Hackett and I went by to administer therapy. John could still drink vodka and ginger ale. Pretty soon we were in the kitchen and got out the guitars. By this time John's speaking voice had come back. His voice had always been a bit gravelly. Now it was just more gravelly and lower. Singing was a different matter. He could sing softly, but sometimes when he opened his mouth nothing came out. It was unsettling to say the least. But we had a good night. We sat around for three or four hours like we used to, strumming and singing. John just kept at. He wanted it. The next day as we were walking around Galway, he stopped and looked at me, "I think it's going to come back. I think my voice is gonna come back."

That Fall John got an acting job in a film that Billy Bob Thornton was making called "Daddy and Them." It promised to be a lot of fun. Andy Griffith was going to be in it and John was looking forward to spending time with him. John didn't have a lot of lines. I think he was the weird uncle. Mostly, he sat in a corner reading the paper and making the odd comment (just like in real life). It was perfect timing. It gave him something to do and got him through the Fall. He got paid, of course, and that didn't hurt. Cancer was expensive. Toward the end of shooting, Billy Bob and Marty Stuart, who was putting together some music for the sound track, asked John if he could come up with a song. He came up with "In Spite of Ourselves." It was supposed to be a duet. They thought they'd get some female "star" to sing it with John, but the lyrics proved to be a problem. "He ain't got laid in a month of Sundays, I caught him once sniffin' my undies." They didn't find any takers. The managers didn't see it as a good "career move." John then said, "What about Iris DeMent?" They said, "Okay. Give it a try." So John called up Iris and sent her a lyric sheet. She called him back and said, "Do you really want me to sing this?" John laughed and said, "Yeah, Iris, I had you in mind all along!" So they did it:

JOHN:
She don't like her eggs all runny
She thinks crossin' her legs is funny
She looks down her nose at money
She gets it on like the Easter Bunny
She's my baby
I'm her honey
I'm never gonna let her go
IRIS:
He ain't got laid in a month of Sundays
I caught him once sniffin my undies
He ain't real sharp but he gets things done
He drinks his beer like its oxygen

He's my baby
I'm his honey
I'm never gonna let him go.

JOHN & IRIS:
In spite of ourselves
We'll end up sittin' on a rainbow
Against all odds
Honey, we're the big door prize
We're gonna spite the noses right off of our faces
There won't be nothin' but big old hearts
Dancin' in our eyes

When I was back in Nashville from Ireland in December, John and I were in his car, and he put on "In Spite of Ourselves." It was just John and Iris, with Marty playing second guitar. I was laughing at the song because it was so quirky, such a John Prine song. I was in tears because John was *singing*. I looked over at him. "You're back! Your voice has come back!" And he smiled his biggest ever John Prine smile. It meant that we were going to be able to finish the duets album we had started over a year earlier and that we had the title song. We didn't waste any time. John came over to Ireland in January and I set up a session at Pat Neary's studio in Galway with Arty McGlynn and James Blennerhassett. I'd been on tour in the fall with Nanci Griffith to celebrate *Other Voices, Too*. We'd played in Dublin, Glasgow, and London with a fantastic lineup, including Odetta, Dave Van Ronk, Tom Russell, Eric Taylor, and Dolores Keane. Every night Dolores came out and did "You'll Never Be the Sun" with Nanci and killed me. I had been talking about it to John, so we asked her to join him on two songs: Moe Bandy's hit, "It's a Cheating Situation," and a new one by Kieran Kane, "In a Town This Size." Dolores's voice had a beautiful smoky, slightly world-weary quality, which worked great with John's lower, grittier, new voice.

As soon as I got back from Ireland in the spring, we headed into Jack's Tracks to finish the album. A couple of the songs brought me right back to my beginning. Patty Loveless joined John on Webb Pierce's "Back Street Affair," which my cousins the Walsh girls found so amusing and gave me hope that girls would like me if I kept on singing. Lucinda Williams came in to sing Hank Williams's "Darlin' Let's Turn Back the Years," the first song I ever played on the guitar. How could I have imagined back then that nearly fifty years later I would love this music as much as ever?

We finished up with Emmylou Harris and John singing Jack Clement's classic "I Know One" and Trisha Yearwood on another classic by Roger Miller and Bill Anderson, "When Two Worlds Collide." The dream list of "favorite girl singers" that John had started more than two years earlier had finally come true. He had come out on the other side of his bout with cancer loving and cherishing every single note he could sing. However, John had one surprise for me. We were getting ready to mix when he said that he had one more singer he wanted to sing with—Fiona. They'd been practicing a song by Bill and Sharon Rice, "'Til a Tear Becomes a Rose." The next day Fiona came in. She was pretty nervous, but I assured her we were all family and there was nothing to worry about. As it happened, Kieran Kane was there to listen to his song "In a Town This Size," so I asked him if he'd like to play mandolin along with John, Fiona, and me. We started running the song, and right away I knew that this was the capstone to all that had gone on in John and Fiona's life for the last four years. They'd had the great joy of getting married and having Jack and Tommy and then having to deal with John's diagnosis and treatment of cancer. They'd come through it and were stronger than ever:

In deepest night
When memories tend to gather
Lay with me
And put your fears to sleep
'Cause there's no pain no dream
Can put asunder
All the love that binds us
You and me
Chorus: Darling I can see the clouds around you
And in your heart I know a sorrow grows
But if you weep I'll be right here to hold you
'Til each tear you cry becomes a rose

In Spite of Ourselves went on to be nominated for a Grammy and became one of John's best selling albums. When John went back out to perform he was overwhelmed by the love his fans showed for him. John was like a family member who had gotten sick and recovered. He was back now, and they wanted to show him how much he meant to them. In spite of everything John and his fans wound up "sittin' on a rainbow." It was good to be alive.

LIFE AFTER
FORERUNNER

Happy as I was to have successfully completed *In Spite of Ourselves*, this was a bittersweet time for me. Once we made our decision to sell Forerunner, the hard work started. From the time we made the decision until we completed the sale, it took us eighteen months. As it turned out, if we'd waited another year or even six months, that door would have closed, and we would have been stuck. The business was changing that fast. It was difficult. We had a staff to tell that they were going to lose their jobs. They genuinely loved their work, so it wasn't just about how many months they would continue on or what the severance terms were. We also met with every writer individually and went over our reasons for selling, so that they would be absolutely clear about why we felt we had to do this. In spite of all the emotional upheaval, however, I still had no doubt in my mind that we were right in our judgment. I didn't know then how right we were.

When you sell a publishing company, the buyer comes in and does what they call "due diligence." They look at your books, all of your contracts for all of your songs, looking for anything that might be out of line. Now we did everything we could to insure that the sale would go smoothly as far as all the paperwork was concerned. We had about 2,500 songs! With so many split copyrights because of multiple writers and publishers on a single song, there were bound to be mistakes, and Terrell and our living saint of a secretary, Mary Todd, did their best to find and correct them, and then we hired an outside accounting firm to take a second look. Only then, after more than a year, did we engage Mike Milom, one of Nashville's most respected music attorneys, to bring the company to market.

Pat Higdon at Universal Music expressed an interest early on. They already had absorbed some of Hal Ketchum's and Pat Alger's songs, and they also had the old Jack Music catalogue, so we decided to sell to them. The time Terrell had taken to get our books in order turned out to be time well spent, because when the lawyers and accountants from Universal in Los Angeles came in, they were finished within three weeks. They told Terrell that they hadn't found as clean a catalogue in years. Although Terrell hadn't wanted to sell the company, it was her thoroughness as an administrator that made it possible in the end. She could be proud of the job that she had done. Looking back, all of us were proud of what we had accomplished. From the beginning we had remained steadfast in our belief that an intimate, independent, and creative atmosphere would enable writers to fully express themselves and to bring into the world songs that would become part of the fabric of literally millions of people's lives. We had set our own standards and done business on our own terms. When we understood that the forces of the digital revolution were irresistible, we chose to capitalize on the success of the company rather than watch its value steadily diminish. We wanted Forerunner to go out on a high, and we had achieved that.

There was definitely going to be life after Forerunner for me. I kept my office in the basement of Jack's Tracks, so I still had a base of operations in Nashville. However, I realized that with the publishing company gone and with me spending more time in Vermont and Ireland, there was a danger that I would lose touch with my musical community in Nashville if I didn't structure something. I booked a gig at the Station Inn and called up a bunch of my favorite pickers. Pat McLaughlin, Pat Alger, Pat McInerney (the "Pat Trick"), Stuart Duncan, Jelly Roll Johnson, Richard Bailey, Dan Dugmore, and Gene Libbea all showed up. There was no rehearsal! We all knew lots of songs between us. I knew what I'd start with and what I'd finish with; the middle was up for grabs. Later, Gene Libbea moved to Colorado and Dave Pomeroy stepped in on bass. Shawn Camp, Pete Wasner, and Bill Kenner joined in. After each gig I'd book another one two or three months later. One morning after one of these gigs I was flying somewhere. I was dozing, and an image of the band on stage came into my mind—Pat McLaughlin hunched over his guitar, Big Bill Kenner towering over his little mandolin, Jelly Roll Johnson's bald head crowning his harmonica. The word "Irregular" came into my mind. I came to, and it was clear—"Rooney's Irregulars." We've been going since 1999, with no end in sight. Still no rehearsals! The band did just what I hoped it would. It kept me close to those in Nashville I loved most. I didn't miss the business a bit, but I would have missed them terribly.

FIGURE 34. Sandwiched between my two mentors and dear friends,
Allen Reynolds and "Cowboy" Jack Clement.
Photograph: © Catherine J. Flanagan.

The "Irregular" gigs insure that I get to Nashville at least four or five times a year. I go for that gig if for nothing else. Sometimes it coincides with an album project, sometimes it doesn't. I try to spend a few days on either side of the gig so I can drop in on Cowboy or Allen Reynolds or Mark Miller and catch up with what they're doing, maybe have a pint with Pat Alger and Tony Arata. Naturally, things are gradually changing in Nashville. People die. Harlan Howard died. John Hartford died. Johnny Cash died. Chet Atkins died. They all left big holes.

Personally, it was going to be impossible to fill the void in my life created by the passing of Eric Von Schmidt in 2007. Since the first day I met him in Harvard Square, I had been swept along by his energy, his endless creativity. Our times creating together were always joyful, intense affairs, whether we were putting together the graphics for The Blue Velvet Band album, working on his record albums, or writing and putting together *Baby, Let Me Follow You Down*. His capacity for work was prodigious, but, for me, it was never so impressive as in the final decade of his life when he turned his focus on a series of immense paintings collectively titled "Giants of the Blues." These paintings, starting with "John Hurt's Dream," were visionary explorations of the entire body of music that had captured Eric's imagination. There were different groupings of the Delta Blues Men—those from East Texas, those from Memphis. There were the great female singers and belters. Ray Charles exploded out of the surrounding group of piano players. Throughout this period Eric was assaulted with a stream of Joblike afflictions, starting with Lyme disease, which resulted in partial paralysis. He kept painting. He fell and broke his hip and needed to use a walker. He kept painting. Eventually he contracted esophageal cancer and lost his voice box. He kept painting. Finally, at the end, he was working on a painting of gospel singers focused on one of his original inspirations—Sin Killer Griffin, from whom Eric had got "The Galveston Flood." "Wasn't that a mighty storm" could have been his theme song. Facing overwhelming challenges, he refused to give in. Not one for "going gentle into that good night," Eric fought tooth and nail right up to the end. His passion was close to rage, and he knew it. Often when I came to visit during these last years Eric would ask me to play John Prine's "Bruised Orange." The chorus spoke to him:

> You can gaze out the window, get mad and get madder
> Throw your hands in the air, saying what does it matter
> But it don't do no good to get angry, so help me I know
> For a heart stained in anger grows weak and grows bitter
> You become your own prisoner as you watch yourself sit there
> Wrapped up in your very own chain of sorrow.

His painting was what kept Eric's anger at bay. All the love he had for this music born of hardship poured itself onto these canvases and finally brought peace to his soul.

A few years earlier, when John Hartford had finally been overtaken by the cancer he had fought for fifteen years, he left the hospital world behind and came home to his house on the Cumberland River to spend his last days. What happened then was one of the most extraordinary musical events I've ever witnessed. For six weeks or so every day pickers dropped by and played music for John. For many years at Christmas time John and Marie would have an open house. The music and the cooking never stopped. This was just like that. There was no plan or schedule. People just came whenever they felt like it. One day Ferg and I drove out. When we arrived, John was still inside, but the weather was fine and he wanted to come out on the porch. Pete Wernick, from Hot Rize, and I picked John up and brought him out and sat him on a big comfortable couch. Others arrived—Maura O'Connell, Tim O'Brien—and we all started to pick and sing. John was pretty weak and often his head was on his chest, but his hand tapped time and at the end of a tune he'd lift his face and give us one of those beautiful John Hartford smiles! If we ever needed it, this was proof that we are all part of a wonderful sustaining stream of music, which was flowing before we came along and will be flowing long after we're gone. It is up to us to flow with it as far as we can.

Producing records continues to be a source of great satisfaction and joy. I like nothing better than to come into the studio with an artist and the songs we have chosen and present them to a group of musicians who are all ready to join us in finding where each song and the artist come together. Over the years I have developed relationships with so many musicians and engineers that we have a deep rapport and understanding between us. I found out late in life that the great film director John Ford was a cousin of my grandmother's. His real name was Feeney and his family was from Spiddal in Connemara, as were the Lydons, my Gammy's family. I saw an interview with Ford where he talked about how he liked to work with a group of actors again and again like Henry Fonda, John Wayne, Maureen O'Hara, Ward Bond, and Barry Fitzgerald. He liked to set a long shot up and let the action come to the camera, trusting in the instincts of the actors and his crew. Not unlike him, I love to let the musicians and the artist find their way together while the engineer and I try to capture the action live. Likewise, my dad worked with a crew of laborers, masons, and carpenters over the years building schools, hospitals, and churches, many of which were designed by my Uncle Jim. I now understood that the satisfaction he took in that process resulting in a useful, well-built, well-designed building was very similar to the satisfaction I get from producing an album of well-played, well-recorded performances by a good artist, which will make its way into people's lives in ways we can only imagine.

In addition to making albums with Tom Rush, Mickey Clark, Naomi Somers, Roberto Bianco ("The Romantic Voice of our Time") and Michael Johnson, Charley Landsborough, Notorious, Hal Cannon, Robin and Linda Williams, and Chris Brashear, I continued to work with John Prine, Iris DeMent, Tom Paxton, Bill and Bonnie Hearne, and Paul Zarzyski.

FIGURE 35. Hanging out with the cowboys at the Elko Cowboy
Poetry Gathering (*l. to r.*: Don Edwards, Jim Rooney,
Paul Zarzyski, Waddie Mitchell).

My connection to the West through music and poetry has been another great source of energy and inspiration for me personally. I keep
returning to the Cowboy Poetry Gathering in Elko to stay in touch with
Paul Zarzyski, Don Edwards, Hal Cannon, and Ian Tyson and to absorb
some of the primal energy which continues to bubble up from the land
and the people who live on the land.

I received the same sort of energy and reinforcement from my life in
Ireland and continued making albums with Sean Keane and The Lee Valley String Band as well as with Chris Meehan & His Redneck Friends and
the Rough Deal String Band. I also play gigs with my Irish "Irregulars"—
Arty McGlynn, Mick Daly, Phillip Donnelly, Paul Mulligan, Tony Trundle,
Mary Staunton and Mary Shannon. Living in Ireland got me back to the
communal aspect of music, which isn't about trying to find a hit song or
produce a hit record or making lots of money, it's about serving a func-
tion in the community, and I'm still very much a part of the community
of Ballinderreen. When we arrived there were fifty or sixty kids in the
village taking music lessons on traditional instruments—fiddle, flute,
box, banjo, and I was asked if I could help them make a tape of the kids,
the "First Friday ceili band" and some of the local singers. We wound up

selling several hundred cassettes and raised a good bit of money, which was used to buy instruments for the kids to learn on. Three years later we recorded a CD at Paul Mulligan's studio in Kinvara. It was a chance for the kids to show how much they had improved since the earlier record-ing. This process helped keep the momentum of the program going. It's something that's special to Ballinderreen, thanks to the commitment and hard work of Sue Fahy, Mary Francis Dervan, and Brendan O'Loinsigh.

When Martin Joe O'Connor, who owned O'Connor's Pub in Ballinder-reen, died, his widow Dolly asked some of us to play at the graveside to give him a proper send off. Another great character in the village, Bertie Flannery, died. In his younger days Bertie had been a fierce dancer. After the funeral we played for a great group of his former dancing partners and mates gathered in the back room of Jordan's for some of the best dancing I've seen since I've been in Ireland. I knew then how much I had been taken into the fabric of this place we had found by accident twelve years earlier. I also can't help but think of my grandfather and great grandpar-ents who left Ireland in dire circumstances. They had to leave, never to return. So, in my own way, I have been able to bring something back on their behalf.

Many, if not most, of the artists and musicians I have worked with over the years have taught me something about how a dreamer can make his dreams come true. I have another teacher closer to home who continu-ally surprises me with the power of visionary thinking—my wife Carol. In the Spring of 1999, Carol's dad Jack Langstaff was visiting. Carol was excitedly telling him about an idea she had for a community-based dance ensemble to be called the Flock Dance Troupe. "Where will you be putting on the shows?" Jack asked. "In the amphitheater," Carol said. I looked at Jack and Jack looked at me. "What amphitheater?" "Let me show you," Carol said, and led us from the pond through the pine woods to what looked to me (and, I suspect, Jack) like a very shaggy pasture that had been let go. Carol's face was shining as she looked at what, to her eyes, was an amphitheater perfect for her new Flock Troupe. Jack immediately joined in her enthusiasm. Carol, after all, was decidedly a chip off an eternally optimistic block.

When I later broached the subject of clearing the pasture, one of Car-ol's suggestions was to let a flock of sheep graze it! However symbolically appropriate, that idea didn't really take hold. I didn't think the dancers would appreciate the little piles of sheep shit! We inquired about brush-hogging it—$300 a time would do it, we were told. That wouldn't work. Carol was busy shaping up her first show, to be called "Elemental." She was culling cast members from local dances, supermarket checkout lines, anywhere she had a chance to buttonhole people. The amphitheater was my problem. On the Fourth of July, I was waist-high in hay and weeds cursing the broken belt on my new (to me) mower. This is the part of show business they never tell you about!

My other task was to figure out a way to provide sound for the performances. Carol was using music from all over the world, and each dance section had a different piece of music—more than twenty in all. I bought a double CD player built for dance DJs, so I could play music continuously. I rented a sound system, built a somewhat rainproof shed in the woods for a sound booth, hid the speakers in the trees, ran a 150-foot extension cord and plugged it in. As it turned out, the shape of the field made for an amazing natural sound, which seemed to literally materialize out of thin air.

Watching Carol work the evening rehearsals was a real education for me. She was demanding, patient, and determined. None of the cast were professionals. A few had done some theater work before or had done contra dancing, but this required them to stretch themselves in every conceivable way. In addition, there were mosquitoes, occasional downpours, and the uneven surface of the field to contend with. Through it all Carol held her focus. The show was about the four elements—Earth, Air, Fire, and Water. Each section would start with a celebration of the element, show how humankind had once integrated life with the elements but in modern times had become estranged from them as a result of greed and arrogance. Each section ended with a ritual placing of a symbol of the element in a beautiful globe created from saplings. The entire show ended with a powerful dance of cooperation and celebration of the elements to the music of Ernest Bloch.

When the final chord sounded of the Bloch Concerto on the opening night, I had tears in my eyes. She had done it. This is what she had envisioned when all I could see was weeds and difficulties. The faces of the cast told it all. They too had had their doubts. How was this ever going to work? Would they be able to physically do what Carol was asking them to do? They had. The meaning of it all came clear that night.

They had succeeded in bringing this vital message about the elements to an audience who could feel their depth of commitment. As the cast took their bow out by the pond, a great blue heron took off and circled overhead. The Flock Dance Troupe had been blessed.

Since then, in Vermont and in Galway, through her Flock productions Carol has explored the issues of consumerism, immigration and migration, death as a part of life, the changing roles of men and women, cooperation as a necessity for survival—all against the backdrop of the four elements. What I like about her shows is how inclusive they are. The casts are large—usually twenty-five to forty people—ranging in age from three or four to nearly eighty! Likewise, the audience is made up of people from all walks of life and of all ages. So much modern dance that Carol took me to seemed so abstract, even cold. There were no stories, no messages to bring away with you. Taking her inspiration from her former teacher, Martha Graham, Carol wants her work to have meaning. She wants to bring the audience along to the place where they will see the need for change and embrace it. Her work is not an abstract exercise; it is part of life. Carol and I are together on this. I feel the same way about the artists I have chosen to work with. Their music becomes a part of people's lives and helps them overcome their difficulties, celebrate their joys, mourn their losses. Art is a necessary part of life, not something apart from it.

Of course, one of the strongest strands in our life together is our family. There is no doubt in my mind that my life is much richer for having Sarah, Matthew, Sonya, and Johanna in my life. Every one of them has presented me with challenges and difficulties to be worked through. I have been forced to get outside of myself and think of ways to make room for each of them in my life. Fundamentally, though, it hasn't been any different than my approach to working with artists. I am trying to help them. I want them to succeed. I want them to be themselves. Sometimes I can help financially; sometimes with advice. Mostly, though, it is a matter of being a constant in their lives, of loving them no matter what and making sure that they understand that.

Now Carol and I are in yet another phase. We're Granny Carol and Grampa Jim (or Grampa Rooney). It started not too long after we went to Ireland when Johanna called to tell me she was expecting a baby. She and Ron had settled in Bend, Oregon, and started a cleaning business. They had found a place with six acres of irrigated land, and they

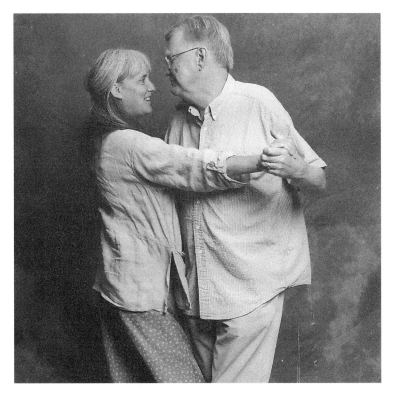

FIGURE 36. Dancing through life with Carol.
Photograph: © McGuire.

started building a nest. So I wasn't totally surprised when Jo told me her news. Nests are for babies. A year later I flew out to Bend and held my grandson James Joseph Ravitch. His birthday was the day after mine, and it meant more than I could say that, like Johanna James, he had been named after me.

For years I carried a picture with me that I had taken of Judy and Johanna on our trip up to Magog to try and show Johanna to Bruno when she was barely one month old. It was my own version of the classic Madonna and child. There was a tiny flame flickering there—a combination of innocence and vulnerability—that I cherished and could not abandon and allow to be extinguished by the ways of the world. That's what kept me hanging in there all those years until finally Jo was strong enough to make a life of her own, and I could end my codependent relationship with Judy. For all of its difficulties that relationship had borne good fruit. That flame lives on in Johanna and now in James.

A few years later Sarah and her partner Angus brought into the world their daughters Maika and Amalia. They live near Boston, less than three hours away, so we can see them pretty frequently and watch them grow. Having three small kids in your life definitely changes your perspective. You begin to understand that you don't have all the time in the world, so you want to make sure you're using it well. There are times in your life when you need to take hold of it a little bit and redirect yourself. One of my little sayings is, "If you don't live life, it will live you." Carol and I both understand that any artistic venture is insecure. There are no guarantees. When you are your own boss you have to dream things up yourself. Then you have to go to work to follow through to make what you've dreamed up happen. As time goes by you do develop some confidence in your ability to achieve your goals, but you're still always aware of the risks. There is not a recording session that I go into that I don't have the feeling in the back of my head that, "I could come out of here today with nothing." You need to have that. If you don't, then, interestingly enough, the chances of getting nothing become more real.

Another great source of perspective in our lives is that we live close to nature. In the summer evenings by the pond we listen to the tree frogs and owls. Birds are continually coming and going—kingfishers, herons, ducks, bats. We see deer in the orchard beyond the garden. Families of wild turkeys cross the hay field. We feel the intensity of the seasons—the florescent green of Spring, the overflowing abundance of Summer vegetables, berries, and flowers, the firestorm of Autumn leaves, the deep silence of Winter snow.

In Ireland the major natural influence on us is the sea and the tides. Each day the bay empties and fills back up. Witnessing that alone can't help but make you wonder at the power and the constancy of nature. Living in a place where people have been living for ten thousand years or more will also give you a bit of perspective on life. One of the songs I got out of *The Sandburg Songbag* was "Clinch Mountain," which I recorded on the first Borderline album. My favorite verse is

You may brag of your knowledge and boast of your sense
It will all be forgotten a hundred years hence

Coming across the ruins of tombs, forts, castles, and churches as we climbed over the hills with P.J. Curtis or Moya Cannon, I would be reminded of those lines. We all think that whatever we are doing and the times we live in are so important that nothing else matters. Time spent in the company of rocks and water will quietly erode those notions.

However we still keep on. I'm still singing, writing, and producing. Bill Keith and I celebrated our more than fifty years of playing together, with appearances at the Philadelphia Folk Festival and the Joe Val Bluegrass Festival where we were honored with the Boston Bluegrass Union's *Heritage Award*, a very special and meaningful honor. Carol carries on with Flock, dreaming up new shows and dances and teaching kids and adults from the surrounding towns. We plant our garden every year.

Life is lots of small steps. One day we look back and see how far we have come and wonder how that happened. One of my schoolmates at Roxbury Latin, Jared Diamond, wrote a book called "Guns, Germs & Steel." It is an interesting book whose roots, I suspect, were in Mr. Whitney's geography lessons. One image from that book that has stayed with me is the image of man walking from Africa, through the Middle East, Europe, Central Asia, the Far East, across to North America, down through Central America to the tip of South America. The journey took hundreds of thousands of years, but we did it one step at a time.

That's how I look at my own life. My parents did their best to steer me in what they thought was the right direction, but the best thing they gave to me was the freedom to be myself. Acting on my Gammy's advice, I've been following my own path—doing it "my own ignorant way"—one step at a time.

Even though I was living pretty close to the bone sometimes, and spent my last dollar more than once, I did manage to stay afloat. Two things kept me going. One was the joy that music brought me personally. It was a way I could express myself. Perhaps more important as far as the work I was to do in music was the emphasis my parents had placed on service. The point of life was to be of service to others. They had thought of teaching as a good way to do that and had pointed us all in that direction. In my own case, I have been motivated by a desire to help artists, songwriters, and musicians get their music out to the world. I did my best to create good conditions of performance at the Club 47, at the New Orleans Jazz Festival, at the Newport Jazz and Folk Festivals, at

FIGURE 37. Celebrating after the Americana Association Lifetime Achievement Awards, Nashville, 2009 (*seated, l. to r.*: Tim O'Brien, Stuart Duncan, John Prine, Nanci Griffith, Pat Alger; *standing, l. to r.*: Dan Dugmore, Pete Wasner, Pat McInerney, Shawn Camp, Roberto Bianco, Jim Rooney, Dave Pomeroy, Pat McLaughlin, Richard Bailey, Bill Kenner, Kirk "Jellyroll" Johnson).

Photograph: © McGuire.

venues and festivals around the world. My motivation was the same at Bearsville or in the recording studios in Nashville or Ireland where my focus was on creating an environment for the musicians and the artists, which would make it possible for them to be at their best. At Forerunner we tried to give the writers the freedom and support they needed to do their best work.

Music is a great force for good in the world. When we send our music out into the world we never know where it will land or who may be touched by it. One night in the pub during Sea Week in Connemara I was talking to a man named Frank Nugent. Frank had been part of the Irish expedition to climb Mt. Everest and had given a fascinating talk about it that afternoon. In the course of conversation Frank asked me what I did. I said that I was in the music business and produced records. He said, "I always take tapes with me on my expeditions." Then, without knowing a thing about me, he said, "Up on Everest I was listening to a song called 'Tecumseh Valley.'" I said, "Really? A friend of mine wrote that song, Townes Van Zandt. Whose version were you listening to?" Without hesitating, Frank said, "Nanci Griffith's." I was amazed. "I produced that record!" There Frank was up on Everest listening in his little tent to a song we'd recorded at Jack's Tracks. Nanci's deeply heartfelt performance had found its way to Frank's heart way up there. You never know.

In 2009 I was surprised and honored to receive a Lifetime Achievement Award from the Americana Music Association at the Ryman Auditorium in Nashville, just a few feet from where Hank Williams used to sing. It seems that by following my heart and putting one foot in front of the other for sixty years or more since first hearing Hank's voice and the sound of the Confederate Mountaineers coming out of my radio, I have created enough of a path to leave a mark. Although I am well aware that I will have been forgotten "a hundred years hence," I have to believe that the music I helped bring into the world will live on in some way in people's hearts and in their genes to be discovered repeatedly by generations to come. That's probably as close to immortality as I will get. That's close enough for me.

DISCOGRAPHY

PRODUCED BY JIM ROONEY

Pat Alger: *True Love & Other Short Stories*, 1988, Sugar Hill Records
    Seeds, 1993, Sugar Hill Records
    Notes and Grace Notes, 1994, Liberty Records
Rick Beresford: *First of One*, 1986, Tirn Records
Roberto Bianco with Michael Johnson: *Always*, 2004, Yellow Rose Records
Chris Brashear: *Heart of the Country*, 2012, Dog Boy Records
Hal Cannon: *Hal Cannon*, 2011, Okehdokee Records
Ceoltoiri An Doirin: *Music at the Crossroads*, 2004, Ceoltoiri An Doirin
  Records (Ireland)
Mickey Clark: *Winding Highways*, 2009, ear-X-tacy Records
Iris DeMent: *Infamous Angel*, 1992, Philo/Rounder Records; 1993, Warner
  Brothers Records
    My Life, 1994, Warner Brothers Records
    Lifeline, 2004, Flariella Records
    The Train Carrying Jimmie Rodgers Home (on the album *Going Driftless:*
      An Artist's Tribute to Greg Brown), 1992, Red House Records
    Big City (on the album Tulare Dust), 1994, Hi Tone Records
    Hobo Bill's Last Ride (on the album The Songs of Jimmie Rodgers:
      A Tribute), 1997, Sony/Egyptian Records

Whispering Pines (on the soundtrack album The Horse Whisperer), 1998, MCA Records

Leaning on the Everlasting Arms (downloadable bonus track on the soundtrack album *True Grit*), 2010, Nonesuch Records

Richard Dobson: *Save the World*, 1983, RJD Records

Don Edwards: *West of Yesterday*, 1996, Warner Western Records

Don Everly: *Let's Put Our Hearts Together* (single), 1981, Polydor Records (U.K.)

Garrison Brothers: *Songs and Stories*, 1980, Boot Records (Canada)
Thinking of You, 1982, Boot Records (Canada)

Steve Gillette: *The Ways of the World*, 1991, Compass Rose Records

Jane Gillman: *Pick It Up* (5 tracks), 1986, Green Linnet Records

David Grier: *Freewheeling*, 1987, Rounder Records

Nanci Griffith: *Once in a Very Blue Moon*, 1984, Rounder Records
The Last of the True Believers, 1986, Rounder Records
Other Voices, Other Rooms, 1993, Elektra Records
Other Voices, Too, 1998, Elektra Records
No Expectations (on the album Stone Country), 1997, Beyond Music Records
If I Had a Hammer (on the album *Where Have All the Flowers Gone? The Songs of Pete Seeger*, Vol. 1), 1998, Appleseed Records
If These Old Walls Could Speak (w/Jimmy Webb, on the album *Red Hot & Country*), 1994, Mercury Nashville Records

Bill and Bonnie Hearne: *Diamonds in the Rough*, 1997, Warner Western Records
Celebration! Live at the La Fonda, 2002, Big Hat Records

Sean Keane: *No Stranger*, 1998, Grapevine Records (Ireland)
The Man That I Am, 2000, Grapevine Records (Ireland)
You Got Gold, 2006, Circin Rua Records (Ireland)

Robert Earl Keen Jr.: *The Live Album*, 1988, Sugar Hill Records
West Textures, 1989, Sugar Hill Records

Hal Ketchum: *Past the Point of Rescue*, 1991, Curb Records
Sure Love, 1992, Curb Records
Every Little Word, 1994, Curb Records
Solitary Man (on the soundtrack album Maverick), 1994, Atlantic Records (all coproduced with Allen Reynolds)

Charlie Landsborough: *Still Can't Say Goodbye*, 1999, Ritz Records (United Kingdom), (coproduced with Arty McGlynn)

The Lee Valley String Band: *Corner Boys*, 1998, Corner House Records
  (Ireland)
   Prolific or What? 2008, Corner House Records (Ireland)
   (all coproduced with Mick Daly)
Pat Mclaughlin: *Wind It On Up,* 1981, Appaloosa Records (Italy)
   (coproduced with Curt Allen)
   Party at Pat's, 1992, Appaloosa Records (Italy) (coproduced with
      David Ferguson)
Dave Mallett: *Vital Signs*, 1986, Flying Fish Records
   For a Lifetime, 1988, Flying Fish Records
   This Town, 1993, Vanguard Records
Chris Meehan & His Redneck Friends: *Dancing in the Kitchen*, 2009, Round-
  stone Records (Ireland)
Andrew Murray: *I Wish My Love Was a Red, Red Rose* (on the album *Hell or High
  Water*), 2005, White Cow Music
Notorious: *The Road to Damascus*, 2010, Black Socks Press Records
David Olney: *Roses*, 1991, Philo/Rounder Records
   (coproduced with Tommy Goldsmith)
Tom Paxton: *Wearing the Time*, 1994, Sugar Hill Records
   Live for the Record, 1996, Sugar Hill Records
   Looking for the Moon, 2002, Appleseed Records
   Comedians and Angels, 2008, Appleseed Records
John Prine: *I Saw Mommy Kissing Santa Claus/Silver Bells*, 1981 (single), Oh
  Boy! Records (on the album *A John Prine Christmas*), 1993, Oh Boy! Records
   Aimless Love, 1984, Oh Boy! Records
   Let's Talk Dirty in Hawaiian/Kokomo (single), 1985, Oh Boy! Records
      (on the album *German Afternoons*), 1986, Oh Boy! Records
   German Afternoons, 1986, Oh Boy! Records
   John Prine Live, 1988, Oh Boy! Records
   In Spite of Ourselves, 1999, Oh Boy! Records
   Souvenirs, 2000, Oh Boy! Records
Rough Deal String Band: *If You Wanna Get Your Fill*, 2006, Rough Deal
  Records (Ireland)
Peter Rowan: *Walls of Time*, 1982, Sugar Hill Records
   The First Whippoorwill, 1985, Sugar Hill Records
   Bluegrass Boy, 1996, Sugar Hill Records
Tom Rush: *What I Know*, 2009, Appleseed Records
   Celebrates 50 Years of Music, 2013, Appleseed Records

Naomi Sommers: *Gentle as the Sun*, 2008, American Melody Records
Oystein Sunde: *Kjekt A Ha*, 1989, Tomato Records (Norway)
Barry and Holly Tashian: *Trust in Me*, 1988, Northeastern Records
    Ready for Love, 1993, Rounder Records
    Straw into Gold, 1994, Rounder Records
    Harmony, 1997, Rounder Records
Ian Tyson: *Eighteen Inches of Rain*, 1994, Vanguard Records; Stoney Plain
    Records (Canada)
Townes Van Zandt: *At My Window*, 1987, Sugar Hill Records
    (coproduced with Jack Clement)
Eric Von Schmidt: *2nd Right, 3rd Row*, 1971, Tomato Records
    (coproduced with Michael Cuscuna)
    Living on the Trail, 2002, Tomato Records
Jerry Jeff Walker: *Gypsy Songman*, 1986, Tried & True/Rykodisc Records
    Live at Gruene Hall, 1989, Tried & True/Rykodisc Records
Robin and Linda Williams: *These Old Dark Hills*, 2012, Red House Records
    Back Forty, 2013, Red House Records
John Lincoln Wright: *Takin' Old Route One*, 1977, Esca Records
    That Old Mill, 1990, Northeastern Records
Paul Zarzyski: *Words Growing Wild*, 1998, JRP Records
    The Glorious Commotion of It All, 2003, JRP Records

ENGINEERED BY JIM ROONEY

Al and Emily Cantrell: *Under a Southern Moon*, 1988, Sombrero Records
Jim and Jesse: *In the Tradition* (mix engineer), 1987, Rounder Records
Alison Krauss: *Too Late to Cry*, 1987, Rounder Records
Edgar Meyer: *Unfolding,* 1986, MCA Records (Master Series)
Nashville Jug Band: *Nashville Jug Band*, 1987, Rounder Records
Mark O'Connor: *The New Nashville Cats* ("Cat in the Bag" track), 1991,
    Warner Bros. Records
Blaine Sprouse: *Brilliancy*, 1985, Rounder Records
Johnny Western: *Sings 20 Great Classics & Legends*, 1985, Americana Records
The Whitstein Brothers: *Rose of My Heart*, 1985, Rounder Records

PERFORMED BY JIM ROONEY

Bill Keith and Jim Rooney:
    Livin' on the Mountain, 1963, Prestige Records; 1997, Blues Interactions
      Records (Japan)

The Prestige/Folklore Years, Vol. 6 (includes 9 tracks from *Livin' on the Mountain*), 1999, Prestige/Folklore Records

The Blue Velvet Band:

Sweet Moments, 1969, Warner Brothers Records; 1999, Warner Music (Japan)

Silver Meteor (anthology including two Blue Velvet Band cuts), 2010, Sierra Records

Borderline:

Sweet Dreams and Quiet Desires, 1972, Avalanche Records; 2000, Liberty Records (Japan); 2013, Real Gone/Razor & Tie Records

The Second Album, 2001, Capitol Records (Japan); 2013, Real Gone/Razor & Tie Records

Jim Rooney:

One Day at a Time, 1975, Rounder Records

Alive and Well and Hangin' Out in Bangor, Maine/Cruisin' Town (single), 1975, Esca Records

No Expectations/South in New Orleans (single), 1979, JMI Records

Ready for the Times to Get Better, 1980, Appaloosa Records (Italy)

Brand New Tennessee Waltz, 1981, 1994 (CD with both albums), Appaloosa Records (Italy)

My Own Ignorant Way (w/Rooney's Irregulars), 2001, JRP Records

Farewell to the Tracks (w/Rooney's Irregulars), 2007, JRP Records

Woodstock Mountains Revue:

Mud Acres: Music among Friends, 1973, Rounder Records; 2003, Beatball Music/Bongrass Records (Korea)

Woodstock Mountains: More Music from Mud Acres, 1977, Rounder Records; 2004, Beatball/Music/Bongrass Records (Korea)

Pretty Lucky, 1978, Rounder Records

Back to Mud Acres, 1981, Rounder Records

Woodstock Mountains: Music from Mud Acres (a compilation CD), 1987, Rounder Records

Live at the Bearsville Theater, Vol. 1 and 2, 1990, Pony Canyon Records (Japan)

Bill Keith:

Something Auld, Something Newgrass, Something Borrowed, Something Bluegrass, 1976, Rounder Records

Banjoistics, 1984, Rounder Records

Beating around the Bush, 1992, Green Linnet Records

SONGS WRITTEN BY JIM ROONEY

One Morning in May (music cowritten by Jim Rooney and Bill Keith; words traditional)
    Recorded by: Bill Keith and Jim Rooney
      Joan Sprung
      Joe Val
      Pierre Bensusan
      James Taylor
      Ian Tyson
Kentucky Moonshiner (music by Jim Rooney; words traditional)
    Recorded by: Bill Keith and Jim Rooney
The Knight upon the Road (music by Jim Rooney; words traditional)
    Recorded by: The Blue Velvet Band
Fond Affection (music by Jim Rooney; words traditional)
    Recorded by: The Blue Velvet Band
Alive and Well and Hangin' Out in Bangor, Maine (music and words by Jim Rooney)
    Recorded by: Jim Rooney
Cruisin' Town (music and words by Jim Rooney)
    Recorded by: Jim Rooney
Do You Think It Will Ever Go Away (music and words by Jim Rooney)
    Recorded by: Jim Rooney
Lonesome in Paradise (music and words by Jim Rooney)
    Recorded by: Rosalie Sorrels
In It for the Long Run (music and words by Jim Rooney)
    Recorded by: Jim Rooney
Only the Best (music and words by Jim Rooney)
    Recorded by: Borderline
      Jim Rooney
      George Hamilton IV
The Girl at the End of the Hall (music and words by Jim Rooney and Lamar Hill)
    Recorded by: Jim Rooney
Interest on the Loan (music and words by Jim Rooney)
    Recorded by: Jim Rooney
      The Woodstock Mountains Revue
Lord Lovell (music by Jim Rooney; words traditional)
    Recorded by: Jim Rooney

Ian Tyson *Ross Knox* (music by Jim Rooney; words by Ian Tyson
and Tom Russell)
Roving Gambler (music by Jim Rooney; words traditional)
Recorded by: Jim Rooney
Pretty Fair Maid (music by Jim Rooney; words traditional)
Recorded by: Jim Rooney
Hello Baby It's You (music and words by Jim Rooney and Herb McCullough)
Recorded by: Jim Rooney
Devil's Level (music and words by Jim Rooney and Herb McCullough)
Recorded by: Jim Rooney
Point of View (music and words by Jim Rooney and Herb McCullough)
Recorded by: Jim Rooney
Sean Keane

BOOKS AND LINER NOTES
WRITTEN BY JIM ROONEY

BOOKS

Bossmen: Bill Monroe and Muddy Waters (1971)
Published by: Dial Press
Hayden Books
Da Capo Press
JRP Books
Baby, Let Me Follow You Down (w/Eric Von Schmidt) (1979)
Published by: Anchor/Doubleday Books
University Of Massachusetts Press

LINER NOTES

Better Days (1973) Bearsville Records
Janis (1975) Columbia Records
Elizabeth Barraclough (1978) Bearsville Records
Emmylou Harris and The Nash Ramblers at the Ryman (1992) Warner Brothers
The Lilly Brothers and Don Stover on the Radio 1952–1953 (2003) Rounder
Records

INDEX

JIM ROONEY is a songwriter and Grammy winning record producer, and author of *Bossmen: Bill Monroe & Muddy Waters* and coauthor of *Baby, Let Me Follow You Down*. In 2009 he received a Lifetime Achievement Award from the Americana Music Association. His web site is www.jimrooneyproductions.com.

MUSIC IN AMERICAN LIFE

Bibliographical Handbook of American Music   *D. W. Krummel*

Goin' to Kansas City   *Nathan W. Pearson Jr.*

"Susanna," "Jeanie," and "The Old Folks at Home": The Songs of Stephen C.
    Foster from His Time to Ours (2d ed.)   *William W. Austin*

Songprints: The Musical Experience of Five Shoshone Women   *Judith Vander*

"Happy in the Service of the Lord": Afro-American Gospel Quartets
    in Memphis   *Kip Lornell*

Paul Hindemith in the United States   *Luther Noss*

"My Song Is My Weapon": People's Songs, American Communism,
    and the Politics of Culture, 1930–50   *Robbie Lieberman*

Chosen Voices: The Story of the American Cantorate   *Mark Slobin*

Theodore Thomas: America's Conductor and Builder of Orchestras,
    1835–1905   *Ezra Schabas*

"The Whorehouse Bells Were Ringing" and Other Songs Cowboys Sing
    Collected and Edited by Guy Logsdon

Crazeology: The Autobiography of a Chicago Jazzman   *Bud Freeman,
    as Told to Robert Wolf*

Discoursing Sweet Music: Brass Bands and Community Life in Turn-of-
    the-Century Pennsylvania   *Kenneth Kreitner*

Mormonism and Music: A History   *Michael Hicks*

Voices of the Jazz Age: Profiles of Eight Vintage Jazzmen   *Chip Deffaa*

Pickin' on Peachtree: A History of Country Music in Atlanta, Georgia
    Wayne W. Daniel

Bitter Music: Collected Journals, Essays, Introductions, and Librettos
    Harry Partch; edited by Thomas McGeary

Ethnic Music on Records: A Discography of Ethnic Recordings Produced
    in the United States, 1893 to 1942   *Richard K. Spottswood*

Downhome Blues Lyrics: An Anthology from the Post–World War II Era
    Jeff Todd Titon

Ellington: The Early Years   *Mark Tucker*

Chicago Soul   *Robert Pruter*

That Half-Barbaric Twang: The Banjo in American Popular Culture   *Karen Linn*

Hot Man: The Life of Art Hodes   *Art Hodes and Chadwick Hansen*

The Erotic Muse: American Bawdy Songs (2d ed.)   *Ed Cray*

Barrio Rhythm: Mexican American Music in Los Angeles   *Steven Loza*

The Creation of Jazz: Music, Race, and Culture in Urban America
    Burton W. Peretti

Charles Martin Loeffler: A Life Apart in Music   *Ellen Knight*

Club Date Musicians: Playing the New York Party Circuit   *Bruce A. MacLeod*

Opera on the Road: Traveling Opera Troupes in the United States, 1825–60
    Katherine K. Preston

The Stonemans: An Appalachian Family and the Music That Shaped
    Their Lives   *Ivan M. Tribe*

The University of Illinois Press
is a founding member of the
Association of American University Presses.

Designed by Jim Proefrock
Composed in 11.25/14 Marat Pro
with Goshen display
at the University of Illinois Press
Manufactured by Sheridan Books, Inc.

University of Illinois Press
1325 South Oak Street
Champaign, IL 61820-6903
www.press.uillinois.edu